Josiah Royce
in Focus

Josiah Royce, Public Philosopher. Collection of The Bancroft
Library, University of California, Berkeley.

Josiah Royce in Focus

Jacquelyn Ann K. Kegley

Indiana University Press

BLOOMINGTON AND INDIANAPOLIS

This book is a publication of

Indiana University Press
601 North Morton Street
Bloomington, IN 47404-3797 USA

http://iupress.indiana.edu

Telephone orders   800-842-6796
Fax orders   812-855-7931
Orders by e-mail   iuporder@indiana.edu

The paper used in this publication meets the
minimum requirements of American National
Standard for Information Sciences—Permanence
of Paper for Printed Library Materials,
ANSI Z39.48-1984.

Manufactured in the United States of America

Library of Congress Cataloging-in-Publication Data

Kegley, Jacquelyn Ann K.
Josiah Royce in focus / Jacquelyn Ann K. Kegley.
       p.   cm. — (American philosophy)
   Includes bibliographical references and index.
    ISBN 978-0-253-35240-8 (cloth : alk. paper) —
ISBN 978-0-253-21959-6 (pbk. : alk. paper) 1. Royce,
Josiah, 1855–1916. 2. Philosophers—United States—
Biography. I. Title.
   B945.R64K445 2008
   191—dc22
   [B]
                                        2008015017
1 2 3 4 5   13 12 11 10 09 08

This book is dedicated to Stephen Charles and Cassandra Elizabeth, my grandchildren, and to my step-great-grandchildren, Calder, Christopher, and Bryson. May they and future members of the family be those "loyal and loving persons" who seek to build "genuine communities" within their own families, communities, and country, and in the broader world.

Our fellows are known to be real and have their inner life, because they are for each of us, the endless treasury of *more ideas*. They answer our questions, they tell us news, they make comments, they pass judgments, they express novel combinations of feelings and they relate to us stories, they argue with us, and take counsel with us. . . . *Our fellows furnish us with the constantly needed supplement to our own fragmentary meaning.*

JOSIAH ROYCE, *The World and the Individual,* II

Contents

Preface

This book had its beginning some years ago when I was a graduate student at Columbia University. There my mentor and teacher, Justus Buchler, suggested that I explore Royce's views on science. I remain eternally grateful for this suggestion as I continue to find in Royce's voluminous writings new and relevant insights for contemporary issues. Interestingly, in my early career I did not, in any extended way, pursue my work on Royce. There were, in fact, few scholars working on Royce. Instead, I turned to technology and related ethical issues. However, as I worked in this area, I soon found Royce's ideas about community, interpretation, and self to be beneficial to the various contemporary public issues I was pursuing. Then, at the suggestion of John McDermott, I pursued the idea of Royce as a public philosopher. This resulted in my book *Genuine Individuals and Genuine Communities*. Another stimulus led me to Royce's writings on religion and several articles on sin, grace, and atonement. Then even more recently, I gave a paper on Royce and race at the first Royce Conference at Vanderbilt University. This led to the most immediate stimulus for this book, which was a suggestion by John Stuhr of Vanderbilt University that I consider a book on Royce for the Indiana University Press series on American philosophers. I extend my gratitude to all those who have sent me back to Royce for a deep and more extended exploration.

My deep appreciation also goes to Frank Oppenheim, John Clendenning, John Smith, John McDermott, and Randy Auxier, who have provided published letters and bibliographical commentary and, most importantly, superb published versions of Royce's work, many of which were unpublished or long out of print. They and a new generation of scholars have also given us critical insight into

Royce's thought through books, essays, and shared dialogue. Younger scholars are adding to this corpus. Royce is deservedly coming into his own as a rich, deep, and exciting philosopher.

In this book, I look at Royce through contemporary interests and needs. I view him as a model philosopher: a scholar and a committed teacher, as well as a philosopher much concerned about public issues and basic human concerns. I deeply admire his amazing breadth of knowledge, his constant concern for criticism, interaction, and open dialogue, his focus on a holistic view of the human being, and his deep interest in science, mathematics, logic as well as ethics, and religion, in addition to the usual topics of philosophy, namely, metaphysics and epistemology. Philosophy today has become hyper-specialized. The interest in public issues is often not featured in the main sessions in the meetings of the American Philosophical Association but rather is found on the programs of the various societies and/or special topics groups that meet in conjunction with the APA. These issues often also are left to the bio-ethicists or so-called applied philosophy groups. In many mainstream areas of philosophy, reductionism is operative and focus is on technical problems within philosophy itself.

Further, science is seen as the only grounding for knowledge claims, and thus many traditional issues in philosophy are reinterpreted through the lens of particular sciences. Thus evolutionary—naturalistic versions of philosophy appear in many areas—epistemology, philosophy of mind, and even ethics. Neuroscience is also seen as providing answers for philosophical problems. Royce understood science very well, but he viewed science as a social, fallible interpretive endeavor; it provided many insights into the nature of the world, but he would turn a critical eye to any claims that it be foundational to all philosophical reflection. Royce was much admired at Harvard for his logic seminar, which drew in scientists from many specialties as well as scholars from other disciplines. Today the philosophical community rarely seeks inter-disciplinary and cross-disciplinary discussion. One exceptional example is the Coss dialogues at the annual meetings of the Society for the Advancement of American Philosophy. However, such interdisciplinary discussions need to be encouraged today; the complicated and complex problems confronting our world can be adequately addressed only in this manner.

Refocusing on Royce also reminds us of the importance of history and of the history of philosophy. A historical perspective, in my judgment, may allow us to see contemporary philosophical issues from new and richer perspectives. Perhaps we will avoid old mistakes or move forward with aspects of past solutions. It is unfortunate, in my view, that today many philosophers either do not know the history of their field or disdain such knowledge as unimportant. Thus, for example, anyone interested in insight on the problems faced today by the state of California would do well to read Royce's history of California and his essays on issues that faced this state in its early development. Further, Royce concerned himself with more global issues, especially with the building of a peaceful world community. This concern is being addressed by a few philosophers such as Martha Nussbaum, but more attention could be given to community building on an international scale. Royce's work certainly could contribute to such efforts.

It has been exciting to engage in a refocus on Josiah Royce, and I hope those who read this book will find it as enriching as I have.

Acknowledgments

Again, my profound thanks goes to those scholars such as John McDermott, Frank Oppenheim, John Clendenning, Randy Auxier, and Scott Pratt, as well as the members of the Josiah Royce Society, who continue to work to bring Royce's thought alive in this time and place and for the future. However, any errors, misinterpretations, or failures of imagination in this book are mine alone.

Josiah Royce
in Focus

1

Royce as a Frontier Californian and Intellectual Pioneer

Forging Self and Thought in a New and Developing Land

This biographical sketch of Josiah Royce will focus on some of his ideas and character traits, centered on two themes: Royce as a bridge builder and as a seeker of "insight." These foci include exploration of the following sub-themes: (1) philosophy as reflection on life as experienced in all its richness, variety, conflict, and unity; (2) philosophy as personal and as a philosophy of life; (3) enrichment of life and thought through the critical exchange of ideas; (4) the philosopher as a "frontiersman"; (5) forging a life and self as a narrative with a central cause or ideal as a theme; (6) the prime importance of the temporal, of history, and of the irrevocability of the past; (7) nature as part of life and as a philosophy.

This approach will, first, set a general context for understanding Royce's thought because, in my view, he lived out his philosophy in his own life. In modern parlance, he "walked the talk." Second, Royce strongly believed that the best sources for understanding a person were reading their books and essays and observing their thought in action. Royce remembered his beloved teacher and mentor, Joseph Le Conte, as his inspiration for this belief.[1] In his tribute to William James, Royce puts his view succinctly: "A great philosophy expresses an interpretation of the life of a man and a view of the universe which is at once personal and, if the thinker is representative of his people, national in its significance."[2] Thus, our biographical sketch will focus mostly on how details of his life illuminate his thought and actions. I believe Royce's thought was also representative of "his people," and thus has broader significance.

This approach is in concert with Royce's view of the goal of philosophy. He writes:

> Philosophy . . . has its origin and values in an attempt to give a reasonable account of our own personal attitude toward the more serious business of life. You philosophize when you reflect critically upon what you are actually doing in your world. What you are doing is of course, in the first place, living. And living involves passions, faiths, doubts and courage. The critical inquiry into what all these things mean and imply is philosophy.[3]

All of the sub-themes enumerated above, in fact, follow from this view of philosophy. Thus, Royce believed his task as a philosopher—although he also believed it was everyone's task[4]—was to forge a "philosophy of life," and if the philosopher was representative of his people (and, in Royce's view, the great philosophers of history were), the philosophy would be "national" in significance. Royce argues that the philosophy of William James is "national in significance."[5] Royce uses the phrase "philosophy of life," primarily in 1911, but I believe it describes well what his life and thought is all about. Royce defines "philosophy of life" as the task of "learning to see life as it is, to know the world as we men know it, and to guide our purposes as we ought to guide them."[6] In terms of his time Royce saw this task as "the effort to see whether and how, you can cling to a genuinely ideal and spiritual interpretation of your nature and duty, while abandoning superstition, and while keeping in close touch with the results of modern knowledge about man and nature."[7] In 1911, Royce's advice to the graduates of Simmons College in molding a philosophy of life was "Be loyal; grow in loyalty."[8]

Life, believed Royce, was a tremendously complicated affair, and thus no one individual could possibly bring to light its inexhaustible treasures. Such richness and depth would produce a variety of views, seemingly conflicting and certainly expressed via an endless variety of modes, whether it be poetry, science, or philosophy. Thus, Royce sought to learn from a broad range of experiences, including the poetic, literary, and musical, and from various fields of science. Doing this was, for him, a necessity. Also important was his readiness to share his fund of experience with others.

Central to his life and thought was the task of **bridge building,** seeking harmony and synoptic vision, believing that "the seeming opposing assertions about the world may, in a deeper sense, turn out to be equally true."[9] Royce thus sought enrichment also through the critical interchange of ideas. As we will see, he welcomed criticism. One needed continually to revise one's vision in light of experience, which was always full of riches.[10]

Douglas Anderson, in his book on Royce, claims Royce was a person of a "tolerant spirit," his openness was an "existential openness"; he "took all persons at face value, as living possibilities."[11] Anderson writes: "Attitudinally and existentially, Royce is a much freer thinker than many who simply endorse freedom propositionally, and it was in part this trait that sustained his long friendships with James and his own students."[12]

Royce once wrote that "a philosopher is by destiny forever a frontiersman."[13] This is an apt description of Royce as a philosopher, and in several senses. First, Royce, of course, was in actuality a "frontiersman"; he came from a pioneer family, and he was himself involved in some seminal moments. Thus, he was in the first undergraduate class at what was to become the University of California, Berkeley, and a member of the first graduate class in philosophy at Johns Hopkins University.

Second, Royce has what Douglas Anderson calls a "frontier attitude." Royce, he says, saw philosophy as "intellectual wandering."[14] The philosopher wanders in the wilderness seeking answers and experiences, always the fearless and unsparing questioner. In a letter to Stanley Hull about the teaching of philosophy, Royce writes: "No philosopher cares, as such, what you say that he merely believes. He cares only to be sure that what he teaches as insight he has seen and hopes to get others to see. The true born student of philosophy, *while* he studies philosophy, should act only as a philosopher,—freely, fearlessly, unsparingly,— questioning solely for the sake of insight."[15]

The philosopher as questioner, then, is a wanderer; Royce was a wanderer, in thought and in action. He sought insight through many different avenues, including travel to such distant places as Australia and New Zealand and to the Caribbean islands of Jamaica and Trinidad. From these visits he gleaned important experiences and insights that found their way into his writings on social and political issues. He explored literature and poetry for insights that might be gleaned there. His approach to history of philosophy was sympathetic and critical. He drew on those resources, but always with a discerning and questioning attitude.

Another aspect of this notion of philosophy as wandering appears in his 1897 interpretation of the story of Job. In this essay he speaks of those wise who wander: "For the triumph of the wise is no easy thing. Their lives are not light, but sorrowful. Yet, they rejoice in their sorrow, not, to be sure, because it is mere experience, but because, for them, it becomes part of a strenuous whole of life. They wander and they find their home even in wandering."[16] For Royce the human self is a being of conflicting desires, interests, and values, and also one who desires wholeness. Royce saw life as a task, an ethical undertaking, requiring adventure, humor, courage, perseverance, and deep reflection. Life is also risk, because, in choosing a life plan one must exclude possibilities and reject certain value and pathways. And evil is an ever-present reality; life is fragile, and human beings lose their way and betray their causes. Thus, there is sorrow and evil, and one must face both courageously, taking them up into one's life with new meaning; as we shall see, it is community that saves, for in serving the cause of community, with our fellow beings, we can achieve unity of self. The community is also the place where inquiry and questioning can be carried on in an endless process of interpretation and search for meaning.

Another aspect of being a frontiersman was also to become, in some senses, a "knower of the wilderness." Later, in his wanderings in Australia, Royce will note parallels between California's experience with the wilderness and Australia's. Thus, both countries learned to reclaim the wilderness and particularly the desert. There was also the developing of mineral resources, especially gold. Royce writes: "In Australia, as with us, the story of exploration goes hand in hand with the story of conquest and of general progress on various frontiers."[17] Nor is it surprising that Royce would argue that geography and climate play a role in one's character development.[18] Further, Royce believed there was a deep affinity between human beings and other beings, and he had a deep respect for nature.[19]

As indicated, philosophy was, for Royce, quest, and particularly a quest concerning self. For Royce, the essence of a self was a life plan, a central theme or cause, and a narrative, a temporal process that involved continuity and change, a clear enrichment as past flowed into present and into the future through an interpretive process that connects the time-elements of one's experience.[20] Royce would seek in his life and philosophy to answer two central questions: "Who am I?" and "What shall I do?" Life would be a search for self and for a worthy life. This self-searching is reflected early in his life in a narrative about "Pussy Blackie," written when he was only eight. Indeed, the notion of "narrative" is a key idea for Royce because he believed all reality is temporal in nature, and narrative captures its development. Randall Auxier argues, in his forthcoming book, that Royce's philosophy is a form of "temporalism."[21] Throughout his philosophical career Royce was concerned with understanding and affirming the essentially temporal nature of experience, of life, of thought. He argued for the significant import of the idea of the "irrevocability of the past" as well as the importance of the past as a ground for the flow from present to future in life, for self, and for philosophy, just as in narrative. This theme is exemplified in his strong argument for the importance of the history of philosophy and in his fascination with the "cult of the dead," which was the subject of his very last writing.[22] He sees in the cult of the dead a continuation of the never-ending story of life.

We turn now to Royce's life experience. This sketch will be theme-based as well as roughly chronological; thus aspects of his later life may appear connected to earlier parts as I pursue the related themes.

Royce the Pioneer in Search of Self and a Philosophy of Life

Josiah Royce was a Californian by birth, born on 20 November 1855, in Grass Valley, the son of Josiah (1812–88) and Sarah Eleanor (Bayliss) Royce (1819–91), whose families were recent emigrants from England. Like their parents, Josiah and Sarah sought their fortune in moving west in 1849. And as hinted earlier, Royce, again like his parents, would see himself as a pioneer, a "philosopher who was by destiny forever a frontiersman."[23] He writes: "The philosopher in the world of thought is by destiny a frontiersman. He may seem the mere wanderer . . . but the solitary labor of the seeker for truth shall in the end be submitted, not only to those theoretical tests which philosophy recognizes . . . but also the social and ethical judgment of the practical man. . . . The frontiersman may wander, but he must some day win what shall belong to the united empire of human truth."[24] Royce was a pioneer in a number of ways. First, he was, it seems, always at the beginning of things, involved with seminal times. The first such seminal experience was to participate, with his pioneer mother, Sarah, in the forging of a new social and political community in Grass Valley. Sarah, in her own recollections, written at the urging of her son, describes this community building and its various struggles, giving a beautiful portrayal of the ways in which women and families were able to "tame" the wildness of this mining town.

Creating opportunities for the appreciation of higher culture and founding institutions was among her important activities. Sarah was the center of much musical activity with her melodeon, the first brought to California. She also helped found a church and served as a teacher of the young, including young Josiah. Katharine Head Royce, later the wife of Josiah, recalls: "She clearly prized the benefits of civilization, not the gaieties or luxuries, but the churches, the libraries, the schools, and the companionship of an enlightened society . . . wherever she went, she made civilization even when it seemed that she had little indeed from which to make it."[25] Under his mother's tutelage Josiah developed his love of literature, reading Milton and other literary works; made his acquaintance with the Bible and religious experience; was given an introduction to music and its beauty; and experienced the joys of a warm, loving community, his family, and particularly his mother and sisters.

Sarah Royce, in her instruction of the children, put much emphasis on writing, and young Josiah began his literary career with a delightful story of the travels of Pussy Blackie, a "Huckleberry Finn cat," who runs away from home; gets bitten by a dog; is captured by an eagle; travels on a railroad car; lives in the house of a rich family; finds a cat companion with whom Pussy exchanges stories; and discusses social issues such as the contrast between the rich and the poor, as well as the treatment of the less fortunate and moral questions such as honesty, shame, killing, and war. In many ways, this story embodies ideas and characteristics of the adult Royce—a continual search for self, a willingness to go against tradition and to take risks, a love for a story, a belief that life and self are narratives, a sense of humor, a love of cats, a concern for ethical and social issues of import, and a belief in the exchange of ideas.

Two later indications in his life of going against tradition are that he commenced his study of the history of philosophy with Spinoza and not Descartes and he introduced "Logic" into the teaching of writing at Berkeley when he was a young professor there. The first was unconventional, the second was a risk. Adventure and risk taking certainly characterized a Royce who left California for the difficult trip to Harvard, with a wife and new baby, leaving a secure job on the slim offer of a sabbatical leave appointment. Like Pussy, Josiah did travel east from the frontier, and his life has been described as "the engrossing story of an intellectual Huckleberry Finn, spiraling outward from the image of a shy village boy in a remote mining town to that of a world-renowned philosopher at Harvard University."[26]

While he was at Harvard, Royce's humor, his fondness for cats, and his love of the intellectual exchange that dominate the Pussy Blackie story all also appear in a story about Royce, William James, and a cat.[27] Standing on his front porch one day in Cambridge and seeing James approaching, Royce is alleged to have said, "Puss, Pussy, here comes a pragmatist." The kitten snarls and James is purported to have said, "Royce, that's no kitten, it's your familiar spirit."[28] The wonderful, loving relationship and many critical exchanges of ideas, always in good humor, between James and Royce are well documented.[29] Royce and James can perhaps be envisioned as Pussy and companion traveling the world of intellectual and practical problems, seeking enlightenment and enrichment and courage from each other.[30]

Royce's pioneer mother, I believe, did indeed leave him a number of legacies, and here I use the term "legacies" to mean "planting seeds," as parents do, consciously or unconsciously, that produce expected or unexpected fruit and flowers in a child's later life. The "seeds" that Sarah planted included a love for music and literature, a deep sensitivity to religious insight, and a concern for community building, whether on the level of family or the broader community. Another legacy may well have been Royce's belief in a vigorous, courageous, committed ethical/religious philosophy of life involving active perseverance against life's many travails and evils. Sarah Royce was a woman who displayed independence and perseverance; she not only endured the trek to California, with her husband and newborn baby, but later lived through many moves from community to community, following her restless pioneer husband. Once she faced down a wild coyote, and at other times she experienced extreme aloneness in the desert. She "met all hardship and rude conditions of living with unfailing energy and cheerfulness."[31]

Josiah also experienced hardships in his own life, including the mental illness and death of his eldest son, Christopher, as well as a "nervous breakdown" early in his own academic career. He carried an enormous workload of teaching, lecturing, and writing, partly to remain solvent financially because of his many family obligations, including the care of a developmentally disabled grandchild. William James is reported as writing to James Mark Baldwin, "Royce is working like three men and thinking like 100."[32] Royce met these hardships with energy and journeyed on, much like the pilgrim John Bunyan, on whose life he reflected.[33]

In addition, Sarah Eleanor Bayliss Royce is described as "the epitome of a woman whose pioneering life intensified rather than relaxed her moral commitments."[34] Royce, too, remained loyal to his commitments, even as he grew personally, intellectually, and socially. His constant concern as a philosopher was to deal with the serious business of life, to reflect critically and earnestly upon "living."[35] The close tie between mother and son is perhaps best exemplified by the judgment that Sarah's "career was an almost perfect expression of Josiah Royce's philosophy of loyalty."[36]

Royce's Educational Experiences

In Grass Valley, young Josiah was schooled entirely by his mother and three sisters, one of whom introduced Royce early to the joys of intellectual debate. His view of thought and self as developing via interaction and contrast obviously had an early origin in his own life. From what one can glean of Royce's early life, the family relationships, especially among Royce, his mother, and his sisters, were rich and interactive. He developed his own sense of self, in both appreciation and rebellion. His mother's deep religious feelings made an impact on Royce, although he did not join a formal religious organization in his later life. His excellent knowledge of the Bible and of religious stories became part of his thought and vocabulary, but, unlike his father, Royce did not hold to any literal interpretation of the scriptures or of the religious stories. His strong love for and belief in critical debate and interaction obviously developed through his intellectual exchanges with his sisters, but he never loved debate just for its own sake, and he cautions against such an attitude throughout his writings.

Further, Royce's early experience in and with nature led to a bond with it and an interest in science. He spent his childhood on Avon Farm, outside of Grass Valley, which was surrounded by woods with ponderosa pine, sugar pine, and fir, traversed by a stream filled with trout and by numerous Indian trails, inhabited by deer, red fox, coyotes, and brown bear, as well as numerous birds, and offering plentiful blackberries, all with a view of the immense Sacramento Valley. An 1865 Christmas gift from his mother, a book on the career and achievements of John Ericsson, the engineer, fed his interest in science. Later, upon enrolling at the new University of California, Royce first selected engineering as his major. He later switched to the classics, but he maintained a lifelong interest in technology and in the industrial arts.[37] He was to grow in this love of nature and science at the university, as he shared hikes with his mentor-teacher Joseph Le Conte and naturalist John Muir in Yosemite. Royce's belief in the influence of geography and climate on character has already been mentioned. Royce's piece "Meditation before the Gate" is a superb reflection on nature and what it might teach. Looking down on the Bay of San Francisco, Royce writes: "That one realizes the greatness of the world better when he rises a little above the level of the lowlands, and looks upon the large landscape beneath, this we all know; and all of us, too, must have wondered that a few feet of elevation should tend so greatly to change our feeling toward the universe."[38] Royce was to offer other such reflections on climate and geography in his two articles on Australia.[39]

In 1866, the Royce family moved to San Francisco, where Royce first attended the Lincoln School. It was here that Royce received his first experience of bullying, and as he matured, he developed a profound dislike for the "self-aggrandizing bully." In spite of the difficulties with bullying (among other things), late in his life Royce observed that his early school experiences gave him his "first introduction to the majesty of community" one that was "impressively disciplinary and persistent." The remarks here about community, we suppose, are partly ironic in light of Royce's later thoughts on community and loyalty. Bullies represent aggressive individualism, with disregard for others or for community in general. Royce had the deepest respect for the individual and for a strong individuality, as will be apparent in his ethics and social and political philosophy, but he argued all his life about the harmful character of bullying and saw it as one of the barriers to developing genuine community and self. Royce saw several prominent public figures as bullies, including John C. Frémont and Theodore Roosevelt. Frémont, in Royce's judgment, sought his own selfish goals, and not the broader goals of a future community called "California," in taking California from the Spanish Californians. Royce would carry on a long controversy with others about his judgments of Frémont, which are expressed in his history of California.[40] Frémont's action, as representative of aggressive individualism expressed in greed and bullying, was, in Royce's estimation, one of the deep failures of the people of California as they sought to build a new state.

Another experience his attendance at Lincoln School introduced into Royce's life was that of a community of discipline, military in nature. Interestingly, Royce also experienced this as an undergraduate at the University of California, where, amazingly, students were required to put on uniforms and march on a parade ground. This was common to land grant schools, one purpose of which was to encourage the development of military sciences and technologies. One wonders how current UC, Berkeley, professors and undergraduates would view this history. In his philosophy-of-loyalty book, Royce would discuss the images of the warrior and of the warrior community. In terms of Royce's views on community and loyalty, these expressions of the military-style community in his youthful life would be less than genuine because they lacked the notion of a "personally chosen cause" and were not aimed at expansion of spirit, self, and community.

Lincoln School would also, however, transform Royce's pioneer spirit. There Royce became, observed his sister, Ruth, "an intellectual pioneer": "He saw each new world with the eyes of a discoverer—made his own observations, cut his own trails, and saw more in the stupendous whole than others ever saw."[41] There he sped through mathematics, developing his own system of logarithms, and began his lifelong journey into literature. Both of these subjects provided resources for Royce's thinking and publications and for his developing philosophy. Royce also attended San Francisco Boys' High School, where he appears to have developed some friendships with his classmates, among whom was the (later famous) physicist Albert Michelson. This venue also enriched further his belief in intellectual interaction, for it is described as a "stimulating place," a "species of educational nirvana where older scholars worked with younger scholars, where projects and research abounded—a place of 'spirited' argument between keen lads and alert men on points of scholarship."[42] Two of Royce's high school essays are also of interest, "A Nocturnal Expedition" and "The Miner's Grave." Both are on the theme of death and grief and perhaps reflect his reading of Tennyson and Poe. They also connect to Royce's strong belief in necessary remembrance of the past, the theme of his last writing.

Continuing his pioneer trek, Royce entered, at age fourteen, an infant University of California, later becoming one of its first graduates, thus participating in the beginnings of higher education in the state. Here Royce began to forge a new identity, moving from the shy, homely, red-haired boy who lived at home to become "Josh," the editor of the college newspaper, the *Berkeleyan*, as well as one of its prolific writers. He found lifelong friendships, though he endured much friendly teasing from his fellow classmates, including a bogus commencement program featuring Josiah as a "fiery-haired Jehovah" with a swelled head and a "capacious stomach."[43] His classmates perhaps saw him as a prophet, as he wrote on many topics of public interest. Also, this description is interestingly apt for the caricature of Royce drawn by a leading nineteenth-century American cartoonist, Homer Davenport, utilized in an essay by historian Kevin Starr in a 1998 article entitled "The Gold Rush and the California Dream."[44] This caricature appears as the frontispiece of this book. As for Royce's red hair, it was much remarked on during his lifetime. In this light, a piece in the *Grass Valley News*, when Royce was only seven, says the following about those with red hair: "A red head is always accompanied with a delicately fair skin and light eyes: these indicate . . . the nervous or intellectual nature, forming when properly regulated, one of the finest organizations in the world; very generous, very affectionate, 'go-ahead-ative' and intelligent."[45]

If we look ahead from these early days, we do indeed see Royce as a prophet.[46] This was illustrated most clearly in 1916, when, in the presence of a great audience in Tremont Temple nearly a year before the United States entered World War I, Royce delivered an address entitled "Duties of Americans in the Present War." Historian Rollo Walter Brown writes about this event as follows:

> His words were electrifying almost beyond belief. Very literally they were heard round the world—so startling were they. They had not been the noisy eloquence of any advertised public figure; they were the outcry of a man who had lived a life of benevolent gentility and now saw a condition of life coming when neither benevolence nor gentility would count. Millions who had never seen his name until yesterday now talked of him as one of humanity's great bulwarks. With plenty of instances before their eyes of what he talked about, they were ready to believe that what he declared was undeniably true.[47]

In traditional terms a prophet is basically a spokesman for God, a person chosen by God to speak to people on God's behalf and convey a message or teaching. Royce did not see himself in this light, but he did see himself as deeply concerned about the ideal and about the ultimate values in life. He writes that a central task in life, a key aspect of any philosophy of life, is "the effort to see whether and how, you can cling to a genuinely ideal and spiritual interpretation of your nature and duty, while abandoning superstition, and while keeping in close touch with the results of modern knowledge about man and nature."[48]

Further, prophecy has always been seen as an instrument of social change. Its purpose is that of changing the group's current intentions, behaviors, cultural or social practice, or structure to conform to higher ethical standards. In this sense, then, Royce's message is rightfully taken as prophetic. His fellow students, in calling him a prophet, obviously saw his fiery passion about social issues.

At Berkeley, Royce also found two mentors as well as two lifelong friends. The first was Joseph Le Conte, who taught him "the architecture of an argument" and stimulated a lifelong appreciation of science and a continuing interest in evolutionary thought. The other key personality was Daniel Coit Gilman, the university's first president, who became Royce's guardian, confidant, sponsor, and friend. Gilman helped Royce get funding to study in Germany, and later, when Gilman was president of Johns Hopkins, he got Royce admitted with a fellowship.

Royce's published works during his university days contain seeds of his developing philosophical ideas, including his views of art and science as complementary and as ideal enterprises—the truth in art always being subordinate to the truth in emotional expression and scientific laws seen as abstractions never realized in our own experience.[49] As a young undergraduate Royce was already the "bridge builder." A fruitful endeavor for Royce's scholars would be to explore Royce's ideas about the bridge between art and science. In addition to his explorations of science and evolution and his immersion in the works of John Stuart Mill and Herbert Spencer, Royce wrote on literature and the arts, becoming something of a Classicist. For example, he wrote on the tragedy *Antigone* by Sophocles. He also produced a baccalaureate thesis on *Prometheus Bound,* a highly sophisticated interpretation of this tragedy by Aeschylus. As we shall see, the Greek heroine Antigone will figure prominently in Royce's later discussions of ethics. She, in Royce's view, represents a "supersexual insight," for she embodies a synthesis of masculine and feminine traits as well as exemplifies the combination of the three ethical ideals of independence, compassion, and fidelity.[50] Royce's undergraduate thesis on the play by Aeschylus is a thorough discussion of a major controversy in interpretation of this play in terms of its fit with Greek religion and the legends of Prometheus. Royce, still a youth, demonstrates his skill at setting out various theories while seeking a reasonable synthesis or unity of view. He argues that, indeed, the playwright intended to place Zeus in a poor light and Prometheus in a positive light, but in the context of Greek religion at the time, this did not offend the sensibilities of his audience. More importantly, Royce interprets the play as an ideal representation of the conflict of freedom against oppression, significant in the context of the Persian War. Again, this youthful work demonstrates Royce's concern for transforming conflicts into harmony and for developing a deep concern for and insight into significant social-ethical issues.[51]

Among the other key influences in Royce's early development as a person and philosopher were his study in Germany and his graduate experiences at Johns Hopkins. In Germany he studied the history of German philosophy with the historian Wilhelm Windelband; learned Sanskrit; studied anthropology, logic, and empirical psychology with Wilhelm Wund; studied Kant with Rudolf Hermann Lotze; and kept up his studies of mathematics and evolutionary theory. This began his lifelong interest in the philosophy of Kant and the various schools of thought relating to it. Returning to Johns Hopkins, Royce taught a course on Schopenhauer, another "pioneering" event, for evidence shows this to be the first graduate course in philosophy to be given at an American university. Royce also gave a course of lectures on "Return to Kant," a series Royce later sheepishly acknowledged as based on "an entire, misinterpretation of Kant's meaning."[52] Royce's doctoral dissertation at Johns Hopkins, on epistemology, contains positions later foundational in his subsequent thought; it is essentially a theory on knowledge, arguing for the constructive nature of knowledge as well as its social import.

In the Desert: The Development and Founding of Royce's Philosophy

Upon graduation from Johns Hopkins, Royce was forced by circumstances to return to California to teach at Berkeley. He believed this was tantamount to exile to an intellectual desert, where neither ideals nor philosophy were present or respected. This negative view of California in no way diminishes the influence that California had in Royce's life. Royce saw California honestly in terms of her flaws as well as her positive features. He learned from the flaws, as is evident in his history of the state. For one who thrived on and believed in interchange and criticism of ideas this would be, indeed, a desert. Yet, during these California years, Royce developed his lifelong friendship with his immediate superior, poet and professor of English literature Edward Rowland Sill, a man who encouraged his philosophical exploration and who provided opportunities for teaching philosophy. Royce also saw Sill as a person who truly lived his ideals, an exemplar of loyalty, as Royce would later develop that concept. With Sill's blessing, Royce even wrote an introductory text in logic in relation to grammar, and taught it (thus pioneering the first course in logic at UC, Berkeley).

It was also during these years that he met and married his lifelong soul mate,

Katharine Head, with whom he was to share a life filled with joy as well as profound tragedy and sorrow. Some scholars have suggested that their relationship was a difficult one. In my judgment, there is no concrete evidence that this was the case, and a careful reading of Royce's letters indicates a deep concern for her welfare and a genuine sharing of common goals and interests.

During these years he also developed foundational ideas in his philosophy, struggling with the difficult question of the nature of time, explicated in his essay "On Purpose in Thought." He also tackled aspects of social philosophy in his essay "The Nature of Voluntary Progress."[53] This essay foreshadows many of Royce's later views and shows that his voluntarism was already well developed. Royce organized Berkeley's Psychology Club, and he produced several papers on aspects of psychology and mental processes, while at the same time reflecting on important differences between his own thought and that of Kant, Hegel, and Emerson. The articles developed during this period give us a clear picture of Royce's views and demonstrate that ideas characteristic of his later writing were already in his thought.[54] It is important to have a sense of these writings from his time in California, so I will briefly describe a representative group of them.

The enduring and connecting theme of these early articles, following up on his Hopkins doctoral dissertation, is a "theory of knowledge and reality which in its essence is activist and social."[55] At the core of his epistemology and metaphysics is his definition of an idea as a "plan of action." Royce wholeheartedly rejects any copy theory of knowledge, arguing that knowledge is a mode of action; it is an active search for the fulfillment of purpose. In an essay on Shelley, he tells us that "thoughts are not dead and finished mind products. . . . Thoughts are living and each thought lives in the most literal sense, but a moment."[56] In this essay Royce also argues for a doctrine of "creative intelligence," positing the essence of thinking as "originality." In the essay "How Beliefs are Made," Royce asserts: "Thus all knowing is, in a very deep sense, acting; it is, in fact, reacting and creation."[57] It is in this essay that Royce focuses, long before James, on the role of "attention" in knowing; he also stresses recognition as another key factor, which would be thoroughly developed by both Royce and James in the 1880s. The essay "The Nature of Voluntary Progress" gives us the idea that "[b]eliefs are always the satisfaction of individual wants. No belief can be said to be forced upon anyone, in any other sense than that it is accepted because it satisfied a conscious want."[58] However, beliefs of the present moment can never satisfy us. In searching for truth, consciousness is "selective: it pays attention to facts that affect some one of our interests," but on the other hand, "consciousness is not merely selective, but also a faculty of organization."[59] We see prefigured here the "phenomenology" Royce provides in his first major book in philosophy, *The Religious Aspect of Philosophy.*

For Royce, knowledge is and must be social. In "Doubting and Working," Royce argues that the aim in seeking truth is to harmonize the conflicting opinions of men, to substitute for the narrowness and instability of views a broadness of view. One does not doubt for mere doubt, but for social, practical, moral purposes. Doubt is a duty in truth seeking because one should not accept an opinion because it "seems pleasing to you," nor, says Royce, should we seek to conform our minds to things "that do not think." The search for truth is a sacred duty because its goal is "the making of human life broader, fuller, more harmonious, and better possessed of abiding belief."[60] Thus, for Royce, truth is not "individual satisfaction." From the outset, Royce is a pragmatist, but more akin to Peirce than to James and Dewey.[61]

These essays, and others, reproduced in the volume *Fugitive Essays* in 1920 thus demonstrate, for those familiar with the corpus of Royce's work, the flow of his thoughts from his early years into his later philosophical reflections. From our viewpoint here, however, the key essays are "On Purpose in Thought"[62] and "Tests of Right and Wrong."[63] These essays set the context for the further discussions of Royce, and thus a brief discussion of their themes is in order; the second of these essays will be discussed primarily in the chapter on Royce's ethical thought.

At the heart of both essays is Royce's view on the temporal nature of self, thought, action, and reality. In his "Thought Diary" of 1880, Royce spoke of developing the "theory of the world of reality as a projection from the present moment." He envisions a new phenomenology in which the opening contention would be: "Every man lives in the present and contemplates a past and future . . . the future and the past are shadows both, the present is the only real."[64] In his "On Purpose in Thought," Royce is concerned with a "teleological" analysis of thought, seeking to understand the final end of "purely theoretic thought" and the relationship of fundamental axioms and postulates of reasoning, such as the axiom of uniformity, which states that "there will be in our experience some kind of regularity and fixity of succession."[65] For Royce, a fundamental axiom is what he calls the well-known time-axiom, namely "that *facta* cannot become *infecta*, that the past can never be undone."[66] This, argues Royce, asserts something vital about the future, that is, that "[i]n all coming time the inviolability of every moment will be secured as soon as the moment is past."[67] This idea is most likely also foundational to his concern for history in all its forms and for historical thinking in general, as well as key to his concern for "the cult of the dead."

Royce continues his exposition by arguing that past and future are constructions of the activity of the present moment. We cannot, argues Royce, ever directly know anything but a present thought. Past and future, as past and future, are never immediately given. The present moment is the foundation, the builder, of both other branches of the conceived time stream. The conclusion of the essay is thus:

> To sum up, from this point of view the end of thought appears to be: That experience past and future, should be conceived as one whole with a necessary connection of parts; that the present and immediately given content of consciousness should be found, not alone significant nor enough, but a moment in a world of life; that the relations conceived as necessary for one part of the time-stream should be conceived as necessary for the whole time-stream. And the end of thought is realized in the act of constructing the image of possible experience. For by experience, we mean, in addition to what is given, that which is conceived as past and future.[68]

In this essay, Royce also hints at a view he will refine and further develop, namely, that the scientific world of experience is not primordial, but represents a modification of primordial experience for the sake of highly specialized interests. He argues that all knowledge of the external world has been and is intimately tied to and dependent upon the social context. For Royce, objectivity is inter-subjectivity: belief in my fellow men is prior to belief in nature. Royce develops these views in a number of places in his corpus but especially in the essay "The External World and the Social Consciousness."[69] I have argued that Royce's view in this essay about time and about knowledge of the external world presages views of Husserl and Heidegger and thus of phenomenology.[70] Here we also have several ideas foundational for Royce's views of self and of ethics. The key is the notion of "time." For Royce, time is the ground of the formation of the self; it is the locus of all human meaning. Our human experience of temporal succession is an experience of a pursuit directed toward a goal. Royce will declare that "[t]ime is the form of the Will" and that "[i]n pursuing its goals, the Self lives in time."[71]

Here, too, is the germ of the idea of self as an interpretive process that combines past, present, and future. The true self, for Royce, is not a datum of experience, but an ideal, a plan of action, a process, a never-finished product. The self, for Royce, is a "life whose unity and connectedness depend upon some sort of interpretation of plans, of memories, of hopes, and deeds."[72] Moral activity, for Royce, transcends the real present and is directed to the service of an ideal time. One cannot, argues Royce, single out my individual future in considering moral acts because my future is as much a mere expectation as is the future of my fellow man. The goal of my moral striving is the active extension of my future until it embraces the future of all conscious beings. In *The Problem of Christianity,* Royce would argue that genuine community depends upon the power of selves to extend their lives without any definable limit.[73] Thus, Royce's discussion of the significance of time and his notion of the twofold extension of the individual, temporal, and social is at the heart of his later notion of community. It is in time that the human person exists, and this is the medium for the creation not only of community, but of knowledge and of self.

As one can surmise, Royce found his sojourn in California a lonely one, a desert place where there was no substantial philosophical thought or critical reflection. Though this was the case, Royce, pioneer that he was, managed to write a series of seminal essays that contain the central ideas of his developed, refined philosophy, ideas that he would retain and enrich and restate in new forms as the contexts demanded. Like Auxier, I believe that Royce's central philosophical ideas were with him from the beginning and were only refocused and refined as he interacted with life, new questions, and the ideas of other philosophers.

Royce the Harvard Philosopher:
History, Bridge Building, and Insight

We turn, then, to Royce at Harvard. Royce joined the faculty at Harvard in 1882 as an instructor, filling in for William James, who was on sabbatical, and then again for another year as a replacement for George Herbert Palmer. He was given his own full-time appointment in 1884. In 1892 Royce became professor of history of philosophy. Perhaps not well known is the fact that in addition to his voluminous writing, teaching, and lecturing, Royce served as a very successful chair of the department and was instrumental in its period of building and expanding.[74] This faculty, consisting of William James, Josiah Royce, George Herbert Palmer, Hugo Münsterberg, and George Santayana, has aptly been described as "one of the most distinguished any university has ever had and by all odds the finest in the history of higher education in America."[75]

Royce's first major philosophical work was *The Religious Aspect of Philosophy: A Critique of the Bases of Conduct and of Faith*.[76] This 1885 book incorporates many of the ideas of the essays written by Royce while teaching at UC, Berkeley. In 1886, Royce published his history of California, entitled *California from the Conquest in 1846 to the Second Vigilance Committee in San Francisco [1856]: A Study of American Character*.[77] This book was followed a year later by a novel about California entitled *The Feud of Oakfield Creek: A Novel of California Life*.[78] This novel is based on a specific historical event, the famous Squatter's Riot in Sacramento in 1850,[79] an episode on which Royce wrote in 1885. Royce's history of California is considered by scholars today as presaging "a great deal of later historiography" and as being "the study that remains for the whole the best one."[80] Contemporary historian Patricia

Nelson Limerick calls Royce "the father of western history."[81] For Royce, the frontier represented the irresponsible society broken by violence and special interests that blocked the natural progress toward order and community. His history was the first to dispel the myth of the romantic pioneer and to bring to light the role of women and of various minorities in forging the state of California. His history was a social history as well as a commentary on social and moral problems. Royce saw the gold rush as testing the American community both socially and morally as it had never before been tested. Royce also saw this period of history as exhibiting both the true nobility and the true weakness of the national character of our people. This history foreshadows his philosophy of loyalty; it exhibits both failures and successes at building community. In this history and in his novel, Royce is expressing his lifelong concern for "building community," while respecting the uniqueness of the individual, a theme he would develop later in *The Philosophy of Loyalty*[82] and *The Problem of Christianity.*[83]

Royce exhibited throughout his life a deep respect for history and for the past. He often bemoaned the tendency of humans to extol the present at the expense of the past. He firmly believed that "originality" in thought and action depended on the past. He writes: "[F]aithfulness to history is the beginning of creative wisdom."[84] In an early essay, Royce observes:

> [T]he general law of the progress of human thought is the Law of Parsimony, i.e. of the greatest adaptation of old methods, principles, theories, dogmas, formulae, terminology, to new needs and to new facts, with the least possible change, in the form of these traditions. . . .
>
> Even revolutions in thought often turn out to be reactions in disguise, conservative efforts to substitute for the traditions of the elders some ancient and authoritative law, not to destroy old truth, but to fulfill it.[85]

As a teacher, Royce was known for his scathing criticism of views that betray culpable ignorance of the history of philosophy. Royce knew the history of philosophy intimately and was an astute interpreter of its figures and path. Richard C. Cabot, in his reflections on Royce as a teacher, asserts: "No other teacher of philosophy in my time has carried into his seminaries so full and living a consciousness of the historic stream of philosophic thought."[86] It is a travesty today how little contemporary philosophers are aware of this history. Further, many others seem stuck in the past, still espousing beliefs, without much if any transformation, from other centuries. Among these are the seventeenth-century belief in a nature that conforms to exact and irreversible laws; a skepticism grounded in Hume's philosophy; an understanding of mind, body, and the self still dominated by forms of Cartesian dualism; and a social and political philosophy still grounded in the views of Hobbes, Mill, and Locke. In ethical thought philosophy remains strangely dominated by utilitarianism and deontology, despite many contemporary criticisms of these views. Royce honored all these traditions but transcended them, viewing nature in evolutionary, probabilistic, fallible terms, and seeing skepticism as self-contradictory and unsatisfactory for the pursuit of science or philosophy as a reflection on life and living.

Royce's essays on mind are well worth reexamination. Thus, Charles Blakewell, in his reflections on Royce's work in honor of his sixtieth birthday, writes: "He has succeeded in cutting under the old Cartesian dualism of mind and matter . . . the unity of consciousness comes into being *pari passu* with the knowledge of the unity of experience; the interpreter is at once on the object as well as the subject side of the subject-object relation."[87]

With *The Philosophy of Loyalty* and related writings Royce brings new insights for social and political philosophy, and with his unification of three ethical ideas of Autonomy, the Good, and Duty, he has much insight to offer for contemporary ethics. About the philosophical thinker as moralist, Royce wrote: "Many moralists are and have been bloodless creatures who have written about life without themselves possessing any temperament for it. . . . The philosophical moralist, above all, should first be a man of experience in a wide range of elementary human life."[88]

Finally, Royce detested those in philosophy who claimed to have any final view of matters. He writes: "Dogma, as such has no place in philosophy."[89] Royce asserted that philosophy was hard work and forever unfinished. A philosophy should exhibit the wealth of life and the treasures of humanity. And good philosophy must respect the past: "[N]o fresh beginning is worth making, unless the ages have fertilized the forest soil where the new saplings are to grow."[90] With his dedication to and keen sense of the historical, Royce wrote a number of articles on key figures in the history of philosophy, and his book *The Spirit of Modern Philosophy,* written in 1892, remains one of the best introductions to this period.

Royce, as a distinguished Harvard professor, was also known, certainly by many, as something of a sage, a bumblebee of thought, and a man with a vast understanding of many things. His great wealth of knowledge made him a great conversationalist, a trait remarked upon by students, friends, and colleagues. He was also known as gentle, humble, and gracious with his time and thoughts. Not only did Royce absorb great treasures of experience, but he graciously shared them willingly with others. In his reflections on Royce, John Jay Chapman recalls several events that reflected this trait. One delight was Chapman's first chance meeting, as a mere freshman at Harvard, of Royce at a lobster bar after a concert. Sitting across from Royce, he was astounded that Royce began talking to him "exactly as if he had known me all my life."[91] For a half hour Royce talked about Beethoven and continued the conversation with a walk back to Cambridge. Chapman noted that it was a bitterly cold night and that Royce wore an overcoat as thin as paper. However, writes Chapman, "my strong impression was that he was extraordinary and knew everything." Chapman notes that Royce was always accessible for people to draw inspiration from him. Chapman reports that one of his sons was at Harvard and taking a course on the *Prometheus* of Aeschylus. Upon his father's request Royce agreed to meet with his son. Chapman reports: "Royce lectured to this single student for half an hour with the same fervor and gravity as if he had been talking before the French Academy."[92]

Royce, throughout his life, read broadly and sought to enrich his life, the lives of others, and his philosophy by these experiences. He wrote on science, psychology, mathematics, logic, religion, and, of course, poetry and other literature. His views on education were much sought after, and he gave lectures and wrote on this topic and about the development of intellectual thought.[93] To the teacher, he communicates this advice: "[B]e a naturalist, loving and, as far as may be, comprehending the life of childhood and youth, just as other naturalists try to comprehend the life of other organisms . . . be a man of rational ideals, knowing what moral and social ends, he wants to serve, and why he regards them as worthy."[94]

Royce believed in building bridges among disciplines. As a young undergraduate at the University of California, we recall, he wrote a number of essays that argued for a close interrelationship of science and literature. While at Harvard, he greatly enriched the intellectual life of the Harvard community by inviting scientists into his seminars to share ideas and critical interchange.[95] The following tribute to Royce was adopted by the Harvard faculty of arts and sciences 7 November 1916:

> His most notable tribute to the teaching of the university was made through his seminar in logic, which became a veritable clearing house of science. Men of widely different training and technique—chemists, physiologists, statisticians, pathologists, mathematicians—who could not understand one another, were here interpreted to one another by Royce, who understood them all. He would do even more than that. He could interpret each man to himself, divine his half-thoughts and render them articulate.[96]

This ability to take shapeless and incoherent views and reissue them "new minted, clean and finished" was a trait of Royce's much admired by his students.[97] Royce was seen as the rare philosopher who welcomed questions and criticism,[98] who was concerned to develop the thoughts of his students rather than to produce disciples.[99] Finally, Royce sought throughout his life to "build bridges," to seek "harmony."[100] The ultimate goal of his philosophy was a unity with variety, a variety in unity. Royce embodied this goal in his marvelous ability to achieve a kind of "synoptic vision." President Woodrow Wilson, in a letter to his wife, describes his experience of Royce, in a Seminary of Historical and Political Science at Johns Hopkins, as follows:

> I wish I could live with Dr. Royce for a few months. He is one of the rarest spirits I have met. His is one of those very rare minds which exist in a perfectly lucid atmosphere of thought, having never a cloud on its horizon, seeing everything with a clear and unerring vision. He talked to us the other night at the Seminary, and the dullest fellow at the board listened with delight—I don't mean myself!—because he has the faculty of bringing masses of detail into a single luminous picture where they are grouped with a perfection of perspective and a skill of harmonious arrangement which fill the novice, the would-be historical painter, with despair.[101]

Royce, indeed, sought the synoptic vision, the "insight" that was the goal of a philosophy of life. In his commencement address, "Loyalty and Insight," Royce writes:

> And again, the question still arises: Is there any place left for religion that can be free from superstition, that can accept just so much of the foregoing modern results as are indeed established, and that can yet supplement them by an insight which may show the universe to be, after all, something more than a mechanism? . . . Is the philosophy of life capable of giving us something more than a naturalism— humanized merely by the thought that man, being, after all, a well-knit and plastic mechanism, can for a time mold nature to this ends? So much for the great problem of modern insight.[102]

One could say that Royce addressed this problem throughout his life and in all of his writings, but especially in *The World and the Individual*,[103] *The Conception of Immortality*,[104] *The Sources of Religious Insight*,[105] and *The Problem of Christianity*.[106]

In what follows, we will sketch out aspects of his search for insight about the self and about the ethical life, about the religious community, and about social and political matters. In the next chapter the focus will be on his understanding of the "self," the "individual," and the "person" and on the nature of ethics.

2

The Self

Living Views for Today

Royce's psychological and philosophical reflections provide us in the contemporary philosophical scene a wealth of fruitful and relevant ideas. Royce's ideas resonate well with the current concern for basing philosophical reflections on empirical matters arising out of the psychological and biological sciences. Royce was recognized in his time for his work in psychology by being elected president in 1901 of the American Psychological Association, and much of his work in this field can be considered cutting-edge. He engaged in psychological experiments and employed empirical and phenomenological methods to study consciousness and the human self. Further, Royce was intimately acquainted with evolutionary theory, using aspects of it for his own philosophical reflections, while providing insightful criticism of some of its conclusions and practical applications.[1]

Royce had a pervasive interest in the concrete and experiential aspects of human experience: he believed that philosophical reflection must draw on and be in touch with this base. I believe that Royce was more empirically based than most of his contemporaries, who often dismissed his thought, falsely perceiving his work as that of an abstract idealist.[2] In fact, I suggest that Royce was even more empirical than many philosophers today.

The first section of this chapter will discuss Royce as a psychologist. This exposition itself does not do full justice to the rich treasure in Royce's psychological works, and scholars would find this material well worth pursuing as a separate endeavor.[3] We will establish Royce's credentials as a psychologist and note the ways in which he was a pioneer in this field, doing new and significant work ahead of Freud and many of the social psychologists of his day. In Royce's psychology, he gives us a clearly novel approach to mental life; namely, he discards the old "faculty" psychology, which divides mental life in terms of three faculties of mind: reason, will, and feeling. In its place Royce discussed three aspects of human mental life: *sensitiveness, docility,* and *originality.* This exposition demonstrates the deep riches of mental life as well as the interrelationship and interconnections of its aspects, not an artificial separation that is perhaps good for some philosophical discussion, but clearly inadequate for capturing human experience. Royce justifies this new approach on the grounds that it demonstrates the particularly close interconnection between intellectual and voluntary processes.[4] Further, *sensitiveness, docility,* and *originality* play a significant role in ethical choice.

Like James, Royce gives a key role to selective attention in conscious experience; this aspect of mental life is, for Royce, crucial to the role of will and to moral choice, but also to choices in other domains, such as science and even philosophy. In addition, Royce, like Baldwin, emphasizes the role of imitation in self-development, but he goes beyond Baldwin, emphasizing its role in intellectual experience, including the formation of general ideas: a human ability crucial to moral and other evaluation as well as to scientific investigation. In this context, we will see his advocacy for both activity and passivity at all levels of human experience, even the most basic. This emphasis, among others, places him as a forerunner of phenomenology. Further, in a novel and insightful manner, Royce reinterprets feeling in terms of a twofold distinction, adding restlessness/quiescence to the old pleasure/pain dichotomy, with the feelings of restlessness and quiescence playing a key role in attention, in initiative, and in moral life.

Finally, I treat Royce's phenomenology of human *inner time-consciousness.* This temporality introduces a sense of unity into human experience and grounds the notion of the self as a temporal process rather than something discoverable either intuitively or by reflective introspection. The self is to self always a question, and meaning is discovered in time and in a social context.

The next section presents a more extensive overview of Royce's views on the human self and the development of his social psychology. Here I make a clear distinction between four terms: the empirical ego, the self, the person, and the individual. The first term, in this context, is primarily psychological; the second relates to sociology and common understanding; the third is ethical; and the fourth deals with the metaphysical, namely, the topic of individuation and uniqueness. The topic of the individual will be treated only as it impacts on ethical issues.[5] Further, although all of Royce's thought, including his psychology, is of one piece, this book will not deal with his metaphysics and epistemology, except very indirectly as it bears on the topics of ethics, social philosophy, and religion. In addition, I believe that Randall Auxier has made a good case that "Royce always held that metaphysics is descriptive and hypothetical in character, and that philosophical hypotheses do not yield ontological knowledge."[6] With Auxier, I cite Royce's own words in an 1881 letter to William James, where he asserts that

> [a]ny positive theory of an external reality as such, is of necessity myth-making; that however, such ontology may have enough moral worth to make it a proper object of effort so long as people know what they mean by it; that philosophy is reduced to the business of formulating the purposes, the structure and the inner significance of human thought and feeling; that an attempted ontology is good only in so far as it expresses clearly and simply the purposes of thought just as popular mythology is good in so far as it expresses the consciousness of a people; that the ideal of a truth-seeker is not the attainment of any agreement with an external reality, but the attainment of perfect agreement among all truth-seeking beings; that ethical philosophy is the highest philosophy.[7]

On another occasion, I have discussed Royce's view of science as an ethical, loyal, and fallible search for truth.[8] Royce was passionately convinced that an adequate philosophical myth—one capable of accounting for human experience with all its passions and conflicts—was a pragmatic and idealistic worldview that emphasized time and personal quest for meaning and unity. This is a vision I believe worth pursuing today, and, in discussing various aspects of Royce's philosophy, I will assume his vision, but I will not engage in arguments about its philosophical validity. Royce writes: "It is worthwhile to live and surely it is worthwhile to know the significance of life. . . . The real business of philosophy . . . is THE ANALYSIS AND CRITICISM OF THE PRESUPPOSITIONS OF HUMAN LIFE BOTH PRACTICAL AND THEORETICAL."[9]

The second section of the chapter treats the question, What is the self? Royce rejects the views of both Descartes and Hume on the nature of the self, although, in his search for harmony and in his mining of what he terms nuggets of value from the past, he incorporates aspects of their thought into his own view. For Royce, the self is a process, not a thing, a process with both public and private aspects. The second question addressed is, How is a self developed? This is partly the question of the origin of the empirical ego, but it also concerns self as social and as viewed through common understanding. For Royce, indeed, the origin of the self is foundationally social, even at a most fundamental psychological level. The self is developed out of a process of social and personal interaction vis-à-vis a contrast effect. Hume and Descartes, in their understanding of the self, were also concerned to address the question, How is the self known? For Royce, the self is never known directly but only through interaction with other beings in a social world and ultimately through a communal process of interpretation, including self-communication or -interpretation.

In the self's search within time and through its social interaction with other beings, personal and non-personal, the self seeks unity and meaning. This quest, for Royce, is answered by means of a life plan, one that is unique, as the self's experience is unique. What gives the self its unique identity is an act of will, indeed, an act of love, coming first from another self and followed by the self uniquely loving another being or by identifying self with a voluntarily chosen personal cause. At this stage in self-development, the self becomes, for Royce, a person, the ethical actor and subject of moral attributes and interpretations. Here, Royce centers on three interrelated notions of self: (1) as an achievement, (2) as a created center of meaning, and (3) as the expression of purpose, or one ideal. The ethical self is realized through a life plan, a philosophy of life, and a life of loyalty.

Royce provides us with a very rich view of the self, based on a psychology that is, in many ways, quite modern. He allows us to view the human self in at least five important ways: (1) the idea of a human self as object of biological, anatomical, and neurophysiologic understanding; (2) the idea of self as a social-behavioral object of understanding, viewed by science, and by others via interpretation; (3) the idea of self as a subject of consciousness, understood via introspection and through phenomenological description; (4) the idea of self as "expressive," that is, through facial and bodily gestures, through cooperative activities such as art, language, custom, religion, understood via a study of the *expressive signs of mental life*[10]; and (5) the idea of self as person, as the locus of moral attributes and as the source of ethical action and values, studied via an empirical-phenomenological-historical method. This fifth notion of the self will be part of the focus in the chapter on ethics. Finally, Royce argues for the affinity of human conscious life with nature.[11] Royce's views provide, as I have argued on other occasions,[12] a treasure of insights and ideas for dealing with a number of our contemporary problems related to self and self-understanding as well as issues of health and illness. With this evaluation, we turn now to Royce's psychology.

Royce as a Psychologist

In his work on psychological issues, Royce makes clear that he is proceeding as a psychologist. Thus, in the introduction to his *Outlines of Psychology*, Royce asserts: "This is not a book upon the Philosophy of Mind, nor does it deal with any philosophical problem. . . . In the present volume I am concerned solely with the natural history of mind; metaphysical issues are here not at all in question."[13] One only wishes contemporary psychologists, especially neurophysiologists, would express such caution. It is fascinating to note the way in which the term "brain" functions in many recent neurophysiology studies just as the term "mind" or even "self" would be used in philosophical texts. It isn't at all clear that anything is gained merely by choosing narrower terminology, since the conclusions drawn about the brain in most psychology texts are doing philosophical as well as empirical work for these theorists. They might as well say 'self' or 'mind' as 'brain,' since choosing a narrow term to avoid the problems associated with broad terminology only succeeds when conclusions drawn are correspondingly narrow. Most psychological theorists who use the term 'brain' do not restrict their conclusions to physiological processes, but rather venture into social and even philosophical domains which could be more clearly discussed with terms such as 'self' or 'mind.' The choice of a physiological term just ends up creating obscurities.

A number of Royce's psychological studies are clearly experimental, including work done with his Harvard colleague Hugo Münsterberg.[14] During Royce's career he published more than forty psychological articles;[15] he gave public lectures in psychology, including his "Topics in Psychology of Interest to Teachers" (1893), and in 1901 his work was honored by his election as president of the American Psychological Association.[16] These materials impressively show Royce's insight and his keen observations of human behavior, both normal and abnormal. His insight into the growth of the self in the child is especially astute, as is evidenced by both his observations of the child and his argument for the importance of play and imagination in a child's life.[17] His comments about the youthful years and the necessity of rebellion and finding of self in a plan of life are also insightful, as evidenced by his 1898 letter to Dr. G. Stanley Hall, president of Clark University, former psychology chair at Johns Hopkins, and a founder and editor of the *American Journal of Psychology*.[18]

One suspects that most philosophers of whatever tradition are unaware that Royce had close interactions and intellectual exchanges with, in addition to his colleagues James and Münsterberg, the founding fathers of American psychology and, indeed, that he influenced the early development of psychology in the United States. For example, James Jackson Putnam, leader of the Boston group of physicians and psychotherapists who introduced Freudian ideas into the United States, used a number of Royce's insights in his own work, *Human Motives*.[19] Frank M. Oppenheim, in his superb article, "Royce's Community: A Dimension Missing in Freud and James," summarizes Royce's contributions as a psychologist: "Royce is an early American representative of the view that social interaction is primary for psychological theory. He was a forerunner of Harry Stack Sullivan's interpersonal approach to psychiatry and George Herbert Mead's gesture approach to social psychology. Royce thus offers some basic alternatives that balance the approaches of Sigmund Freud and William James, which focus more on the individual."[20]

I strongly concur with these judgments: Royce's views on abnormal consciousness and problems of the self, like his other psychological insights, are valuable to any study of self as well as to an understanding of social and ethical behavior in general. Royce discussed anomalies or abnormalities in two early essays, "The Case of John Bunyan" (1894), and "Some Observations on the Anomalies of Self-Consciousness" (1895).[21] The most interesting aspect of the latter essay is that Royce discusses maladies of social consciousness, namely, the ways in which "the social self above all can come to be the object of a morbidly depressed or exalted inner estimate."[22] Oppenheim notes that the theoretical significance of these maladies "surely seems worthy of a closer consideration than it customarily receives."[23] I agree, and I believe that Royce scholars would find in Royce's psychological studies a wealth of insights and materials relevant to issues today in ethics, social philosophy, and psychology. For social and political philosophy, one needs to explore in detail Royce's exposition of the "conditions for achieving, maintaining, and enhancing a group's consciousness of the meaning of a genuine community."[24]

As for Royce's contributions, relative to the work of Freud and James, Oppenheim correctly writes: "Royce somehow was strangely more on the 'cutting edge' of advancing psychology than was either Freud or William James."[25] His understanding of the social and communal as well as the individual made his psychological observations far richer. More specifically, with regard to Freud, Royce discussed such topics as a censor-like conscience (addressed here in chapter 3), various self-identification processes (addressed here in chapter 3 especially in terms of community recognition of a self), sexuality, and even taboos before Freud's own published thoughts on these issues. In his article on anomalies, Royce writes: "[W]e may expect to find self-consciousness especially deranged in disorders involving the sexual functions. This expectation seems to be abundantly verified, even in ordinary cases of disorder."[26] Sigmund Freud published his *Totem and Taboo* in 1912–13, but Royce had already presented his own observations on this phenomenon in his 1902 lecture, "The Intellectual Significance of the Primitive Taboo," to the Berkeley Club. Royce, like Freud, believed that practical *no*s associated with warnings or threats clearly and significantly mold the ethical and religious thought of primitive people. Royce argues for the fundamental role of contrast in forming a self as well as a key role for non-Ego in forming a conscience. Most surprising of all, Royce argued that although taboos often block intellectual curiosity, nevertheless, they remain indispensable for the growth of science. In his argument, Royce is developing a notion of theory and hypothesis testing quite similar to that of Sir Karl Popper, eminent twentieth-century philosopher of science.[27] In fact, Royce's articles on negation and the logic related to nay-saying are well worth further exploration. Royce, again the bridge builder, also saw a close connection between logic and ethics. Indeed, his work in this area led Charles Sanders Peirce to acknowledge Royce's influence on his thought in this regard; Peirce writes: "I now see more clearly the fundamental dependence of logic upon ethics."[28]

Finally, I concur with Oppenheim that Royce planted the seeds of a gesture theory of social-consciousness and self-consciousness, a theory that was later tested and technically elaborated by George Herbert Mead.[29] In his history of California, Royce establishes how the use of different instruments for gold mining changed social and self habits and attitudes. When miners began using the cradle and later the Long Tom, they were compelled to work together, resulting in a sense of *we at work* community in which they consciously shared a common purpose and engaged in practical coordinated deeds to achieve their goals. The instruments demanded "synchronized cooperative gestures from each miner," which, argues Oppenheim, educes and develops many ingredients of social consciousness: "It fosters a sense of each one's role in the work, a sense of mutual expectations and trust, a sense of shared hope of future gains, and a shared memory of past less effective methods."[30] Again, I agree with Oppenheim that Royce maintained a mutual-gesture theory of community formation throughout his philosophical career. Royce, in fact, used the notion of "synchronized cooperative gestures" in the example of "two men in the same boat" to demonstrate the social origin of the idea of "externality."[31]

In his psychological work, Royce again is clearly a pioneer, and in ways additional to those cited above. Especially important for our concerns about ethics is the fact that Royce gives a significant role to feelings in conduct. As we shall see, feeling is the basis for attention, and attention, for Royce, is the essence of will.

Royce discards the standard division of mental life into the three faculties of feeling, will, and intellect. He writes:

> The treatment of mental phenomena under the three heads of Sensitiveness, Docility, and Initiative, is especially characteristic of the plan of my book. This arrangement and classification of well-known facts involves a point of view, which seems to me to possess a certain relative novelty. The entire subordination of the usual distinctions of Feeling, Instinct, and Will, to these deeper distinctions . . . is intended to emphasise, [*sic*]—the persistent stress that I lay upon the unity of the intellectual and voluntary processes.[32]

Even more novel and also important for ethics, in my judgment, is the fact that Royce disagrees with the traditional view that makes "Pleasure and Displeasure the sole elementary qualities of Feeling."[33] Royce provides what he calls a two-dimensional scheme of the elementary feelings, dividing them into pleasure/pain and restlessness/quiescence. This division, he believes, is needed to make an intelligent statement about the relation of feeling and conduct.[34] Royce writes: "[B]y feeling we mean simply our present sensitiveness to values of things in so far as these values are directly present in consciousness."[35] About restlessness, Royce writes: "We are restless in so far as we are actively dissatisfied with a present experience and are so disposed to change the experience."[36]

Royce discusses the manner in which this two-dimensional view of pleasures can result in various mixed kinds of feelings; for example, "despair, which is a union of unpleasant feelings with predominantly quiescent feelings."[37] Further, Royce believes his twofold classification explains with more clarity and depth the role of attention in focusing our thought and action. It can explain attention to indifferent objects; it can explain why both pleasure and displeasure tend to make us actively attend; and, most of all, it can explain inattention. He writes: "From our point of view, the explanation lies in the fact that active attention involves feelings of restlessness, while feelings of quiescence tend to the cessation of active attention."[38]

Indeed, for Royce, attention is related to the general instinct to persist in trying, which is experienced as a "feeling of restlessness": "What occurs in mind whenever we are actively attentive is attended with a feeling of restlessness, which makes us dissatisfied with all those associative processes that do not tend to further our current intellectual interests."[39] In paying attention to both the active and passive characteristics of human sensitivity to environmental and internal stimuli, Royce's psychology bears parallels to the work of Erwin Straus and Maurice Merleau-Ponty, who focus on the activity of the human organism even at the most primitive and instinctual levels.[40]

Royce connects restlessness also to an instinctual persistence and ultimately to mental initiative. Royce writes: "*The restless over-activity of the organism in carrying out its instinctive processes* or in seeking opportunity for the establishment of new functions is the principal condition of every significant form of mental initiative."[41] The impulse to play comes from this restless overflow of energy in the organism. Royce writes: "As any close observer of childhood knows, children play not merely because it pleases them, but *because they must play.*"[42]

Royce argued for the significance of play in a child's life; it provides the necessary context for the imitative activities that will lead to self-development, but just as importantly, the restless instinct is largely responsible for initiative, new ideas, and the development of skills in the child. "*Mental initiative* is the self-activity of an individual dependent on general instincts which manifest themselves in the form of a restless tendency to a certain overwealth of persistent activities. . . . In their highest and subtlest form they shape the processes of *active attention.*"[43]

Finally, Royce makes this observation about restlessness, human character, and conduct: "The restless men may prove to be failures, but *the most successful of human beings are the men who are in some respects prodigiously restless.*"[44] In this context, Royce connects "restlessness with individualism."[45] He writes, "Now our social initiative depends upon constantly using our social arts, upon continually employing socially acquired habits. On the other hand, the wisely persistent, the restless, although rational desire to be, as we say, 'ourselves,' to call our souls our own,' this is *the continual mother of invention in all our social activities.*"[46] This again is evidence of Royce's deep concern for individual initiative and for individualism as a key aspect of human experience. This will become clearer as we discuss his ethical theory and his admiration for Nietzsche.

Royce, like James and Dewey, asserted the central role of habits in human intellectual and ethical life. Habit is related to docility, the third member of Royce's triad (along with sensitiveness and originality). An organism exhibits docility by "its power to exhibit, in the activities of any moment, the results of former experiences, of what has happened to the organism in the past."[47] Docility, like the other aspects of mental activity, functions at all levels of human experience. As one example, Royce refers to the law of the conservation of cerebral habits, namely, that "*Any function of the brain tends, within limits, to be performed with more facility the more frequently it has been performed before.*" In terms of consciousness, this means that "*any conscious process, which is of a type that has occurred before, tends to recur more readily . . . and to displace rival conscious processes, according as its type has frequently occurred.*"[48] Thus, docility is, for Royce, also related to the processes of assimilation, to perception, to habits of conduct, to the processes of imitation. Docility explains a strongly conservative element in human nature and development: the stability of the past grounds the movement forward; it depends partly on generally productive habits acquired in the past. In terms of ethics, docility also explains the human ability consciously to obey ethical guides as well as the tendency to follow authority.[49] Docility is, of course, also related to the central role of the past and of temporality in human experience. It is also related to one's general tendency to obey, to follow authority, a capacity certainly crucial to ethical action as both a positive and a possibly negative factor.

Another important aspect of Royce's understanding of habit is his analysis of the genesis of general ideas. It is a crucial part of his theory of imitation and the coming to consciousness of the human being. Further, among the four types of general ideas enumerated by Royce are our notion of the relations of things, such as motherhood and equality, as well as scientific conceptions such as causation, law of nature, life and mind.[50]

He writes: "Conscious general ideas are simply conscious habits of conduct in the presence of the objects to which these ideas apply." Further, he states that motor consciousness plays a key role and notes that a real test of a general idea is the presence of "that element of motor consciousness, that awareness of the thinking being concerning what he proposes to do with the objects and characters that he thinks about."[51] Here Royce anticipates phenomenology with a notion of *motor intentionality.* There is clearly a behavior-pragmatic element in this analysis. He writes: "*[T]he whole general idea involves what one may as well call 'a plan of action,' that is, a way of behaviour which is fitting to characterise and portray an object of the class in question.*"[52] However, there is also for Royce clearly an inner personal element, that of individual interest and attention, as well as a social element. He writes:

> The most important of rational general ideas relate to aspects of things that can only be observed when we most decidedly intend to observe them.[53]
>
> A rational general idea is just a habit of response to the general aspects of things, accompanied by a consciousness of what you do as you make this response, and consequently accompanied by awareness that there is, in the object of your general idea, that character which guides your interest and your attention to make this response.[54]

The stress here is on the individual and unique aspect of human experience even as it is embedded in habit and imitation.

Imitation, for Royce, plays a key role, along with social influence in the formation of general ideas. Royce asserts that the essentially "*imitative* character of all complex general ideas appears in all our most thoughtful processes, namely, in our more elaborate scientific ideas."[55] He points to the expression of these ideas in diagrams, in the processes of scientific experiments, and in writing formulas and describing objects. Thus, "one might declare that *higher conceptions,* just in proportion as they are thoughtful and definite, *involve conscious imitations of things."*[56] Finally, he asserts: *"But it is our social life that has made us conscious of our actions, and that has thus taught us how to form abstract ideas."*[57]

This has implications for Royce's theory of self as well as for his ethical theory. His views on feeling and particularly on "restlessness" also have interesting consequences. First, his division of feeling into a dyad of pleasure/pain and restlessness/quiescence partly explains why Royce finds any hedonistic ethics inadequate for a rich human life. The division of feelings into pleasure and pain is just not sufficient to explain the complex feelings and emotions that make up human experience. Further, it does not capture the subtle interconnections between sensitiveness and attention, or sensitiveness and initiative. Second, on the basis of his analysis of feelings, Royce concludes that in our conscious response to stimulation there is adjustment to our situation, but also expression of our desire. Evaluation takes place at the most fundamental level of experience, providing a ground for higher levels of evaluation. Royce writes:

> There is a general sense in which *we can speak of all consciousness as an inner interpretation of our own attitude toward the world.* Of whatever I may be conscious, I am always aware of how something is consciously estimated with reference to my needs and desires. There is, therefore, a good general ground for declaring that *the whole of our consciousness involves will, that is, a collection of attitudes which we feel to be more or less responsive to our world.* . . .
>
> But, as a fact, this our conscious response to our world takes the form *of being aware of objects, and of feeling pleasure and pain, restlessness and quiescence, in the presence of these objects and our own acts.* . . .
>
> In brief, while we are far from denying the presence of will in consciousness, our own view is that, in one aspect, *the whole consciousness of any moment is an expression of the will of that*
> Moment.[58]

Another aspect of Royce's discussion of feeling is his connection of restlessness and quiescence to *"the changing or temporal aspects of our consciousness states."*[59]

Royce associates restlessness with those emotions associated with "future," that is, with expectation, curiosity, hope, suspense, and fear. This future orientation, of course, is essential to action in general, but certainly to ethical action and to "hope," as it might express itself in social and political reform, or even revolution, and in religious "hope," for some "future life" or end. Quiescence, on the other hand, is connected with lack of change and with lack of interest. Such feelings, argues Royce, predominate is the attitude toward life called "fatalism." The fatalist tends to take the same quiescent attitude to the future as to the past. Thus "the fatalist views the future as having the same value for his feelings that the irrevocable past already has."[60]

Quiescence can be a powerful factor in human thought and life, and docility is the foundation of our habits and our close grounding in the past. Royce explores the implications of this aspect of the human psyche in an early essay, "The Nature of Voluntary Progress." Royce argues, in fact, that there is a universal human desire to do all things with the least expenditure of energy.[61] Even more interestingly, he argues that both the conservative and the radical desire new things and that both desire to economize effort. The question that distinguishes them is, Will labor be saved by this change of tradition or institution?[62] Royce defines "conservatism" as "the tendency to change old conditions to meet new needs, in such a way as shall involve the least expenditure of energy."[63] The radical, the revolutionary, confronts new experiences or new demands that he believes will not fit with the present forms of thought or institutions and thus decides that the expenditure of energy needed to make these changes is worth it. However, Royce cites historical examples of the fact that many revolutions claim to be returns to old and forgotten or neglected traditions. This, says Royce, was true of the Protestant Reformation. It is true of philosophers who claim the authority of Plato or Aristotle or some other historical figure as the base for their new ideas. This observation, in Royce's view, is an empirical one, and has nothing to do with evaluative judgment. Royce treasured the past and the history of philosophy precisely because he knew that there was to be found the basis for moving forward to new ideas and insights.

In two essays, Royce explored the issue of "originality" or "inventiveness."[64] His major claim is that "the most characteristic processes of the conscious intellect are, in the main, imitative, assimilative, and, in so far, uncreative."[65] Originality comes to displays itself in three ways: (1) in the style or form given to a work, for example, our voice, our handwriting, our choice of colors; (2) in the selection of the objects I imitate; and (3) in the invention of relatively novel combinations of old material.[66] Yet, Royce urges one to "consciously aim toward effective individuality."[67] This appears contradictory on the surface, but we need to recall that for Royce, every imitator is also an originator. Each organism, he says, inevitably colors its imitations with its own individual qualities. Each imitator begins to contrast self with the model and to develop its own version of the model.

More importantly, since self-development occurs in the contrast-effect between self and others, it is crucial that the social context provide encouragement of individuality and opposition. One typical motive of all individualism, for Royce, is decidedly sharp contrast with the environment. Royce cites the periods of great individualism as also being those of great inventiveness, such as the Renaissance. Royce observes that in the ages, invention occurs among all kinds of people and not just those considered great innovators. This leads to the important point that balance is a key aspect in promoting inventiveness and originality; unique individuality and originality occur in the context of habits, past traditions and ideas, and so a good understanding of these is essential to movement forward. Deep reflection is also needed to determine when change is necessary and worth the extra expenditure of energy. Further, the new is not valuable in itself, and "progress" for Royce is a judgment about value; thus, "voluntary progress" is "change that realizes the purposes of men." In our drive today for newness and more and more invention, we do not pause to ask: "And for what purpose?"

Royce clearly believes temporality to be central to life, thought, and all reality.[68] The concept of temporality is a constant theme in Royce's pursuit of understanding ethical obligation and values. He writes: "Whoever says 'I ought to do thus or thus' stands in a present moment of time and looks forward to a future. . . . In a world where there was no succession, there would be no morality."[69] From his earliest work Royce was exploring a phenomenology of the human inner time-consciousness.[70] In his 1880 essay "Tests of Right and Wrong,"[71] Royce closely examines concrete mental activity. In focusing on the act of judgment, he first stresses the notion of data and makes the point that "the content of feeling or perception or idea in the present moment is absolutely forced upon me."[72] This passive aspect of consciousness is then complemented by a partially active two-fold activity element that works on the data, "evolving from them what is not in them. . . . The data by themselves signify nothing at all. All real significance is given them by the activity which postulates that they stand for a reality not contained in themselves."[73] The first aspect of this activity is related to memory and involves an admittance of the past as real. There is an acknowledgment that something is so and so, that this data is experienced as received. It is "acknowledged or accepted as real or valid over and above what is directly given. . . . Whatever we acknowledge we regard as absolute and unchangeable. The past does not alter."[74] Here, of course, we see Royce's notion of the "inviolability of the past."

The second aspect of the activity is what Royce calls expectancy. The active expectation of the future enters into the experience of the actual present moment. Royce writes: "It is plain that without expectation of a future, my acknowledgment of past time would have little worth. Unless I acknowledge something more than a datum of the present moment, there is no real world for me to work in."[75]

Temporality, then, for Royce, is central to human experience and consciousness. This analysis of time is not that objectively measured by science, clock time, but it is time lived from the inside, concretely and experientially.[76] This is Royce's phenomenological analysis of the self's inner time-consciousness.[77]

Thus, in viewing some aspects of Royce's psychology, we have discovered that it provides the grounding for several important aspects of the ethical life. First, there is the role of feelings in conduct and the notion that evaluation takes place at the most basic level of experience in the form of feelings and/or attitudes taken toward stimuli of various sorts. Second, the basic feeling of restlessness is crucially interconnected to an instinct for persistence, which, for Royce, will prove extremely valuable to the imitative activities of the human being. Third, restlessness is also connected to mental initiative. Fourth, quiescence and docility also play a key role in human thought and experience and account for the basic conservatism and the desire to expend the least amount of energy in seeking to change things. Fifth, there is the clearly temporal nature of experience, which gives ground for the seeking of ends, but which also seems to demand social extension of self as well as temporal extension. Again, Royce's psychology is rich in insights; some of those relevant to ethics have been discussed, and more will be discussed as we turn to his notions about self, especially the question of how the self develops. Finally, we have seen how the individual's interest and will contribute to experience as well as imitation, habit, and social influence.

Royce's Self: A Being-with-Others

In discussing Royce's notions about the empirical self, we begin with the question, How is the self known? Royce affirmed throughout his philosophical career that there is no direct experience of the self: "Never in the present life, do we find the self as a given and realized fact."[78] "Our idea of the individual self is no mere present datum or collection of data."[79] There is no intuitive certainty about self, as Descartes argued. Royce emphatically rejected Descartes's *cogito ergo sum* as either a tautology or inconclusive,[80] and he likewise rejected any Cartesian notion of the self as an independent substance, only temporarily embodied and involved with the realm of nature. "Whatever the self is, it is not a Thing. It is not . . . a Substance."[81]

Nor was Royce happy with identifying the self as a subject of experience: "Whatever the Self as Subject is, it is nothing immediate, like a pain, or like a stone, that you stumble upon."[82] Royce endorses Hume's well-known statement that when he enters most intimately into what he calls himself, he finds only contents of experience, some impression or idea.[83] Royce writes: "When, in an empirical search for my true Self, I 'enter into myself,' I discover, so to speak, that I am not at home,—not to be found there, as Identical Subject, in the world of ex-

perience."[84] Royce argues that any "immediate knowledge" of inner life is knowledge "of the content of this moment." He continues:

> Your present pain or pleasure, the peculiar and indescribable quality of any sensa-
> tion, of the odor of a rose, or of the tones of a violin, or of a private grief, or of a per-
> sonal love of your own, such experience, I say is of this immediate character. . . .
> There is something peculiar and individual, meanwhile, about this immediate con-
> tent of each moment, something unique, which can never be repeated. The moment
> dies, the flavor is gone. *This* feeling you shall never feel again, *this* immediate knowl-
> edge you shall never repeat. In the phrase of Heraclitus: Into the same stream no
> one twice descends. And consciousness, in so far as it is immediate, is this sort of a
> Heraclitean flux.[85]

Thus, for Royce, the self is not a substance, not a "thing," nor can the self be directly known. Rather, for Royce, the self is a process. What one discovers in the
human consciousness is movement. In describing the general features of conscious life, in his *Outlines of Psychology,* Royce, in fact, like James, speaks of a *stream
of consciousness.* However, Royce had, in fact, already published this idea of a stream
of consciousness in *Religious Aspect* in 1885, five years before James's *Principles of
Psychology.* Thus, in this stream, says Royce, we can generally distinguish many
states or different contents of consciousness. He writes: "We live in a state of constant inner change, so that no portion of our consciousness ever remains long
without some alteration, while most of our contents are always changing pretty
rapidly."[86] Here, again, Royce agrees with Hume. However, in contrast to Hume,
Royce argues that in addition to the obvious variety of mental states, there is also
a "unity of consciousness," which means that, at any time, *"whatever is present tends
to form an always incomplete but still, in some respects, single conscious condition."*[87] Royce
continues: "The unity of consciousness is a fact constantly forced upon us whatever our point of view. For *no one can observe a mental variety of inner states without
finding these states together in his once inclusive condition of mind."*[88] Thus, says Royce,
"The one conscious state of the moment is always a unity consisting of a multiplicity."[89]

This unity with variety can best be observed, notes Royce, in cases where there
is a certain harmonious effect. This occurs especially when we listen to music
and are aware of several harmoniously related facts, such as tone, harmony, and
rhythm. This can also be seen in art with a complex of lines, forms, and colors
forming a pleasing totality. Yet, says Royce, even with disharmonious and dis-
tracting states of consciousness there are present contrasting aspects of unity and
variety, "in so far as the most painful and distressing complications of the moment are experienced at once."[90] Royce's ideas here are significant in a number of
ways, including a sense of the aesthetic of experience and an emphasis again on

harmony and on a deep psychological need within humans to harmonize. The self is "process," but it is a process that has a public and physical aspect as well as a private and inner aspect.

Royce does affirm that I am an object to myself in numerous ways, a so-called Empirical Ego. He writes:

> As so-called Empirical Ego, I exist in all kinds of immediate and derived forms as an object. As an object of merely immediate knowledge, a mere mass of organic sensations, I exist for myself, whenever I think of my own general state of personal well-being and of ill being. As Empirical Ego, I include also, very often, this body as a part of me. My life, my calling, my fortunes, my powers,—yes, my children or even my country, I can regard as part of my Empirical Ego. And in such senses I am for myself a vast mass of empirical objects and conditions which form in a greater or less degree one whole.[91]

Royce asserts, "The concept of the human self, like the concept of Nature comes to us, first, as an empirical concept, founded upon a certain class of experiences."[92] The empirical self is constituted by both public and private experiences. The self is a totality of facts. Among such facts are the predominantly corporeal ones, such as countenance, body, clothing, and physical actions—facts that both the self and the other may observe and comment on.[93] Royce acknowledges that if these facts radically change, so does the self.[94] He recognizes bodily continuity and the sense of a body as a criterion of self-identity, though not the ultimate criterion.[95]

Further, Royce fully recognizes the importance of the neurological. He writes: "The organic condition for all these manifestations of mind is the presence of the nervous system. . . . The externally observable discriminating sensitiveness which everywhere accompanies all the higher manifestations of mind is, physically speaking, a property of nervous tissue."[96] The self expresses itself physically in many ways, for example, through gestures, words, and habits. All of these, for Royce, as physical events are *"determined by physiological processes that occur in our nervous systems."*[97] In Royce's time, one could not observe the nervous system and its processes, but it is, in Royce's view, a proper subject for the psychologist. Today, of course, we can, in many senses, observe our brain and neurological processes, although a central question is, What is it that we are, in fact, observing? In the field of neuroethics, there is much concern about the nature and validity of observations made of areas through an fMRI while a subject is engaged in certain behaviors.[98] In this regard, Royce's views on memory are very contemporary.

Further, Royce saw growth and development as a central concept for the self, and this included the brain. In his view, the brain develops for a long time after birth and especially during the first seven years of life. He believed there was good evidence that new connections, structural and functional, form among its various parts. Further, these connections are determined not merely by the inherited tendencies of the organism, but also by the laws of habits and interactions with the environment and by "the actual conduct of the organism in question."[99]

In his *Outlines of Psychology,* Royce names four proper psychological methods: (1) the study of expressive signs of mental life; (2) the study of the relations between brain and mind; (3) introspection; and (4) psychological experiment. Royce would have been enthusiastic about the contemporary advances in neurophysiology and neuropsychology, and I am sure he also would have investigated with interest the field of neuroethics, yet he writes: "Psychology is by no means a branch of neurology."[100]

Royce is concerned to distinguish psychology and brain science for several reasons. First, he was concerned about reductionism of all psychological matters to neurological ones. Thus, in his time, the practice was to treat psychological dysfunctions as "nervous disorders." This reductionism is with us today in other and more insidious ways; mental illnesses today are primarily treated through the use of various drugs or now through new forms of brain stimulation and manipulation of brain functions. Royce's holistic view of psychological function is an excellent counter to these attempts to reduce the experiences of the human self to manifestations of brain processes.

Second, Royce's viewpoint would see neurological functions as an important component of human experience and behavior, but by no means the only or the most significant component. He would view very critically the attempts today to understand human behavior via manifestations of activity in certain areas of the brain.[101] Any psychological function, from his view, would need to be viewed from all aspects of the self, brain, body, mental activities, external behavior, and, above all, social context and functioning. I recommend again his essay on "Some Observations on the Anomalies of Self Consciousness."[102]

Royce's comments about the methods of a psychologist are, I believe, very instructive for contemporary psychologists and philosophers. First, about introspection, he writes:

> If carried on alone, without constant reference to the physical conditions of the mental life observed, and without a frequent comparing of notes with one's fellows, introspection can accomplish little of service for psychology. But, in union with other methods, introspection becomes an absolutely indispensable adjunct to all serious psychological study. The man who has never observed within will never be able to interpret the minds of others.[103]

The method of the study of the expressive signs of mental life, as indicated earlier, includes art, language, customs, faiths, but also the naturalist's study of the minds of animals through an observation of their behavior and skill. About this method, Royce writes:

> A pyramid or a flint hatchet, a poem or a dance, a game or a war, a cry or a book, the nursery play of a child or the behaviour of an insane person may be a physical expression of mental life such as an appreciative psychologist can both observe and more or less fully comprehend. The study of such facts, and of their physical causes and results, throws light both on what goes on in minds and upon the place which minds occupy in the natural world.[104]

Here Royce anticipates ethnology and anthropology, as well as phenomenology. In connection with this method, Royce makes a most insightful judgment. He writes:

> The facts to be studied are very numerous and complex, and easily misjudged, especially in the case of minds that are markedly different from our own. A good example of this difficulty is the common failure of even very intelligent men to understand a good many among the expressive functions of women, or the similar failure of women to comprehend a great many among those of men. The barrier of sex will probably prove a permanent hindrance, in some important directions and regions, to the progress of the scientific study of the human mind, so far as that study seeks to make the mental life of one sex fully comprehensible to psychologists who belong to the other.[105]

Royce was thus well ahead of his time in terms of contemporary psychological research on gender differences, reflected somewhat in popular books such as *Men Are from Mars, Women Are from Venus*.[106] Thus, we also find a contemporary leading researcher in sex differences telling us that "in girls, emotion is processed in the same area of the brain that processes language. So, it's easy for most girls to talk about their emotions. In boys, the brain regions involved in talking are separate from the regions involved in feeling. The hardest question for many boys to answer is: 'Tell me how you feel.'" Further, "Girls and boys respond to stress differently—not just in our species, but in every mammal scientists have studied. Stress enhances learning in males. The same stress impairs learning in females."[107]

A self, then, for Royce, is a certain totality of facts. In addition to the public facts available to the psychologist, other scientists, the self, and others, there is, for Royce, also a set of inner private facts of equal empirical status and importance for the self: "In addition to the external or corporeal Self of the phenomenal world, there is the equally empirical and phenomenal Self of the inner life, the series of states of consciousness, the feelings, thoughts, desires, memories, emotions, moods. These again, both my neighbor and myself regard as belonging to me, and as going to make up what I am."[108]

Aspects of this inner life have already been discussed: (1) the three aspects of sensitiveness, docility, and originality; (2) such feelings as pleasure and pain and restlessness and quiescence; (3) the roles of attention and habit; (4) an evaluative element at the most fundamental level, an attitude or response, an indication of will; and (5) temporality with its implications of self-extension and social extension. This empirical ego, the ordinary or empirical self-consciousness, is, for Royce, a product of experience. He describes this ego at its fundamental level as follows.

> If you ask what inner experiences form a basis for the formation of my idea of myself, the answer is, first of all, my experiences of my own internal bodily sensations, in particular of my "visceral" and my "muscular" sensations, including many masses of skin and joint sensations. . . . So far, the self is a relatively stable group of what are called the sensations of the common sensibility. To these get early joined my experiences of my emotions, and my feelings of voluntary control.[109]

For Royce, then, the self is a complex phenomenon, having various physiological and psychological aspects united and interrelated in many different ways. Thus, for example, Royce interweaves and interrelates human imaginative capacities with the sensory capacities. He holds that mental imagery is dependent both on sense perceptions and on motor responses to the environment. Deprivation of environment, in Royce's view, would lead to deprivation or stunting of the imaginative capacity. In fact, Royce argues that the Puritans, in the fear and thus denial of attractive sense experiences in worship, may have impoverished religious experience. He writes: *"[W]hatever the form of religious training, it ought deliberately to make use of a proper appeal to the senses."*[110] Further, *"the training of the imagination cannot occur apart from a fitting training of the senses."*[111] Not only does Royce integrate the sensory and the imaginative, but he also integrates the imaginative with conduct. *"The whole normal life of our imagination has almost intimate connection to our conduct."*[112] This connection between imagination and conduct relates to contemporary arguments about the role of imagination in moral judgment and argument.[113]

This connection between imagination and conduct is also why Royce, like many contemporary psychologists, recognizes the importance of "play" and the "play attitude" to human development, whether for children or adults. Play develops a person's abilities to integrate and to experience joy and fulfillment in integrative experiences. Play brings together sensory, motor, intellectual, and imaginative elements of the self, and it synthesizes habit and originality. As we recall, habit and spontaneity are, for Royce, integrative, interactive components of human experience. In play, these two aspects of the self come together. Combined with the habits and rules of play is a deep human restlessness, a feeling that exhibits itself in a desire to achieve both unity of experience and a sense of uniqueness, of placing one's own mark on the experience. This restlessness is linked to mental initiative, to originality, and to individualistic tendencies.

Thus, again, for Royce, the self is a very complex phenomenon, a process that involves temporality and growth and the interaction of numerous aspects: neurological, physiological, psychological, and social. Further, Royce does not believe the self can be reduced to any of its aspects. In regard to all facts of the self, he would oppose any reduction to any of the other facts, and particularly to the brain only. In addition, with regard to inner facts, he would no doubt agree with the following statement by a contemporary philosopher: "It is also questionable whether the first-person phenomenological feel of subjective experience can be entirely captured by third-person description of brain functions."[114]

And to all of the facts of self, Royce adds another fundamental factor, the social. In connection with habits, he argues that "a great deal of my natural consciousness of myself depends upon certain habits that grow up in me in connection with my early *social experiences*."[115] Throughout his philosophical career, Royce argued that self-consciousness arises out of a social contrast between self and non-self, between what is mine and what is not mine. Royce writes: "I affirm that our empirical self-consciousness, from moment to moment, depends upon a series of contrast effects, whose psychosocial origin lies in our literal social life, and whose continuance in our present conscious life, whenever we are alone, is due to habit, to our memory of literal social relations, and to an imaginative idealization of these relations."[116] The child recognizes early that there are in the world the experiences, intents, and interests of other people—his parents, siblings, playmates. At an early age the child experiences a contrast between his own desires and those of others, between what he can control and what others seem to control. And there is the strong imitative aspect of the self. Royce writes:

> Nobody amongst us men comes to self-consciousness, so far as I know, except under the persistent influence of his social fellows. A child in the earlier stages of development . . . shows you, as you observe him, a process of development of self-consciousness in which, at every stage, the Self of the child grows and forms itself through Imitation, and through functions that cluster around the Imitation of others. . . . And his self-consciousness, as it grows, feeds upon social models, so that at

every stage of his awakening life, his consciousness of the Alter is a step in the advance of his consciousness. His playmates, his nurse or mother, or the workmen whose occupation he sees, and whose power fascinates him, appeal to his imitativeness and set him copies for his activities. He learns his little arts, and as he does so, he contrasts his own deeds with those of his model. . . . *Now contrast is, in our conscious life, the mother of clearness. What the child does instinctively, and without comparison with the deeds of others, may never come to his clear consciousness as his own deeds at all.* What he learns imitatively, and then reproduces, perhaps in joyous obstinacy, as an act that enables him to display himself over against others—this constitutes the beginning of his self-conscious life.[117]

It should be noted that selective attention and the interests and desires of the organism play a role, for Royce, in imitation. I focus on what is familiar and thus the importance of past experience. But I also am attracted by what my friends, parents, siblings, and teachers have been interested in, and herein is the social influence. However, there is also what uniquely attracts the individual. Reflecting on his own experience in the mining camps, Royce notes that he was quite familiar with mining, but the activities of miners never attracted his imitative tendencies. He writes: "As I happened to dislike nearly all the miners whom I saw, my imitativeness was never excited by them. I accordingly formed no apperceptive masses of ideas about gold or about mining, and always heartily despised the whole enterprise."[118] In chapter 1, we did note Royce's interest in engineering, but that interest developed from the book on the career and achievements of engineer John Ericcson given him by his mother.

Further, Royce argues for a tendency in the human self to "deliberate idealization of our imitations, to deliberate deviations from the literal." "One's play is one's own original fashion."[119] Children, says Royce, often mock a model in a way that is more or less consciously untrue to the model and will even engage in a pretend imitation, an exaggeration.[120] As will become evident shortly, in imitating there is also a desire to contrast and to be other than merely what one finds in one's social models.

Another part of the delicate play between ego and non-ego is the development of a self-evaluation process. As a child, I soon become aware that the other person is also aware of me and has an opinion of me. My neighbor approves me, and now I take note and value myself. When the other person expresses dislike in some way, I note this, and it arouses in me some kind of response: a response of resentment, of contempt, of shame, of obstinacy, of a desire to reform, and even of a wish to be someone else. Consciousness of self takes on a new flavor and complexity. What emerges, says Royce, is a notion of my ideal self, the self that I want to be, and this occurs in contrast to what I appear now to be.

In addition, there emerges a desire for some kind of unity, for some kind of clearness about who I am. Royce writes:

> Hereby the contrast between Ego and Alter, no longer confined to the relations between my literal neighbor and myself, can be refined into the conscious contrast between my self-critical Self and my naïve Self, between my higher and lower self, or between my conscience and my impulses. My reflective life, as it empirically occurs to me moment to moment, is a sort of abstract epitome of my whole social life, viewed as to those aspects which I find peculiarly significant. And thus my experience of myself gets a provisional unity.[121]

But the unity is provisional and unsatisfactory. Your empirical self, in one aspect, is purely social; you take yourself to be whatever the world has made you. But the self is restless, willful, and a dreamer. One can begin to think about an ego that might have been or could be; one seeks a meaning, a purpose, an ideal.[122] You are a temporal being, moving toward the future; restlessness drives you forward to new experiences and to something more. You are a seeker, a being seeking ever-enriched meaning and satisfaction. You seek a different kind of unity.

This unity is achieved by giving oneself to an ideal, to a life plan. To achieve a unity of one's life there must be selective attention, exclusion, and committed seeking. You give your attention to a specific ideal to the exclusion of all barely possible ideals, which you now reject. Your ideal provides harmony, organization, and unity of life. "Now, also, whatever happens to you, you live one life; namely, the life of aiming towards that goal."[123] You are a seeker, but more importantly, now you have an ideal that expresses the meaning of your unique experience, and you can rightly contrast yourself with all the rest of the world's life. Royce writes: *By this meaning of my life-plan, by this possession of an ideal, by this Intent always to remain another than my fellows . . . by this, and not by possession of any Soul-Substance, I am defined and created a Self.*[124] Royce adds emphasis as follows:

> I, the individual, am what I am by virtue of the fact that my intention, my meaning, my task, my desire, my hope, my life, stand in contrast to those of any other individual. If I am any reality, whatever, then I am doing something that nobody else can do, and meaning something that nobody else can mean. I have my relatively free will that nobody else can possess. The uniqueness of my meaning is the one essential fact about me.[125]

For Royce, the true Self is the totality of the empirical consciousness viewed as having unity of meaning, as exemplifying an ideal, and as seeking to fulfill a life plan. Royce declares: "A plan in life, pervading and comprehending my experiences, is, I say the *condition sine qua non* of the very existence of myself as this one, whole, connected Ego."[126] The self who achieves this plan is, for Royce, an ethical self, and thus a person. A person is the moral individual viewed as meaning or as aiming toward an ideal. This person becomes a subject of value, one to whom moral attributes can be given. And these, for Royce, need not be positive. He writes: "[T]he term 'person' . . . can mean only the moral individual, i.e., the individual viewed as meaning or aiming towards an ideal, good or relatively bad, angelic or relatively diabolical, lawful, or relatively anarchical."[127]

I become a person by choosing my ideal, by being loyal to it, by loving it. I have made a decision to exclude other ideals and causes because they do not realize my true self. I engage in a journey toward self-discovery and self-definition in contrast to other beings and ideals. For Royce, this journey is continuous since ideals may change in light of experience and causes may broaden, but also because Royce believes there is in time no satisfied will. The future is always ahead of us. "The true or metaphysically real Ego of a man . . . is simply the totality of his experience *in so far as* he consciously views this experience, as, in its meaning, the struggling but never completed expression of his coherent plan in life, the changing but never completed partial embodiment of his own ideal."[128]

Each self, as a temporal finite being, embodies a limited perspective, and thus our meanings and our goals can be only partial. This is why there must be self-transcendence via community and a seeking of wider and wider perspectives and goals and ideals. This brings us then to Royce's ethics and ultimately to his philosophy of loyalty, the subjects of the next chapter.

Royce's Ethical Theory

3

This discussion of Royce's ethical theory begins with his 1880 essay "Tests of Right and Wrong"[1] and treats various expressions and refinements of his main ideas up and through his 1916 course on ethics, further exploring the continuity and flow of Royce's thought as well as the interconnections among his various concerns—scientific, ethical, metaphysical, epistemic, social-political, and religious. The 1880 essay establishes several key themes: (1) Royce's use of various methods, including the historical and the analytic, to deal with ethical issues; (2) his lifelong concern about various ethical conflicts: ethical realism–idealism; egoism-altruism; and autonomy-duty; (3) his sympathetic, yet critical, attitude toward ethical skepticism and ethical pessimism and an attempt to overcome their negatives; (4) his conviction that human beings desire unity and harmony; and (5) his refinement and continuation of the need for both self-development and moral action to extend one's view temporally and socially, and thus to include the concerns of others in one's ethical considerations. In discussing *The Religious Aspect of Philosophy* we will highlight another of Royce's lifelong concerns, namely, to critically yet sympathetically assess naturalism and evolutionary ethics.[2]

Royce's concerns are amazingly contemporary. The ethical conflicts remain with us today, particularly the ethical realism–idealism debate and the conflict between deontological ethics (autonomy) and utilitarian ethics (social good). Royce's treatment of these conflicts provides insight relevant to contemporary ethical discussions. Another example of this is his concern with ethical skepticism and ethical pessimism. The relevance of Royce's ideas will be fully addressed in the final chapter.

Further, "naturalism," in a variety of forms, is common in contemporary philosophy, and naturalized ethics is very much the philosophical topic. Royce believed evolutionary thought had much to offer for understanding human experience and life, but believed it could not provide a ground for "ethical theory" nor for establishing "free will." And in his writings on science and on the "uniformity of nature" he establishes excellent grounds to question the basic assumption of all these endeavors—the "truth" of a strictly deterministic position, supposedly a truth based on the physical sciences.[3] Royce argued that it is social motives that lead us to postulate a uniform, predictable natural world. Man's basic interest in nature, argues Royce, is to win control over it. Thus, "the uniformity of nature" is a socially useful notion. It reveals no absolute truth; it can never be fully verified in human experience.[4] Royce's insights on these issues will also be addressed in the final chapter.

In his 1880 essay "Tests of Right and Wrong," Royce distinguishes two methodological approaches to ethics: the historical and the analytic.[5] The "historical" method, says Royce, studies the genesis and development of the moral ideas of men. The "analytic" method seeks to understand the moral as it is.[6] Royce believes each method appropriate and necessary, and yet not quite adequate for developing an ethical theory. His own thought will draw on both but will supplement them. The central question addressed in the 1880 essay is, What is the ground of a distinction between right and wrong, a distinction assumed by the moral agent and the common world of moral action? In pursuing the question, Royce explores the nature of judgment and then of conduct. He concludes that an adequate account of judgment and conduct requires extension of self temporally and socially and a notion of "possible experience."

In 1885 in *Religious Aspect*, Royce continues to probe the question of the nature and ground of the distinction between right and wrong. Royce critically examines answers provided by the moral realist and the moral idealist. He finds both valuable but also inadequate and seeks to go beyond their insights in his search for an answer. In addition, Royce uses the analytic (phenomenological) method to explore the human experience of moral skepticism and argues that its accompanying desire is for harmonization of values.[7] In this spirit Royce examines the history of ethical theory for adequacy of expression to human moral experience[8]

Again, as the systematic bridge builder he is, Royce seeks to find kernels of wisdom in each theory and to harmonize them in a more adequate understanding of human ethical life.

Royce presents extensive exploration of concepts of self, of moral agent, and of moral person in *The Conception of God* (1897) and *The World and the Individual* (1899 and 1901). In 1908, he broadens his discussion of the self as moral seeker by focusing on the following set of questions: "For what do I live? Why am I here? For what am I good? Why am I needed?"[9] This, says Royce, is the hardest of human practical problems. The answer to this central life question is loyalty.

In 1910, Royce's future daughter-in-law, Elizabeth Randolph, wrote a letter to him with a series of questions, the central one being "Why *must* we live?" Royce refers Elizabeth to his book *The Philosophy of Loyalty,* but also provides this clear answer: "[T]he great principle of the art of giving sense to life, is the principle:— Have a cause, choose it, and having chosen it, be fearlessly and steadily faithful to it."[10] This moves us forward to Royce's *Philosophy of Loyalty* and the harmonization of values and the unification of the self through loyalty to a cause and to serial extension of self and community in the commitment, loyalty to loyalty. In this context we will briefly discuss Royce's ethics from the vantage point of his 1915–1916 Extension Course on Ethics. In this final work on ethics, Royce continues the argument for the harmonizing of values, for balancing self-interest, autonomy, and duty, and for uniting self-fulfillment and communal fulfillment. He proposes three ethical leading ideas—freedom, goodness, and duty—and argues for a balanced synthesis of all three. In this work Royce also discusses loyalty as exemplified and illustrated in family relations. These issues will be treated more fully in the chapter on social and political philosophy; however, the exposition of Royce's later ethics by Oppenheim in his book *Royce's Mature Ethics* is excellent and need not be restated here.[11]

Royce's ethical thought is rich indeed and well worth exploring in terms of our new, contemporary ethical landscape. He develops a highly sophisticated concept of loyalty that synthesizes both the serving of one's own very personal causes and the transcending of mere self-interest or sterile benevolence. His careful balancing of individual and communal interests could provide a much-needed solution to concerns in international bioethics and in health care ethics about how best to deal with the conflicts between Western individualistic ethics and other views, such as the Confucian familial ethic. Another significant contribution to discussions in contemporary ethics is Royce's notion of the moral self. The moral self is a self dedicated to a unique cause that unifies its own life and provides self-realization, and yet at the same time this self serves the principle of loyalty to loyalty, which promotes loyalty in all beings and thus also their self-realization. This unique notion of a moral self adds new insight to the contemporary debates about the relationship between personal identity and ethics, issues that will be explored further in our final chapter.

Royce's Ethical Ideas: Conflict and Pessimism

In his first excursion into ethical theory in his 1880 essay "Tests of Right and Wrong," Royce sets out two major ways to study ethical phenomena: a historical examination of their genesis and an analysis of their structure as they now exist.[12] Insightfully, Royce notes that each method embodies a basic postulate or assumption about the nature of the phenomenon it studies. (If only philosophers today were more alert to the assumptions of their methods.) The postulate of the historical method is "The forms of things are determined by the growth of things."[13] This method has general confidence in the uniformity of nature. The historical method seeks to give a complete account of how the moral ideas of men grew up. This method is, of course, that of evolutionary ethics. The analytic method assumes certain permanent elements of the world and has relationship to the science of mathematics and the "world of ideals." This method seeks to distinguish, describe, and criticize certain ethical tendencies in human character and moral consciousness.

Royce points out the central weakness of each method. About the analytic method, Royce observes: "[I]t is plain that if one determines to base his system of ethics on an analysis of his own moral consciousness as it is now, he will probably fail for lack of a sufficient variety of illustration. . . . His code will be provincial in the narrowest sense . . . or not be based on an intelligent appreciation of the diversity of human life."[14] In assessing the historical method, Royce argues that it can, on the one hand, lead to a social relativism, a kind of moral principle that "as a rule, the truly civilized man does not steal." Royce writes: "Historically . . . there is no moral fact discoverable that makes my theft bad for me unless I just now happen to regard it as bad. . . . [T]his study of evolution does not get rid of the fact that what makes the call of morality binding on each of us is his own inclination to be moral."[15] "History is powerless before the fact that whatever the moral consciousness of men has sprung from it is more than enlightened selfishness."[16] Essentially, evolutionary study cannot demonstrate the binding force of individual obligations; it cannot answer the individual question, Why be moral? This seems an important claim to be explored in light of the contemporary concern for "naturalized ethics." In fact, it is a major objection to contemporary "moral realism."[17]

Royce believes that both the historical and the analytic methods are necessary and that they are in no conflict. Further, they give us certain key insights. About the analytic method, Royce writes: "To be sure each man's self-analysis must be the foundation of all his philosophy. Nothing can be more certain than what we really observe in ourselves. But for suggestions as to what we should seek in ourselves, this process of historical analysis is invaluable."[18] The historical method keeps us in touch with experience.

In continuing his analysis, Royce formulates a crucial assumption, namely that we must begin with this given: *a world of moral agents, required to define most generally their mutual relations as moral agents, and the kind of work morally devolving upon each.*[19] Royce then provides us with a definition of a moral agent as "a being not hindered by external interference, acting solely according to the laws of his own nature, and possessed of the sense that distinguishes between right and wrong."[20] There follows a description of plain instances of the distinction between right and wrong, including rescuing a shipwrecked crew, not exploding dynamite under the house of someone you dislike, speaking kindly to a crying child, and not beating a dog just to hear him howl. This discussion reminds one of the work of contemporary ethicist Charles Taylor, who argues that the self's ability to have moral intuitions and to articulate them presupposes the existence of evaluative frameworks provided by a community.[21]

Further, in this section of the essay, Royce exemplifies his belief that philosophy is the critical inquiry into living. Royce valued common human experience and "the common mind," unlike many philosophers of this and the past century. In a letter to Arthur O. Lovejoy, he asserts: "The popular mind is deep and means a thousand times more than it explicitly knows. The philosopher's endless task is to find out what this deep mind means, and to tell what it means."[22]

An essential aspect of the common moral world and human mind is the assumption of a distinction between right and wrong. The central problem of the essay is to find a foundation for this distinction. Royce addresses the problem by a phenomenological analysis of consciousness and of the nature of judgment and conduct. Royce asserts: "To distinguish right from wrong is to perform an act of knowledge, to make a conscious judgment."[23]

Royce's analysis of the act of judgment leads to the identification of three elements. First, there is a fact or datum given that I passively receive and cannot, *at the time*, alter.[24] Royce identifies the second element as a "persuasion" that a present judgment has some sort of "objective validity," which the datum itself cannot carry; involved in this is recognition of the past as given and as having once been actually present. "Expectancy" is the third element: "I actively expect future experience. It is plain that without expectation of a future, my acknowledgment of the reality of past time would have little worth."[25] Expectancy, for Royce, is the most immediate important element for action.

The inability to deal with the future and expectancy is Royce's main criticism against Schopenhauer and his pessimism. Royce had great respect for Schopenhauer, and he himself struggled early in his life with pessimism; for Royce it is a fundamental aspect of inner life, of a phenomenology of moral experience, and, indeed, of religious consciousness.[26] However, Royce believes "ethical pessimism must be transcended because it constitutes a major hindrance to leading an ethical life." Pessimism results in a fatalist attitude, and "[t]he fatalist views the future as having the same value for his feelings that the irrevocable past already has."[27] Pessimism gives no credence to the possible.

"Time" is an essential concept in Royce's philosophy, and it is certainly crucial to any ethical theory. Royce writes: "Whoever says 'I ought do thus or thus' stands in a present moment of time and looks forward to a future. . . . In a world where there was no succession, there would be no morality."[28]

Royce now focuses on the relationship between temporality and morality. Conduct, argues Royce, is actively directed toward an end, and in order to form the idea of an end, it is necessary to have a synthetic experience of time. Royce writes:

> In a present moment of experience there must be at least one desire, i.e., a certain sort of feeling, itself apprehended as a datum. There must also be a simple judgment of expectation. For when we act we expect future experience of some sort, and wish to affect that experience. There must also be a judgment of possibility, i.e., an acknowledgment of some fixed objective relation of which we propose to avail ourselves, coupled with expectation of some particular case under that relation which may occur if our act is properly directed.[29]

Royce writes again: "To act for a purpose is to seek satisfaction for a momentary desire, by making real one of several possible experiences."[30] Conduct or action for an end, then, is made possible through (1) desires, (2) judgments of expectation, (3) judgments of possibility, and (4) the "the entirely unique moment of choice or conquest of one desire over opposing ones."[31] Royce names this moment "will."[32]

Royce continues his analysis of an act of conduct and moves on to claim that the greater the time span involved in our conduct, the more complexity there will be. Thus, says Royce, consider an act of the simplest form. Each act has three conditions, and in this case these are as follows: (1) at the moment of choice only one desire is in consciousness; (2) there is but one possible way of fulfilling it; and (3) the expected experience fills a single future instant.[33] An example of such a simple kind of conduct would be my extending my arm in order to grab something to eat. But, if I stop to consider whether the edible item is "good in the long run for me," my temporal horizon becomes expanded both into the future and also into the past because I now consider the memory of a disagreeable experience with this item. Royce argues that after considering various complexities of conduct, we would observe that the further the horizon recedes in both directions of time, the more are the elements integrated and the more complex is the conduct. "The general principle follows: That conduct is as a rule more and more complex according as the future experience that is expected at the moment of acting is more and more extended."[34]

Royce then asserts that the morality of an act is likewise related to extension, in this case, extension of consideration of consequences: "An act is complex according to the extent of time that was taken into account in performing it. It is good or evil in similar ratio, according to the extent of conscious experience that it is designed to affect, and according to the way in which it is designed to affect that experience."[35]

Royce illustrates this idea with an interesting case, that of pulling the trigger of a gun. In this case, I can conceive of the amusement that may be expected by pulling the trigger and feeling the power of the effect, but I presumably also note the harmful consequences that may follow from a careless discharge of the gun. I decide to pull the trigger. The result is a serious injury. In terms of judgment, says Royce, one focuses not on consequences but on expectations. Royce writes: "My act was wrong because, conceiving as I did of two possible experiences, one of slight pleasure, the other of great pain, I chose to make both real, because the little pleasure seemed worth more to me than the great pain could overbalance."[36] Again, Royce affirms that acts are approved or disapproved according to the expectation with which they are performed, not according to results.[37]

From this analysis, he proposes the following rule of conduct: "In thy acts treat all the future as if it were present."[38] In other words, in performing an act subject to moral judgment, one must consider all possible results of the act in question; all future consequences remote or near, in the most desired aggregate. Further, in considering the right and wrong of acts, one must avoid, says Royce, "the illusion of perspective in time." In Royce's view, temporal extension implies social self-extension. "When I estimate the consequences of my acts, for whom are these consequences? Do I mean consequences for me, or for my fellows, or for all of us?"[39] It is not *my* momentary interest that matters, but *our* interests. "I must include my neighbor's future with my own, and order my conduct accordingly."[40]

This insight into the intrinsic temporal and social character of moral acts is barred, notes Royce, by the "illusion of selfishness," which tells us that some expected experiences, our own, have more reality than those of our neighbor. Thus we want to place a higher premium on pleasing ourselves and on following our separated interests than on harmonizing them with those of others.[41] However, argues Royce, sticking to the experiential and to our empirical analysis of our conscious life, we can dispel the illusion of selfishness: we examine consciousness as it is, not as it grew; and we find in it no absolute ego given, no organized self who must be served above all. Here we recall Royce's arguments that the self is not a datum and his criticisms of the views of Descartes and Hume on knowledge of the self. Thus, says Royce, my selfhood is no more a datum of consciousness than is that of my neighbor. Royce writes:

> My existence as a permanent real entity is no more and no less given in consciousness than is the experience of my neighbor. . . . The lack of feeling of self-interest in conceiving them does not make these conceived experiences less acknowledged and expected realities. The difference is an emotional one, not one of thought. I know my neighbor to be as real as myself. His experiences are no more given to me than my own past and future experiences are now given. Yet none the less I posit their reality.[42]

What does this insight mean? It means that all should be viewed equally. "Every present act should, therefore, be ordered for the welfare of all future conscious life, in case it should be ordered for the welfare of any future conscious life at all."[43] Royce argues that an analysis of conscious life reveals that my own life and my neighbor's life must be posited as equally real and equally worthy of consideration in moral acts. This is a worthy ideal and an excellent statement of what it means in practice to take a moral attitude. This notion will appear throughout Royce's philosophical career and is embodied in his philosophy of loyalty. Royce will refine his notion of the "moral attitude" as he develops his moral philosophy, and the most mature version of it will appear in the attitudes involved in the process of interpretation.

We turn now to *Religious Aspect*. This work follows up directly on Royce's excursion in the 1880 essay and in several ways.[44] First, it makes the same fundamental assumption of common human experience, namely, "we will suppose a moral agent in the presence of this concrete world of human life in which we all believe ourselves to exist."[45] Second, the central question of this essay is the same as that of "Tests," namely, "What is the real nature and ground of this distinction between right and wrong?" Third, Royce employs both the historical and analytic methods. Fourth, in this work Royce also deals with the "illusion of selfishness."

Royce reframes the central question in terms of the conflict between the ethical realist and the ethical idealist. The ethical realist, like the historicist, is one who seeks to find the basis for the distinction between right and wrong, good and evil, in the real world. The ethical idealist, like the person of the analytic method, is the person who seeks to demonstrate if possible an ideal as the true and only ideal, without in any way making it depend upon physical reality. These methods and views are for Royce opposites. He writes: "The judgments: *This is*, and *This is good*, are once for all different; and they have to be reached by widely different methods of investigation."[46] Further, neither view is adequate. To base our ideal on the real is to betray the distinctive thrust of the moral ought, and yet pursuing the ideal in an ideal world alone ends in caprice and ultimately in falling back on an external justification.[47] In contemporary ethics, this would be the position of "subjectivism," and perhaps several other forms of "non-cognitivism." These views will be discussed and criticized, via Royce's ideas, in the final chapter.

Royce asks: How shall we decide between these two views, ethical realism and ethical idealism? He writes: "Alas! The decision is the whole labor of founding a moral doctrine. We have not yet seen deeply enough into their opposition. They may both be one-sided. The truth may lie in the middle. But as yet we have no right to dogmatize."[48] Again, if only we in philosophy today proceeded in this manner. The debate between moral realism and moral non-cognitivism (ethical idealism) continues today, in a dogmatic fashion and without any awareness of Royce's work on this issue in the 1880s.

In his search for a solution to the conflict, Royce turns first to the history of philosophy and various speculations about the ideal. His motives in this pursuit probably are manifold, but several have been identified. Harry Cotton notes that the excursion demonstrates that moral idealists are unable to supply a moral criterion that will justify itself.[49] This is certainly one of Royce's conclusions. Second, Peter Fuss believes that Royce's "polemics" against other ethical theories are designed primarily to show that realist and idealist theories, given their starting points, must reach conflicting conclusions about the nature of moral distinctions.[50] This seems plausible given Royce's assertion that "[t]he controversy that the last chapter considered is a controversy endlessly repeated in the history of moral doctrines."[51] Another aim, as we shall see, is to reach the conclusions of the 1880 essay and a notion of a "moral insight." Finally, in this excursion into history, Royce provides us with insights into the theories that are examined, and some of the central ideas are carried forward into his own ethical thought.

Royce first critically examines Greek ethics, primarily the views of Plato and the Stoics. Royce argues that each fails to establish their ideals on a firm ground; their ideals appear ultimately to be a matter of caprice in choice. Each theory, for Royce, reveals a "living idea" that should be carried forth in any ethical theory. Plato, he notes, provides us with the concept of justice. About the Stoics he writes: "The Stoics have a new thought to offer, one that would have been

Evolutionary . . . if they could but have grasped and taught its full Meaning. . . . Their new thought, which gave foundation to their moral ideals, was the thought of the perfect equality of all men in the presence of the universal. Reason to which all alike ought to conform."[52]

Turning to the ethics of Jesus, Royce hints at themes that will later appear in *The Problem*. Jesus provides us with a morality based on a principle of Infinite Love: "Act as one receiving and trying to return an Infinite Love. To thy neighbor act as it befits one so beloved to act toward his brother in love."[53] Involved in this ethic is the grounding of the idea of duty to one's neighbor in the consciousness that his neighbor is his brother.[54] Here is the notion of the necessary social expansion of consciousness, already a concern in "Tests of Right and Wrong," and a theme continuous in Royce's philosophy.

Royce's next critique is directed toward "moral sense" theories. These fail because they oscillate between equally unsatisfactory forms of ethical realism and ethical idealism and thus cannot give an adequate ground for moral choice. Royce writes: "We insist then that one of the first questions of the moralist must be, *why conscience in any given case is right*. Or, to put the case otherwise, ethical doctrine must tell us why, if the devil's conscience approves of the devil's acts, as it may well do, the devil's conscience is nevertheless wrong."[55] As we discovered in chapter 2, Royce was exploring the notion of "conscience" before Freud published on the subject. Royce's own view on "conscience" is quite interesting, and relevant to ethical theory and to our present discussion. The most obvious connection to Freud is evident in an 1895 essay. Royce writes:

> Conscience is a well-knit system of socially acquired habits of estimating acts—a system constituted as to be easily aroused in conscious presence by the coming of the idea of any hesitantly conceived act. If conscience is aroused in the presence of such a hesitant desire to act, one has purely as a matter of social habit, a disposition to have present both the tendency to the action, and the disposition to judge it, standing to one another in the now familiar relation of Ego and non-Ego.[56]

How the act is estimated depends on the passion associated with the act. If the desire for the act is strong and a vigorous temptation, then, says Royce, the reproof appears as "the colder non-Ego, the voice of humanity or God." I want to have my own way but the "authoritative inner non-Ego will not let me go free."[57] If, however, the desire for the act is less passionate and I am resolute, then I personally identify with the "voice of humanity" and disdain the incipient "less righteous act."[58] More importantly, in neither case, for Royce, do I reach autonomous moral consciousness. In the first case I am controlled by the pleasure-pain drive, and in the second by an unexamined conformism to outside standards. Royce believes that true moral behavior is neither. This notion of conscience also contains another idea, namely, that the social context, although crucial to self-development, also inflames self-will and in fact trains the self for self-assertion. This will be discussed later in this chapter.

In his 1893 essay "On Certain Psychological Aspects of Moral Training," Royce contends that there are two dispositions or motives found in the developed conscience of any civilized man. These are: "Live for the general good" and "Always be true to your own rational higher self." Royce then argues that "these motives ought to be somehow completely harmonized. . . . It is our ignorance of how to harmonize them which makes our actual consciences such variable and complex products of imperfect experience."[59] The answer to the dilemma, asserts Royce, is to "[b]e always mindful of the will and the needs of other men, but have a universal plan, a life-rule, for the guidance of the will." "No man without a plan is moral."[60] The conflicting two motives are, of course, those involved in the discussion of egoism/altruism in "Tests" and in *Religious Aspect*. Again, harmonization is the urged resolution. These issues will occur more explicitly in his 1916 ethics, where he will bring together the three ethical ideas of freedom, goodness, and duty. The theme of a life plan has already been discussed but will be central to *The Philosophy of Loyalty*, and in his *Pittsburg Lectures* of 1910 Royce writes: "My philosophy of loyalty . . . is an endeavor to harmonize individual right with social duty, private judgment with a willingness to accept a certain sort of external authority, the personal consciousness with the voice of our wiser moral traditions."[61]

In his 1894 article "The Imitative Functions and Their Place in Human Nature," Royce discusses the formation of a "social conscience." He writes: "Our social morality . . . is in one direction dependent upon our regard for the will, the interest, the percepts, or the welfare of our fellows. Now such regard is, in its turn, dependent upon our power, by imitation, to experience and to comprehend the suggested will, interest, harmony, and desires of those about us. So, then, without imitativeness, [there is] no chance for the development of the social conscience."[62] Imitativeness is a basic human instinct, and thus not only does it provide grounds for a social conscience, but it also accounts for our human ability to expand consciousness in a social direction to include our fellows' interests and values. As evident from our discussion of Royce's belief that self-consciousness develops via a contrast-effect with others, it is correct to say that self-interest appears later than the social connection with others, and is, in fact, learned and promoted by the social. It is the habits and states of self-consciousness, not social consciousness, that are derived and secondary. The essence of the human self is, at the deepest level, "being-with others."

In fact, turning back to Royce's discussion in *Religious Aspect,* we find him dealing with the conflict between altruism and egoism. In this context Royce examines, in some detail, the evolutionary ethics of Herbert Spencer. The central idea of this ethics is the notion that once we discover the goal toward which the evolutionary process tends, this goal will become our moral ideal and be thus grounded in evolutionary fact. Royce gives us two critiques of this view. First, this view confuses the notion of progress, the conception of growth in complexity and definiteness of natural phenomena, with the conception of growth in moral worth. This is a confusion of what will be with what ought to be. Royce again points to the inadequate move from fact to ideal: "Why should I work for future ages, if it is not already quite plain, apart from any knowledge of evolution, that I ought to do what I can just now for my brother here?"[63] Unfortunately, this confusion of natural progress and moral progress is very much with us today in various forms and certainly is embodied in a technological imperative that if we can do it, we ought to do it.

The second criticism against evolutionary ethics raised by Royce is the failure to distinguish between moral and prudent motives for action. Spencer, says Royce, argues that it is in our enlightened self-interest to be altruistic because unless we cooperate with our fellow men in furthering the evolutionary goal inherent in the social order we shall fail to attain our own ends. Royce argues that appraisal of moral worth has primarily to do with motives and not consequences; the actions of the clever selfish man and the man motivated by regard for the well-being of others may have the same results, but the second man is "generally regarded as deserving of moral praise" even when his actions fail to bring about the intended result.[64] Ultimately, Royce's evaluation of evolutionary ethics is that it can inform us about available means of action and for the realization of ethical ideals, but it cannot judge the moral worth of the action or find an ethical ideal.[65] Royce's extensive discussion of evolutionary ethics is worth reexamination today; some of the issues will be discussed in the final chapter.

Finally, in continuing the examination of the conflict of egoism and altruism, Royce criticizes ethical theories founded upon pity or sympathy. In an interesting psychological analysis, Royce critiques Schopenhauer's view that a genuine feeling of pity for another's suffering always leads one to try unselfishly to alleviate it. Royce argues that pity is an indeterminate impulse and that, in fact, for most people the first impulse is to get rid of the pain that the neighbor is causing you to feel. Sympathy can lead to recoil in terror from the pathos of the sufferer's condition, and pity can end in hatred of suffering and contempt for the sufferer. But finally, Royce says, the foundation provided for the worth of this moral principle seems to be solely in the fact that it exists.

Another insightful comment on the role of sympathy in moral action is made by Royce in his essay on John Fiske, a philosopher and historian and author of *Outlines of a Cosmic Philosophy,* published in 1874. Fiske did much to promote evolutionary theory in America. To fully understand Royce's comment on sympathy in moral behavior, we need a brief discussion of its context. Fiske argued for the development of moral consciousness via a series of widening communities, evolving in four stages. The first stage is the emergence of the first essential community, that of mother-child, which, in turn, requires the development of the community of family to preserve family and race. Subsidiary communities then develop to protect the family: clan, tribe, nation, and humanity. Each community develops a shared consciousness, which includes shared values. This evolves into virtues of loyalty to clan and courage to help the community withstand the eliminating selection of evolutionary nature. At a third stage there develops a shared meaningful worldview and group tradition and participation in skills. At this level science, religion, and philosophy serve as instruments for developing that meaningful worldview.[66]

In this context Royce identifies the origin of the sympathetic aspect of human behavior: "Thus all civilization develops, in a sense, about the bed of the helpless infant. And the sense of duty grows from the same root. In consequence, our idea of duty is primarily an idea of helpfulness to those whom we love. And this accounts for the evolutionary origin of the sympathetic aspect of morality. All ideals of kindliness thus have their source in an unselfish fondness for fellow beings that need help."[67]

In this passage Royce gives us yet a third foundation for the natural social expansion of human consciousness, namely, an evolutionary one, based in the nature of our human social world. This is added to the revelation that the reality of ego finds no base in human consciousness, and thus the assumption of the equal reality of self and others appears justified. Finally, there is the basic biological/psychological instinct for imitation[68] and the evidence that self-consciousness arises out of social interaction, making social-consciousness prior to self-consciousness.

Ethical Skepticism

In his discussion of ethics in *Religious Aspect,* Royce sought to answer the question, What grounds the distinction between right and wrong? He found that both ethical realism and ethical idealism fail to provide such a ground. Their ideals fall on the stake of the caprice of personal whim or only provide means for realizing moral action through factual assertions. The inevitable outcome of Royce's search for an answer appears to be ethical skepticism. This problem, this instability of ideals, is shared by ethical theorists, but it is also exemplified in the genuine modern pessimism of a Schopenhauer, who despairs as he finds life restless and aimless, or in the poetry of many of the Romantics. This whimsy of ideals is, says Royce, even one of daily life.

Royce believes he finds a satisfactory answer to the conflicts he has analyzed and the resulting skepticism. The answer lies within our own moral experience of the conflict of wills. Skepticism comes about when we contemplate two opposing aims in such a way as momentarily to share them both. The conflict is in us, and we feel skeptical indecision because both aims represent our will. "[M]oral skepticism is itself the result of an act, namely, of the act by which we seek to realize in ourselves opposing aims at the same time."[69] Thus, Royce is specifying three conditions for the experience of moral skepticism: (1) the existence of conflicting aims within us; (2) our belief that both are equally worthy of fulfillment; and (3) our feeling of the conflicting ends within as *our ends*.[70]

Royce moves forward to argue that in the experience of moral skepticism one also comes to the realization that in the desire to realize these conflicting aims all at once, one also desires their harmony, and this becomes a higher end that one aims to realize. One achieves a "moral insight." One has found an ideal, the ideal of "harmonization" or "unity." In today's philosophical parlance, this is a second-order ideal. Further, this ideal becomes a practical one because one can say: "I will act as if all these conflicting aims were mine. I will respect them all."[71]

Having established the moral insight, Royce then confronts the question, Why is it easier for me to be selfish? Royce essentially repeats the discussion in "Tests of Right and Wrong," of the illusion of selfishness and of its solution, though he casts his discussion in a different perspective. This priority to selfishness exists on the level of our everyday contact with others, where we are conscious of others only as loosely organized masses of behaviors or attitudes that affect us. We see them as train conductors, grocers, business rivals, and so on, displaying qualities such as industriousness, laziness, politeness, deceit, and the like.

On this plane, I consider the others in the outer aspect of their conscious lives as a power affecting me. However, if I reflect on our interpersonal relations, I discover that I cannot consistently regard the other as a "dead fact" of nature, since many of his actions force me to an awareness of him as a conscious and voluntary agent much like myself. I realize, "As he is real, he is as much an object for my effort as I myself am, in case, I can affect him."[72]

Further, as I become aware of the extent of my neighbor's reality, I may come to the following realization and resolution: "We see the reality of our neighbor, that is, we determine to treat him as we do ourselves."[73] Royce addresses the egoism-altruism conflict by arguing that it is not a matter of impulses either way, since impulses do not make a moral man. It is insight. Once a man gets to know his fellow men as well as he knows himself, if he is rational and consistent, he will condemn his own selfishness as immoral. Selfishness is blind. This kind of insight would seemingly have great moral gains. If we could see the world through our neighbors' eyes, we would be relieved of the sin of treating them blindly, of mistaking their motives. This is the principle of "walking in the other's shoes." Again, this idea is not based on some impulse to sympathy but rather is the result of an insight into what consistent behavior to self and others requires.

Finally, Royce introduces the argument that to act for an end is to postulate future states of myself, and thus I extend my concerns beyond the present moment. Critical reflection finds no rational warrant for regarding my own future states that I do not now experience as any more or less "real" than the present and future states of my fellow men that are not now my own. I begin to appreciate the oneness of life: "As the prudent man, seeing the reality of his future self, inevitably works for it, so the enlightened man, seeing the reality of all conscious life . . . at once and inevitably desires, if only for that one moment of insight, to enter into the service of the whole of it."[74] In his exposition of the moral insight, two things are clear. In our human life this insight, with its accompanying resolutions, is easily clouded by passions and lost in long stretches of delusion and selfishness. Second, Royce asserts that we must not assume this moral insight is, in any sense, actual. Royce writes: "Not because these aims are already in themselves one, but because we, as moral seers, unite in one moment of insight the realization of all these aims, for that reason alone is this life one for us. . . . The moral insight discovers harmony not as already implied in the nature of these blind, conflicting wills, but as an ideal to be attained by hard work."[75] This harmony is a goal and a vision for moral life, one that, Royce believes, seeks to be as adequate for the richness and fullness of human moral experience and human moral needs.[76] It is a goal to be worked for—a hypothesis to be tested. Like his stance on ontology, Royce retains a hypothetical stance on ethical theory; he believes his moral insights provide the best answer to human moral dilemmas, but he makes no claim to infallible truth. I believe his hypothesis of the moral insight very worthy of full consideration as viable and testable in life, especially as we see it refined and deepened in his philosophy of loyalty.[77]

Indeed, at the end of his discussion of the moral insight, Royce asserts that "our ideal must be made to do work in the world." He adds that "in seeking an ideal for life, one does not want a barren abstraction, but such an ideal as can also be our guide." The guidance to be given is as follows: *"Get and keep the moral insight as an experience, and do all that thou canst to extend among men this experience,"* and *"Act out in each case what the moral insight bids thee to do.* "[78] In others words, Royce urges all of us to strive for moral insight and to keep it as our principle despite the trials and tribulations of life and, further, to extend it as much as possible among our fellow beings. This would mean to engage in moral education, to respect one another as rational and voluntary agents, and to work for interpersonal harmony, in a common effort. Royce writes: "It would demand all the wealth of life that the separate selves now have; and all the unity that any one individual now seeks for himself." And finally, *"the universal will of the moral insight must aim at the destruction of all which separates us into a heap of different selves, and at the attainment of some higher positive organic aim."* [79] These central ideas inform all of Royce's philosophy and will be discussed when we turn to *The Philosophy of Loyalty.*

Person: The Moral and Loyal Self

In his ethics of loyalty, Royce, in fact, brings together a number of our themes in this chapter as well as threads from his psychology, both cognitive and social, and his ideas about self. Thus, in 1908 in his *Pittsburgh Lectures on Loyalty*, Royce declares:

> My doctrine starts from the obvious fact that a moral individual, a person with rights and duties, is not born, but made. He is the product of a long process of social adjustment and of inner consciousness. . . . His moral freedom, his private judgment, his rights, his conscience is not the root, not the source, it is rather the result, the flower of his moral life. He is not born self-conscious. Not at birth is he free, or dutiful, or conscientious. He wins these qualities, if at all, only through the aid of a long social training. On the other hand, no social training can make a moral personality, unless, at each step in the process, the embryonic moral individual himself cooperates in the process—becomes, as they say, *self-active*, takes over the moral motives and makes them his own,—wins individuality through somehow coming into a voluntarily chosen unity with his *social world.*[80]

There is, for Royce, as we have already observed, a constant interaction in the development of the individual self between passive elements, represented in the datum of experience, the inexorability of the past, and social conformism, and active elements, represented in restlessness, mental initiative, self-assertion, and selective attention. How then does the moral individual come into "voluntarily chosen unity with his social world?" It begins with the self and the development of a life plan and thus with at least a minimum unity of self.

In the 1914 Berkeley Lectures, Royce declares: "A self is a life living according to a plan, which, of course may be extremely ill known to the self. . . . But so far as there is no plan whatever . . . one is not a self."[81] I need a plan to be a self, but often I have no clue about it. How then do I find my life plan? This is a basic human process of discovery, with deep roots in the human psyche. The search for a self begins with a deep-seated need to live and be. Royce writes: "We long to live, we long to be active. For life means activity; and activity . . . means longing, striving, suffering, lack."[82] Recall that a central aspect of the human psyche is the feeling of restlessness, which, in turn, is at the base of attention and mental initiative. Attention, in turn, plays two fundamental roles. It provides clarity and choice. Attention, notes Royce, makes clear to consciousness what otherwise would not be observed. Second, attention is selection. It is "our choice to narrow the field of our consciousness in a particular way at a particular moment."[83] Further, in terms of life plan, attention becomes manifest as a *"deliberate and free dwelling upon, or ignoring of, plans of action which we are supposed already to possess."*[84] As we shall see in our chapter on religion, error and sin lie in this very ability to deliberately focus our attention.

Further, for Royce, individuality depends upon selective attention. In logic, Royce interprets "selective attention" as a disposition to regard the individual object as identifiable throughout a process of investigation so that no other can take its place.[85] The temporal nature of this designation should be noted; the temporality of the self and its ability to interpret itself to itself play a key role in its "personal identity" and the ability to carry a plan into the future through action, and commitment is essential to loyalty and ethical action. Attention involves temporality and the future.

Further, it involves choice and exclusivity. In *The World and the Individual*, Royce declares: "The individual is, primarily, the object and expression of an exclusive interest, of a determinate selection."[86] Further, says Royce, "it is the ethically organizing interests of life" that are individuating, and "they all involve an exclusive element."[87] Organizing life around a specific goal individuates. "It is by an individuating and exclusive interest in living life for one purpose that a man becomes a moral individual, one Self, and not a mere collection of empirical contrast-effects."[88] For Royce, the self is basically an ethical category because what we are is what we choose to be. We choose this plan from the possibilities of plans and thus decide that there shall be no other. We "love" our cause, and for Royce "love" is exclusive and individuating. Love is to "this one" as an object of an exclusive interest. The finite self must will this and no other.[89]

But how then do we find a life plan? Royce claims that "[m]y duty is simply my own will brought to clear self-consciousness."[90] Yet, I am a collection of impulses with no clear direction, and "by nature I am a sort of meeting place of countless streams of ancestral tendency. . . . There is no one desire that is always present to me. Left to myself alone, I can never find out what my will is."[91] I must learn to have a will of my own and to have a life plan. This, claims Royce, is the principal task of one's life. But he notes that immediately one confronts a paradox: "Here, then, is the paradox. I, and only I, whenever I come to my own, can morally justify to myself my own plan of life. No outer authority can ever give me the true reason of my duty. Yet, I, left to myself, can never find a plan of life. I have no inborn idea naturally present within myself. By nature I simply go on crying out in a sort of chaotic self-will, according as the momentary play of desire determines."[92]

Whence, then, can I derive a plan of life? Royce's answer is "imitation": "One gets various plans of life suggested through the models that are set before each one of us by his fellows. Plans of life first come to connection with our endless imitative activities. These imitative processes begin in our infancy, and run on through our whole life. We learn to play, to speak, to enter into our social realm, to take part in the ways and so in the life of mankind."[93] Thus our ideas for plans of life get suggested to us by the social order.[94] "It is our social existence, then, as imitative beings,—it is this that suggests to us the sorts of plans of life which we get when we learn a calling, when we find a business in life, when we discover our place in the social world. And so our actual plans of life, namely our callings, our more or less settled daily activities come to us from without. We in so far learn what our own will is by first imitating the will of others."[95]

But this cannot be the whole story, for Royce, like Nietzsche, clearly believes in moral autonomy and self-assertion.[96] Though there are various social pressures to conform to various ideals of personal life and to accept divergent standards of moral excellence, it is imperative, in Royce's view, that the individual choose a life plan and a system of moral standards of his own. In his *Philosophy of Loyalty,* Royce writes: "So far as moral values are concerned, it is therefore indeed certain that no ethical doctrine can be right which neglects individuals, and which . . . disregards their duty to centralize their lives, and so their moral universe, about their purposes."[97] One's cause must be uniquely one's own.

The explanation for this seeming paradox in seeking a cause is in a clear understanding of Royce's theory of imitation. First, self-assertion is learned and is secondary and derived. Royce writes: "Take away the Alter from consciousness, and the conscious Ego, so far as in this world we know it, languishes and languishing, dies. . . . Hence, I am not first self-conscious, and then secondarily conscious of my fellow. On the contrary, I am conscious of myself, on the whole, as in relation to some real or ideal fellow, and apart from my consciousness of my fellows I have only secondary and derived states and habits of self-consciousness."[98] Further, self-assertion and imitation are not opposed. "The normal relation between the two is that we constantly use our imitativeness to give us opportunities for self-assertion. Having followed a given model, I can make use of the power thus acquired to display myself in the presence of other fellow beings."[99] Thus, social imitativeness stimulates the will of the individual and also teaches the self customs and devices for self-expression. "Teach men social customs, and you equip them with weapons for expressing their own personalities. . . . Social conformity gives us social power. Such power brings us to a consciousness of who we are and what we are. Now for the first time, we begin to have a real will of our own. And hereupon we may discover this will to be in sharp conflict with the will of society."[100]

Thus the groundwork for the development of the moral self is in Royce's theories of attention, imitation, and self-development. However, to attain moral selfhood we must move beyond this base. Royce clearly saw that imitation can lead to mindless collectivism or self-assertive individualism. Loyalty is the solution to this conflict because it combines commitment to a social world and others with self-expression and self-fulfillment.

In *The Philosophy of Loyalty*, Royce initially offers three criteria for a cause to be a fitting object of an individual's loyalty. First, the cause must personally engage me. It must "have some elemental fascination for me. It must stir me, arouse me, please me, and in the end possess me."[101] Royce notes that "I should serve causes such as my natural temperament and my social opportunities offer me. I should choose friends whom I like. My family, my community, my country will be served partly because I find it interesting to be loyal to them."[102] Second, a cause must be capable of *holding* my interest. Since the cause defines my life plan, it must be rich enough to fulfill over a long period of time my growing and changing desires and needs. It must provide the self with indefinite future extension, a cause that can never fully be achieved, and only then, says Royce, can it truly unify my life. And, of course, the cause, in addition to temporal extension, must provide social extension. It must tie me to some "larger whole." The cause, says Royce, will "unite him with other persons by some social tie, such as personal friendship, or his family, or the state."[103] It ties me to community. Ultimately, as we shall see, it becomes loyalty to a universal community.

In 1915, in his Extension Course on Ethics, Royce discusses three types of loyalty as exemplified in the family, which, we recall, Royce considers humankind's most basic community: each type of loyalty is related to the relationships between siblings, between friends, spouses, or lovers, and between parents and child or across generations. Connected to each relationship is also a central ethical idea: autonomy between siblings, goodness or happiness for friends or spouses and lovers, and duty between parent and child. In this analysis Royce is concerned with building community and overcoming discord and estrangement that occurs between people, between dyadic pairs. Again he seeks harmony through loyalty. He writes: "Loyalty, as you remember is an effort to bring into union, into a sort of synthesis and cooperation, the three leading ethical ideas: the idea of independence, the idea of the good, and the idea of duty."[104]

Finally, loyalty is an intrinsic good for the self. Royce writes: "[L]oyalty is for the loyal man not only a good, but for him the chief amongst all moral goods of his life, because it furnishes to him a personal solution of the hardest of human practical problems, the problem: 'For what do I live?'"[105] Loyalty unifies a life, gives it a center, fixity and stability. "Whoever is loyal . . . is devoted, is active, surrenders his private self-will, controls himself, is in love with his cause, and believes in it."[106] Further, the cause individuates because the cause that the loyal self loves is a personal being. Royce, in his Berkeley Lectures, asserts that a cause cannot be defined by abstract nouns, or by words that end in "-tion" or "-ism." People who view a cause in this manner, says Royce, "refuse to think of a *cause* as a live being, with blood in its veins, with a concrete and lovable existence belonging to it."[107]

Loyalty, writes Royce, "is the universal form in which the human Self fulfils its individual and social function."[108] The principle of loyalty asserts that the realization of self as a whole necessarily involves the fulfillment of social obligations. Again, Royce writes:

> In our philosophy of loyalty there is only one cause which is rationally and absolutely determined for the individual as the right cause for him as for everybody—this is the general cause of *"loyalty to loyalty."* The way in which any one man is to show his loyalty is, however, in our philosophy of loyalty, something which varies endlessly with the individual and can never be precisely defined except by and through his personal consent. I can be loyal to loyalty only in my own fashion, and by serving my own special personal system of causes.
>
> The general principle of loyalty to which all special choices of one's cause are subject is the principle: Be loyal to loyalty, that is, do what you can to produce the maximum of devoted service of causes, a maximum of fidelity, and of selves that choose and serve fitting objects of loyalty.[109]

In Royce's ethics of loyalty we find all of our themes incorporated. Loyalty overcomes the conflicts of egoism-altruism and autonomy-duty; it provides a positive theory in answer to skepticism and pessimism; it provides unity and fulfillment of self as well as temporal, social extension and a moral attitude that takes into account the needs and interests of others. There is in this ethic a universal intent and concern for the moral life and growth of all selves; there is one common moral obligation, with room for individual freedom in fulfilling it; there is self-unification and self-fulfillment within the context of a social and moral world; and there is an emphasis on morally productive action, on bringing about a loyal world filled with loyal selves.

In *The Problem of Christianity*, we find that the encompassing goal of the furthering of universal loyalty is now given a concrete object, "the community," but a community viewed as a personal being. In this work, Royce defines loyalty as "the practically devoted love of an individual for a community." The community is a person by the same criteria that identify the life of the human self. Royce, then, asserts, "In brief, my idea of myself is an interpretation of my past,—linked also with an interpretation of my hopes and intentions."[110] The self is essentially a temporal, meaningful, time-process. Likewise, a genuine community for Royce is both a *community of memory* and a *community of hope*. Royce describes the first aspect as follows: "A community constituted by the fact that each of its members accepts as part of his own individual life and self the same *past* events that each of his fellow-members accepts, may be called a *community of memory*."[111] As for the future dimension, Royce asserts: "A community constituted by the fact that each of its members accepts, as part of his own individual life and self, the same expected *future* events that each of his fellows accepts, may be called a *community of expectation*, or upon occasion, a *community of hope*."[112] Further, communities have causes and plans that unify them as "persons," just as a plan unifies individual selves. Royce writes: "[F]or our purposes, the community is a being that attempts to accomplish something in time through the deeds of its members."[113]

Royce's notion of the community as a "person" will be discussed more fully in the chapter on social and political philosophy. For ethical theory such a concept is crucial, for it allows moral assessment of communities as communities. Too often, contemporary communities and institutions dismiss responsibility for harms inflicted on persons, animals, and communities by the excuse that "one can hold only individuals responsible" and not communities or institutions as such. Further, dysfunctional communities or sociopathic communities harm their individual members by not providing them the nourishment and guidance they need to be fully functional moral selves. As I have argued in my earlier book on Royce, genuine individuals and genuine communities need each other.[114] Genuine communities foster genuine, morally responsible selves by providing the conditions for unity, loyalty, and self-expansion. Further, genuine communities equally need genuine individuals. Royce writes: "How rich this community is in meaning, in value, in membership, in significant organization, it will depend upon the selves that enter into the community, and upon the ideals in terms of which they define themselves, their past, and their future."[115] Thus a community that fails its individuals will ultimately harm itself as its members will have little to contribute to the quality of the community.

In positing loyalty to loyalty as now loyalty to an individual community, Royce also gives the human self and the human race an even higher and more encompassing goal, namely, to build a universal community. Royce writes: "Judge every social device, every proposed reform, every national and every local enterprise by one test: *Does this help towards the coming of the universal community?*"[116] And, more significantly, Royce asserts this as an ongoing task; we can look forward to no final form of the universal community. The moral commitment is, in a real sense, an eternal one. Royce writes:

> *The best world for a moral agent is one that needs him to make it better.* The purely metaphysical consciousness, in vain, therefore, says of the good, *It is.* The moral consciousness insists upon setting higher than every such assertion, the resolve, *Let it be.* The moral consciousness declines to accept, therefore, any metaphysical finality. It rejects every static world.[117]

4

Religious Insight, the Spirit of Community, and the Reality of Evil

In *The Religious Aspect of Philosophy* Royce writes: "Religion invites the scrutiny of philosophy, and philosophy may not neglect the problems of religion."[1] We recall from the first chapter that Royce's father and mother were religious people, although their temperaments in this regard were quite different. Josiah's mother, Sarah, practiced religion through music, worship, and reflection on scriptures, while Josiah Sr. tended toward dogmatism, often quoting scripture passages for various occasions. Sarah also wrote about her mystical experience in the desert during her trek to California.[2] Although Royce's early reading included the Christian scriptures, he read widely on religion, including the Hindu scriptures in Sanskrit, and his undergraduate thesis concerned Greek religion.[3] However, during his lifetime, Royce had no formal religious affiliation. In a 1904 article Royce clarified what he believed to be the correct relationship of a philosophy teacher to organized religion, namely, that "one should conscientiously avoid all connection with any sect or form of the visible church."[4]

However, Royce also asserts that "[r]eligion . . . constitutes the most important business of man."[5] The philosopher cannot neglect religion, but the greatest contribution of a philosophy teacher to the improvement of religious life, in Royce's judgment, would be to bring "(1) Clearness of thought about religious issues; and (2) a judicial spirit in the comparison, in the historical estimate, and in the formation of religious opinions."[6] These constitute the philosopher's task. Royce followed his own advice and did write about religious philosophy, religion, and religious ideas, producing four major works as well as a series of articles.[7] I believe these works contain a number of valuable ideas relevant for us in our contemporary time. His works speak to two central themes of our time: (1) vigorous religious plurality, which often produces warfare rather than tolerance and community, and (2) a perceived conflict between religion and science, taken up as a serious battle by at least one major contemporary philosopher.[8]

The first section of this chapter will focus on Royce's discussions of the Absolute, or God, as set out in *The Religious Aspect of Philosophy* and *The Spirit of Modern Philosophy*. These early works set out the pattern of his ideas on this topic as well as a number of the central ideas present in all his attempts to provide an adequate account of reality, an adequate conception of the infinite or absolute. Royce's metaphysics will not be discussed here, as others have provided an adequate overview of many of his metaphysical ideas, particularly as related to philosophy of religion.[9] Indeed, the primary approach has been to focus on metaphysical-epistemological issues and his supposed absolute idealism. Unfortunately, this approach has also led to both a misunderstanding of Royce as a philosopher and a neglect of the riches of his work. Others are now looking at Royce's metaphysics-epistemology from a new perspective,[10] and I fully endorse and applaud these efforts. I believe that Royce's philosophy is of a rich, interconnected whole, and his work on metaphysics and epistemology, as well as on logic and philosophy of science, plays significant roles in comprehending that whole.

Royce's understanding of the Absolute (God) (Infinite) (Eternal) is, of course, particularly relevant to his understanding of religion, of the religious attitude, and of the interconnections between a religious attitude, a moral attitude, and a theoretic attitude. In discussing Royce's expositions on the Absolute or God, I will draw on the ideas of the twentieth-century philosopher-theologian Paul Tillich and on the book *Your God Is Too Small* by philosopher J. B. Phillips.[11]

In the second part of the chapter, I will discuss Royce's approach to the study of religion. Again his approach is empirical, historical, and phenomenological and is also concerned with philosophical reflection. The focus of this section will be the two articles, "What Is Vital in Christianity?" and "Monotheism," as well as sections of *The Sources of Religious Insight*. In the first article, Royce clearly affirms his understanding of Christianity as a philosophy of life and discusses in detail his understanding of the person, life, and work of Jesus. In both articles, Royce asserts his belief in God as a Spirit and Person, and not as an external creator. Throughout his writings on religion, Royce argues against any causal notion of the Absolute or God and, indeed, views the idea of God as external as a clear barrier for anyone dealing with the problem of evil. The "Monotheism" encyclopedia article is especially insightful in interconnecting concepts of God with three cultural influences, those of Greece, Israel, and India. I will also briefly discuss his "Outline and Text of 'Religious Experience and Religious Truth,'" an unfinished draft recently published in *Josiah Royce's Late Writings*.[12] This will allow us to connect with Royce's psychology as well as his work on religion.

In the third section of the chapter, we will address the problem of evil. Two essays, "The Knowledge of Good and Evil" and "The Problem of Job," will be discussed and related to the discussion of this issue in *Religious Aspect*. This allows us to turn to Royce's explication of the problem of evil in *The Sources of Religious Insight*, where he introduces the idea of the religious mission of sorrow. This, in turn, directs us toward the work of the Interpreter-Spirit of the Universal Community who reconciles good and evil as an ongoing process that works in concert with the human conquering of evil step by step.

The fourth section of the chapter will focus on Royce's answer to the question, "In what sense, if any, can modern man consistently, be in *creed*, a Christian?"[13] This discussion primarily focuses on *The Problem of Christianity*, although the article "What Is Vital in Christianity?" is also relevant. Royce reiterates his theme that Christianity has two principal characteristics, contrasting, and perhaps opposing. First, it is a religion that was taught and first lived out by an individual person, Jesus, and thus appears to be a religion of the Master, concerned with his teaching and with living out, in example, his way of life. Second, however, argues Royce, Christianity has also "always been an interpretation of the Master and of his religion in the light of some doctrine concerning his mission and also concerning God, man, and man's salvation."[14] Royce will focus on the latter aspect and on three essential ideas: (1) the salvation of the individual self as determined by some sort of membership in a certain spiritual community; (2) the idea that this individual is by nature subject to some overwhelming moral burden that, if unaided, he cannot escape; and (3) the idea of atonement. We will also discuss Royce's ideas on sin, guilt, and salvation and will discover that these are communal as well as individual. Central to Royce's discussion of atonement are the concepts of grace and of the traitor. The traitor betrays her own cause and finds herself in the hell of the irrevocable, having done a deed that can never be erased, one that will mark her life forever, but that can be redeemed and given new meaning by a suffering servant on behalf of the community that has been betrayed. The chapter will end with a discussion of Royce's reinterpretation of the exhortation of the Master that his disciples should so act that the Kingdom of Heaven may come.

A God Adequate Enough for the Moral-Religious-Loyal Self

In *Religious Aspect*, Royce asserts that a religion must have three essential elements: "A religion must teach some moral code, must in some way inspire a strong feeling of devotion to that code, and in so doing must show something in the nature of things that answers to the code or that serves to reinforce the feeling. A religion is therefore practical, emotional, and theoretical."[15] This threefold characterization became a standard model for texts on religion. One such text asserts that "all religions, regardless of the times or places of their existence, must involve three fundamental factors. These are: (a) belief, (b) feelings, and (c) action."[16] In his book *Dynamics of Faith*, Paul Tillich defines faith as "an act of total personality," a centering act, and "state of being ultimately concerned."[17] Ultimate concern, for Tillich, unites the subjective, the one who believes in all his feelings and actions, and the objective, the faith that is believed.[18] The integration of personality that Tillich sees as central to faith is certainly similar to that unification of self that Royce posits for loyalty. Tillich writes: "The ultimate concern gives depth, direction and unity to all other concerns and, with them, to the whole personality."[19]

In *Religious Aspect*, Royce connects the three essential elements of religion with the interrelationship between philosophy and religion. He writes: "Philosophy is not directly concerned with feeling, but both action and belief are direct objects of philosophical criticism. . . . Kant's fundamental problems: *What do I know?* and *What Ought I do?* are of religious interest no less than of philosophic interest. They ask how the highest thought of man stands related to his highest needs, and what in things answer to our best ideals."[20] It is my judgment that in *Religious Aspect*, Royce intends to closely connect moral insight, religious insight, and what I will call theoretic insight. His intent further is to answer the question Tillich poses in describing faith as ultimate concern, namely, "What in the idea of God constitutes Divinity?"[21] I believe that Royce would phrase the question in the following terms: "What hypothesis about the nature of reality most adequately addresses the need of man for depth and unification of the self as believer and evaluator?" I believe this question is central to *Religious Aspect, The Spirit, The Conception of God*, and *The World and the Individual*. The unification of self is also a key idea in *The Philosophy of Loyalty* and is reformulated in terms of religious need in *The Sources of Religious Insight* and *The Problem of Christianity*.

In addition to their shared concern for an adequate hypothesis about the reality of the world that would provide deep unification of the self and its needs, Royce and Tillich share the conviction that doubt is an essential component of faith. Like Royce, Tillich does not believe doubt is about propositions. He sees this form of doubt leading to cynicism or despair. Genuine skeptical doubt is "an attitude of rejecting any certainty" and "serious doubt is a confirmation of faith."[22]

In "Doubting and Working," Royce affirms the significant role of doubt in the formation of beliefs. He writes:

> I think it is wrong to say that in seeking for truth we desire, first of all, to duplicate in our own minds the things and relations outside of us. . . . The thinking mind ought not to have as its sole object conformity to things that do not think. That is not our highest aim. Mistake and disagreement and cruel intolerance and superstition are evil states of mind. . . . They mean injury and anguish to the mass of mankind. Therefore, [there is] the desire for ideal harmony of belief. . . . If this be the purpose of our truth-seeking, an evident consequence is that we ought in fact to reverence the business of truth-seeking as we reverence all toil for the good of mankind. We ought to regard truth-seeking as a sacred task.[23]

Thus, for Royce, doubting is crucial to genuine thinking. Further, one must not remain just satisfied with his own creed, but rather must be concerned about the truth for all mankind. All must be devoted to one end—"the making of human life broader, fuller, more harmonious, better possessed of abiding belief." Seeking truth is, then, an ethical duty. We want to make human life better, says Royce, because we see "that men want large-mindedness and peace, where error means narrow-mindedness and war."[24] Finally, in *Religious Aspect*, Royce asserts: "We claim, then, the right to criticize as fearlessly, as thoroughly, and as skeptically as may be, the foundations of conduct and faith."[25]

Further, Royce and Tillich argue that openness and fallibility must be attached to all religious beliefs. Royce, in my judgment, would agree with Tillich that every type of faith (including the philosophical and scientific) has a tendency to elevate its concrete symbols to absolute validity. For Tillich, in the area of faith, this is idolatry. Tillich, relying on religious history, formulated what he called the "Protestant Principle," "[t]he principle that no church has the right to put itself in the place of the ultimate. Its truth must be judged by the ultimate. . . . The same criterion is valid with respect to the whole history of religion and culture. The criterion contains a Yes—it does not reject any truth of faith in whatever form it may appear in the history of faith—and it contains a No—it does not accept any truth of faith as ultimate.[26] This attitude toward the history of religion is certainly Royce's own attitude to both the history of religion and the history of philosophy. From each philosophy and religion studied, Royce sought to bring forth a kernel idea that was valuable for developing a more comprehensive view, one that unified and also probed the depth of human experience. Royce expressed this attitude and view in an early essay on "George Eliot as a Religious Teacher." He writes:

> She was too intensely skeptical to accept easily any one formula . . . this skeptical element is one of the most significant features of her works. Nothing has done more harm in the history of religion than the dead formula. . . . And even the successful formula, the true expression of life, is dangerous as soon as we try to substitute it for the life. . . . The skeptical spirit is the Mephistopheles of the religious consciousness, the companion that Faust "no more can do without." . . . If ever we have a religious philosophy, the poets on the one hand, the skeptics on the other, will have helped the speculator at every step in his search for a theory.[27]

Royce, as we know, had deep respect for poetry. He called it molten thought. In arguing that poetry must be a companion in a search for an adequate theory, he is tipping his hat to the need for religion to address the emotional, feeling side of the human person. Tillich offers insight into this when he speaks of religious symbols as alive or dead. Religion for him, and one assumes for Royce, is the response of a person to the manifestation of the holy, and thus any symbols or expressions of faith must, if they truly address ultimate concern, create reply, action, and communication. Symbols have a lifespan; the relation of the person to the ultimate undergoes changes, and the contents of faith must likewise change or vanish. "A divine figure ceases to create [a] reply, it ceases to be a common symbol and loses its power for action."[28]

Royce understood this very well, and indeed, his central question in *The Problem of Christianity* is the question of the aliveness of the Christian creed. To those who fault Royce on the lack of religious feeling in his concept of the absolute, I urge that they recall the clear distinction Royce makes between religion and philosophy in *Religious Aspect*, when he writes: "Philosophy is not directly concerned with feeling, but both action and belief are direct objects of philosophical criticism."[29] Tillich makes a similar distinction when he writes: "Philosophical truth is truth about the structure of being; the truth of faith is truth about one's ultimate concern. . . . In both cases, ultimate reality is sought and expressed—conceptually in philosophy, symbolically in religion."[30]

Turning to the question of the ultimate, I believe we must see Royce's search for an adequate statement of this ultimate reality in terms of making the concept adequate to the depth and breadth of human experience and to addressing various human needs. In discussing this, I begin with a brief reference to *Your God Is Too Small* by J. B. Phillips. In this book Phillips takes issue with the many inadequate conceptions of God promoted in the contemporary world. He argues that such false conceptions are damaging to faith; they put "god-in-a-Box," shrinking God to fit our notions of what He is like and where He is." His titles for these "limited" concepts are most amusing: "Grand Old Man," "Policeman," "Absolute Perfection," "Heavenly Bosom," "Managing Director," "Projected Image," and "Pale Galilean."[31] Royce might add "Progress" and "Survival Success."

What for Royce constitutes an adequate concept? It must satisfy man's need for harmony of beliefs and harmony of warring ideals. In *The Sources,* where religion is the central focus, Royce adds that it must meet man's need for salvation. Again, I draw on the work of Paul Tillich to broaden this perspective. In the book *The Courage To Be,* Tillich addresses four central anxieties of man: (1) fate and death, (2) emptiness and meaninglessness, (3) guilt and condemnation, and (4) despair. He also addresses examples from the history of philosophy that consider philosophies of life that focus on courage: (1) the Stoics and the courage of wisdom, (2) Spinoza and the courage of self-affirmation, and (3) Nietzsche and the courage of life. Tillich's anxieties can be seen as similar to Royce's emphasis on human needs. Royce discussed all four in one form or another. And we recall that Royce expressed respect both for the Stoics and for Nietzsche in terms of their philosophies of life. Finally, we recall Royce's assertion in *The Spirit* that "life involves passions, faiths, doubts, and courage. The critical inquiry into what all these things mean and imply is philosophy. We have faith in life; we want to reflectively estimate this faith. . . . Such a criticism of life, made elaborate and thorough-going, is a philosophy."

An Absolute for the Believing, Valuing, and Feeling Human Self

As we learned from our earlier discussion of Royce's ethics, in *Religious Aspect,* Royce first addresses the notion of conduct and discovers the need for both temporal and social extension of one's perspective. He writes: "I must include my neighbor's future with my own, and order conduct accordingly."[32] He then addresses man's moral experience, especially the experience of ethical skepticism, of conflicting and warring ideals. In this experience, a moral insight is achieved that highlights the desire for harmony and the higher-order ideal: "I will act as if all these conflicting aims were mine. I will respect them all."[33] I will "to act as if my neighbor and myself were one being that possessed at once the aims of both of us."[34] Finally, Royce leads his reader to discard the illusion of selfishness and to embrace the realization that we must "see the reality of our neighbor" and make the resolution to "treat him as we do ourselves."[35]

Having addressed the conduct aspect of religion, Royce now turns to its theoretical, belief aspect. He discusses the world of doubt, noting that *"doubt is the insight partially attained."* He discusses various concepts of the eternal world, including the popular notion, which he calls innocent faith, and the world as viewed through science, namely, the world as progress and evolution. Royce argues, rightfully I believe, that both the commonsense notion and the scientific notion are based on faith. The commonsense view is an innocent, noncritical faith that expresses itself in "the will to have an external world." The scientific world, asserts Royce, is a world of postulates. Scientific faith is not blind, and postulates are "voluntary assumptions of a risk, for the sake of a higher end. . . . The postulate is deliberate and courageous volition. Blind faith says: 'I dare not question.' The postulate says: 'I dare to be responsible for assuming.'"[36] Royce then proceeds to an argument already defended in an 1882 essay, namely, that our own activity is constantly modifying our experience through the processes of attention, recognition, and construction.[37] He concludes:

> Since all active inner processes are forever modifying and building our ideas; since our interest in what we wish to find does so much to determine what we do find . . . it becomes us to consider well, and to choose the spirit in which we shall examine our experience. Everyone is certain to be prejudiced, simply because he does not merely receive experience, but himself acts, himself makes experiences. One great question for every truth-seeker is: In what sense, to what degree, with what motive, for what end, may I and should I be prejudiced? . . . We are responsible for our own creed.[38]

Thus, we see the need for critical doubt and for Tillich's Protestant Principle in all attempts by man to build a system of belief. Royce's message is: Believe, but be responsible for your belief and make no claims to the final belief and final validity.

What Royce is addressing here is our theoretical need, the desire for a complete and unified conception; the greatest fullness of data with greatest simplification of organization; the greatest richness of content with the greatest definition of organization. His conviction is that it cannot be based on a notion of causation but rather must be based on the idea "that external reality is a counterpart, not a cause."[39] Here is the germ of Royce's later exposition of the internal and external meanings of ideas.

Royce turns to his now infamous argument from the possibility of error. His conclusion is *"All Reality must be present to the Unity of Infinite Thought."*[40] In this regard, I offer the following interpretation by postulating a theoretic insight parallel to the moral insight. For Royce, the theoretic insight involves the recognition that I and my neighbor seek truth rather than error and thus we shall act as if there is a harmony of belief, a truth that satisfies each of our purposes in thought. This is a direct parallel to the moral insight. For Royce, the only alternatives to the "moral insight" are ethical dogmatism and ethical skepticism. Likewise, the alternatives to the theoretic insight are dogmatism in thought, that is, believing there is one truth, mine, and skepticism, that is, that all is error and no truth is possible. The reconciliation and harmony of belief occur in the Infinite Thought.

Royce now addresses the question "Is this the conception of an Infinite Thought of religious value?" He asserts that this is not just theoretic idealism but practical as well. "We have found not only an infinite Seer of physical facts but an infinite Seer of the Good as well as the Evil." The Infinite Thought must have knowledge of all wills and their conflict and know the outcome of that conflict. He is the Judge of our ideals and our conduct. In the last section of *Religious Aspect*, Royce discusses the human moral experience of evil. In doing a good act, I make a choice and thus exclude and overcome my evil or lesser impulses. Royce writes: "The moral insight condemns the evil that it experiences; and in *condemning and conquering this evil it forms and is, together with the evil, the organic total that constitutes the good will. . . . The good act has its existence and life in *the transcending of the present evil*."[41]

Royce believes his conception of the infinite addresses both our theoretic and our moral needs. Further, Royce asserts:

> And so consciousness has given us in concrete form solutions to our two deepest philosophic needs. The possibility of error, necessitating an inclusive thought, is illustrated for us by our conscious thought, which can include true and false elements in one clear and true thought at any moment. And the possibility and necessity of moral evil, demanding a real distinction between good and evil, a hateful opposition that seems at first sight fatal to our religious needs for the supremacy of goodness in the united world, is illustrated for us in a way that solves the whole trouble, namely, in the unity of the conscious moral act. There at the one moment are good and evil, warring, implacable, yet united in the present momentary triumph of the good will. It is a world of the true Life of God.[42]

One notes the parallel here between human and divine consciousness, and this parallel between the human moral consciousness of evil and that of the divine will remain a theme throughout Royce's career. The Absolute, in this sense, is a Person. Further, Royce here characterizes Absolute Thought as a life of infinite rest, but not apart from endless strife. This, too, is characteristic of the human self, whose life is an infinite quest for fulfillment and meaning.

This notion of a suffering God has parallels with process thought, especially the thought of Charles Hartshorne.[43] Another parallel to process thought, and particularly to the work of Alfred North Whitehead,[44] is Royce's reference to a "lure," when he writes: "Herein lies the invitation of the Infinite to us, that is, it knows us. No deeper sanction is there for true righteousness than this knowledge that one is serving the eternal."[45] And this concept of the Infinite also calls us, states Royce, to practical activity. First, "Live out thy life in its full meaning; for behold it is God's life." And join in the highest activity, the *progressive realization by men of the eternal life of an Infinite Spirit.*"[46] In my judgment, what we have here are hints of the principle of loyalty to loyalty and the infinite community of interpretation.

We have argued so far that Royce, in *Religious Aspect,* is seeking an adequate concept of the Infinite, and this entails fulfilling the deep human need for unification of will and belief, for fulfillment of the theoretic and moral insight. This search continues in *The Spirit.* In this book, Royce approaches the infinite via a study of the history of philosophy, seeking insights into a whole that will satisfy our theoretic needs.

> What I here want to suggest is that the truth about this world is certainly so manifold, so paradoxical, so capable of equally truthful and yet seemingly opposed descriptions, as to forbid us to declare a philosopher wrong in his doctrine merely because we find it easy. . . . For grant that the philosophers are all in fact expressing not dead truth, but the essence of human life, then because this life is many-sided, the individual expressions cannot perfectly agree. It is the union of many such insights that will be the one true view of life.[47]

However, Royce will not focus just on beliefs and the theoretic. He asserts: "[T]here is after all, no beauty in a metaphysical system, which does not spring from its value as a record of spiritual experience."[48] In this book he is concerned with spirit as a "plenitude of experience." He explains: "Life is throughout a complicated thing; the truth of the spirit remains an inexhaustible treasure house of experience; and hence no individual experience, whether it be the momentary insight of genius recorded in the lyric poem, or the patient accumulation of professional plodding through the problems of philosophy, will ever fully tell all the secrets life has to reveal."[49]

In fact, his excursion through the various philosophical periods is a search for their insights on the richness of the human and universal spirit. Royce begins with Spinoza, a most interesting choice and a philosopher also of interest to Tillich. Royce focuses on the religious aspect of Spinoza's philosophy when he identifies the essence of Spinoza's religion as the determination to cease to love finite things and to seek to possess "his own soul in knowing God," and therefore to enter into the "divine freedom, by reason of a clear vision of the supreme and necessary laws of the eternal world."[50] In his later article on "Monotheism" Royce will cite Spinoza as an illustration of the Hindu approach to God, which insists equally on the "sole reality of God," and "the unreality of the world."[51]

Continuing the search for the fullness of spirit and experience, Royce concludes his review of the seventeenth and eighteenth centuries with this judgment: "And, this, namely, the inevitableness and true spirituality of genuine doubting is the great lesson that the enlightenment century, in its transition to Kant, teaches us."[52] As for Kant, God "reveals himself to your conscience."[53] Turning to Fichte, we find the assertion that "our world is the expression of our character."[54] Again, in his article on "Monotheism," Royce connects both Kant and Fichte with the ethical monotheism of Israel. "This Kantian-Fichte order is . . . not the Hellenic order, either of the realm of Platonic ideas or of the natural world. It is the order of 'the kingdom of ends.' . . . Monotheism according to this view, cannot be proved, but rationally must be acknowledged as true."[55]

He moves next to Hegel, and in his commentary on Hegel's life and diary, Royce writes: "[N]ever does one learn of an inner experience of any significance."[56] About Hegel's concept of the Absolute, Royce asserts: "Hegel, as we see, makes his Absolute, the Lord, most decidedly a man of war. Consciousness is paradoxical, restless struggling. Weak souls get weary of the fight and give up trying to get wisdom, skill, virtue, because all these are won in presence of the enemy. But the absolute Self is simply the absolute strong spirit who bears the contradictions of life, and wins the eternal victory."[57] Royce then turns to Schopenhauer. He believes Schopenhauer's pessimism is but "another aspect of the paradoxical passion which we have discovered in the heart of Hegel's doctrine."[58] Royce does find logic in Schopenhauer's World-Will, but he finds this logic fatal and gloomy as well as paradoxical. Royce writes: "I think that the best man is the one who can see the truth of pessimism, can absorb and transcend that truth and can be nevertheless the optimist, not by virtue of his failure to recognize the evil of life, but by the virtue of his readiness to take part in the struggle against this evil."[59] This is again the notion of unifying good and evil in the moral experience of conquering evil by the good act.

From his excursion into history, Royce gleans insights, seeking to bring into "synthesis the thoughts that the history of modern philosophy has suggested to us."[60] Thus, in his chapter on optimism and pessimism and the moral order, he posits a genuine synthesis of these two views of the world, one that does not deny the reality and gravity of evil, but that makes it a part of the larger moral goodness; evil is conquered and possessed. This is, of course, also the solution he offers in *Religious Aspect*. This solution and Royce's struggles with the problem of evil will be discussed in the next section.

What appears new in *The Spirit* is Royce's description of two aspects of human experience, which he calls the "World of Description" and the "World of Appreciation." The world of description is that world needed by science, namely, the outer order viewed as one of well-knit and universal law, structure, of definite forms, subject to categories, and independent of momentary caprices.[61] The world of appreciation is the world of *interconnectedness* among minded beings. It is a world where I would truly communicate with other beings; a world we can imagine to exist if all our human lives were directly open to us together and viewable by all; it would be one "of intimate spiritual communion, so that the experience of each was an open book for all of them." In other words, conceive of beings who were mutually perfect mind-readers one of another.

This world, argues Royce, provides the foundation for the descriptive world of science and for our moral world. It is a world of publicity, and thus the very presupposition of the world of description. He asserts that "[i]f I cannot really communicate with my neighbor, and think of meanings that are like his, there is no truth in our descriptions."[62]

As we have already seen in our discussions of Royce, concepts such as externality and objectivity and postulates such as the uniformity of nature are all grounded in social experience and social needs.[63] Royce writes: "Destroy the organic and appreciable unity of the world of appreciative beings, and the describable objects all vanish; atoms, brains, 'suns and milky ways' are naught."[64] Further, "The whole Moral World presupposes a sharing of definite and express appreciations of one by another, a 'realization' of the life of one by another."[65] Both the world of science and the moral world presuppose this World of Appreciation, this world of appreciative, spiritual oneness. This highest spiritual world would be "a world of one undivided soul of many a soul." Again, an adequate concept of the Infinite is one that can unite and fully express both of these worlds. It satisfies at once our theoretic needs and our moral needs. It will be the richest embodiment of experience. Royce provides this summary of his theory as portrayed in *The Spirit:* "This theory is that the whole universe, including the physical world also, is essentially one live thing, a mind, one great Spirit, infinitely wealthier in his experiences than we are, but for that very reason to be comprehended by us in terms of our own wealthiest experience."[66]

In two of his other works, *The Conception of God* and *The World and the Individual,* Royce again is seeking an adequate conception of God and of the nature of ultimate reality that fully accounts for the theoretic needs of man, as well as his moral needs. In these works, Royce also focuses more intently on the need of the self to find meaning and unity in life and to combine autonomy and duty—the individual and the social-communal. Thus, the concepts of the Infinite, the Absolute, or God that he offers in these works address the particular problem of the book as well as the other human needs. In *The Conception of God,* Royce is concerned with the development of the human consciousness via the contrast of self and other and the achievement of a true sense of self, which Royce defines as *"having a unity of meaning, and as exemplifying, or in its totality fulfilling an idea."*[67] Accordingly, in this context, Royce speaks of the "Absolute Unity of Consciousness," which

> [c]ontains, involves, includes, not merely finite types of self-consciousness, not merely finite contrasts of Self and Other, but the contrast and the consciousness of its own Being as Thinker, Experience, Seer, and as Love or Will, and all of these as essentially interrelated aspects of itself as Unity. . . . I regard the Absolute Unity as essentially inclusive of various interrelated forms of Absolute Self-Consciousness. The Unity transcends these forms only in so far as it is meanwhile constituted by and through them.[68]

In *The World and the Individual* Royce's concern is to unite and incorporate three conceptions of being, one representing realism, the next mysticism, and third, Kant's view. His ultimate concept is of a fourth conception of being.[69]

However, Royce does not neglect the feeling human being in his search for an adequate concept of the Infinite. In both *Religious Aspect* and *The Spirit,* Royce addresses suffering, especially the suffering that comes from the presence of evil in the world. In *The Spirit,* he tells us the Absolute Experience is also the Spirit who conquers our despair over the tragedy of brute chance, the capricious evil events of the world. He is our true Self and we can hear from him the following word: "Oh ye who despair, I grieve with you. Yes, it is I who grieve in you. Your sorrow is mine. No pang of your finitude but is mine too. I suffer it all, for all things are mine; I bear it and *yet I triumph."*

We turn now to a brief excursus on Royce and the problem of evil.

Conquering Evil through Inner Transformation

The problem of evil was a lifelong concern for Royce. In 1893, in an article, "The Knowledge of Good and Evil,"[70] Royce asks, how can the knowledge of evil contribute to moral perfection? Royce posits that moral goodness, unlike innocence, is won only through struggle with the forces of evil, and it involves a rather deep knowledge of evil—a knowledge that unfortunately can lead to sin. Moral choice, argues Royce, is conscious choice and thus it involves knowing that *against* which one chooses, as well as that in favor of which one decides: "[M]oral choice is essentially a condemnation of the rejected motives, as well as an approval of the accepted motive."[71] Sins, argues Royce, are possible conditions of a deep intellectual knowledge of certain very common and momentous human experiences, for example, the "extreme loneliness of guilt," that Royce will later illustrate through the poem "The Ancient Mariner" and the novel *Crime and Punishment*. Further, they provide opportunity for extraordinary heroic moral deeds. Thus, says Royce, nobody has harder work to do than a sinner who has repented. He writes: "Sin, when past, furnishes especial opportunities for future virtue. . . . When we once have sinned, our exceptional opportunities to atone, may encourage us to begin afresh with zest the moral task."[72] However, one should not thereby think that one should sin, seek repentance, and thus attain a higher virtue. "Such a person sins because he wants to sin, not because he wants any new moral function to be determined by his previous moral deficiency."[73] In sum, Royce argues that the knowledge and presence of evil are a necessary part of human consciousness and of the experience and act of goodness.

This thesis is further explored in his essay "The Case of John Bunyan" (1894),[74] where Royce presents a case of an actual good man triumphantly struggling with his own profound problem of evil. Royce continually stresses the personal and experiential in dealing with the problem of evil. A consistent theme, both philosophically and practically, is the necessity of a courageous struggle against evil in all its forms. For Royce, individuals can achieve genuine spirituality and morality only by detesting and subordinating evil. Thus, for Royce, good is not a simple concept but rather an idea inseparable from the idea of evil. Further, the essence of moral life is not to seek a pure good or a distant ideal God but rather to find God in the present within the mix of good and evil and to see the truly good man as one who takes his part in the struggle with evil.

In "The Problem of Job" (1897), Royce presents a fairly succinct overview of the traditional statement of the problem of evil and various standard solutions. Job views God traditionally—namely, as wise, omnipotent, all powerful, and all good—and sees his own situation as one of universal unearned ill fortune and a raining down of evils on a good man. For Royce, Job represents the fundamental psychological fact about the problem of evil, namely, the universal experience of unearned ill fortune. This, asserts Royce, is the experience of every person; it is the kind of evil that people can see for themselves every day if they choose, and this fundamental experiential and psychological perspective grounds Royce's own answers to the problem of evil as well as his dismissal of the various traditional answers. One example of this is his response to the view that the purpose of the world is soul making and that pain teaches us the ways of the world and helps us develop our higher potentialities. Royce believes this answer inadequate because it presupposes a greater evil, namely a world that allows evils as the only way to reach given goals. Such an answer, Royce believes, is unacceptable to a sufferer of evil and undeserved ills.

Another answer to the problem of evil is the infinite worth of agents with free will. Royce finds value in this view in that it acknowledges evil as a logically necessary part of a perfect moral order, but he believes this answer ultimately fails, particularly for the innocent sufferer. Such unearned ills may be partly due to free-will actions, but, asserts Royce, the unearned ills are also due to a God who declines to protect the innocent.

Royce believes that as long as one views God as an external power, as Job did, the problem of evil cannot be solved. Rather, one must recognize God as internally present to us and as suffering with us to produce the higher good. When we suffer, our sufferings are God's sufferings, and this is the case because without suffering, evil, and tragedy, God's life could not be perfected. Further, asserts Royce, personally overcoming evil is the essence of the moral life. Thus, in *The Sources of Religious Insight,* Royce presents man as a destroyer of evil, a being who uses every effort to get rid of evil. Conquering evils and oppressions provides man's greatest opportunities for loyalty—the source of religious insight and spiritual triumph. The encounter of human selves with the problem of evil is, for Royce, the most important moral aspect of the world. One must see the problematic situation into which human selves are immersed as part of the atoning process that tends toward an ultimate reconciliation of finite conflicts. Confronted with evils, one needs to trust, within one's limited view, that the Spirit of the Universal Community will reconcile all.

Finally, for Royce, in life relationships are of ultimate significance, and good persons are called to build community. In *The Problem of Christianity,* Royce focuses on the idea of atonement—the work of individuals and community to restore unity to aggrieved and shattered relationships. Indeed, Royce saw the universe as an ongoing interpretive, reconciling process, and each individual as a courageous pilgrim overcoming evil and engaging in creative, reconciling deeds while placing trust in the far wider and deeper wisdom of the Interpreter-Spirit of the Universal Community. Royce believed such a teleological and purposive universe necessary to account for a moral point of view. It is because he holds to this belief that he finds evil, represented in the anti-teleological elements of the world, to be a serious metaphysical problem. Ultimately, Royce sees evil as an eternal part of both human and divine life, and the human conquering of evil step by step as the most important moral fact of the universe.

The Nature of Religion: Practice, Belief within Cultural Contexts

In the essay "What Is Vital in Christianity?" Royce approaches religion with a historic-empirical approach akin to that of modern anthropology. He views religion as it has developed within human history. He writes: "any religion presents itself as a more or less connected group: (1) of religious practices, such as prayers, ceremonies, festivals, rituals, and other observance, and (2) of religious ideas, the ideas taking the form of traditions, legends, and beliefs about the gods or spirits."[75] The term "vital," says Royce, is metaphoric, as in the vital features of an organism. If these changed, the organism would not necessarily be destroyed but would be an essentially different type of organism, and Royce illustrates this with the examples of gill breathing and lung breathing.

But "vital" also connotes "alive" for the persons who are followers of the religion, and this usage is similar to Tillich's understanding of religious symbols as alive or dying. Further, this term means also "primary" in practice. Thus, Royce says his first question is "What is more vital about a religion: its religious practices, or its religious ideas, beliefs, and spiritual attitudes?"

Royce distinguishes between more elementary and more complex forms of religious experience. More elementary forms emphasize religious practices rather than the conscious beliefs that accompany the practice. Here Royce makes two significant points. First, he notes that persons may share religious practices, while being far apart in religious ideas and interpretations of the reasons for the practices or the god(s) to whom the practices are addressed.[76] Philosophers and others who study religions primarily in terms of beliefs often do not recognize this important fact. Royce then observes that, on the whole in human history, religious practices precede "at least the more definite religious beliefs."[77] As people engage in practice they begin to consider why they thus engaged in these practices.

With great "tongue in cheek," Royce applies his principles to the group of pigeons in the Harvard Yard who cluster around those who feed them. He imagines the pigeons coming to consciousness and beginning to regard this way of getting food as a sort of religious function and thus to also begin to worship the feeder. Royce then writes as follows:

> If they did so, what idea about this god would be to them vital? Would their beliefs show that they first reasoned abstractly from effect to cause, and said, "He must be a being both powerful and benevolent, for otherwise his feeding of us in this way could not be explained?" Of, course, if the pigeons developed into theologians or philosophers they might reason thus. But if they come to self-consciousness as . . . men generally do, they would more probably say at first: "Behold, do we not cluster about him and beg from him and coo to him" and do we not get food by doing this? He is, then, a being whom it is essentially worth while to treat this way. He responds to our cooing and our clustering. Thus we compel him to feed us. Therefore, he is a worshipful being. And this is what we mean by a god; namely, some one who it is practically useful to conciliate and compel by such forms of worship.[78]

In this passage, Royce critiques the causal approach to God that is represented in many of the proofs for God's existence, and he is also clearly expressing a pragmatic attitude to beliefs and ideas.

Royce goes on to argue that as religion grows, practices easily pass over from one religion to another and with every transition seem to preserve, or even increase, their sacredness. Most importantly, as they enter a new religion, a new explanation is offered and new ideas develop to fit each change in setting. Royce illustrates this point with the example of the adoption of the Christmas and Easter festivals by Christianity. He points out that these were not initiated by Christianity. Rather, writes Royce, "It [Christianity] assimilated them, but then explained why it did so by saying that it was celebrating the birth and resurrection of Christ."[79]

Royce next turns to those cases where beliefs become primary. Here sincere profession of belief becomes significant and the unbeliever is seen as an infidel, an enemy not only of the true faith, but also perhaps of mankind. And, writes Royce, "[i]n consequence, religious persecution and religious wars may come to seem, at least for a time inevitable means for defending the faith."[80] If you believe not rightly, you have no part in the religion and are labeled a heretic, whereas if you do not participate in the practices, you are called a dissenter. With regard to these two emphases in religion, Royce astutely observes that "the appeal that every religion makes to the masses of mankind is most readily interpreted in terms of practice."[81] However, as religions become more complex the conflict between right practice and right belief becomes a crucial question.

Royce, however, believes that those who seek genuine religion would seek "an affair of the whole man, not of deeds alone, nor of the intellect alone, but of the entire spiritual attitude,—of emotion and trust,—of devotion and of motive,—of conduct guided by an inner light, and of conviction due to a personal contact with religious truth."[82] What is wanted is a unity of faith and practice, a "reaction of the whole spirit in the presence of an experience of the highest realities of human life and of the universe."[83] This is what is vital to a religion, and yet, says Royce, it is today a problem. "How can such a solution be any longer an object of reasonable hope, when the faiths have become uncertain, the practices largely antiquated, our life and our duty so problematic, and our environment so uninspiring to our religious interest?"[84] Here, in my judgment, Royce expresses, in general, our situation today.

Next he turns to the question, What then is vital to Christianity? This, of course, prefigures his discussion in *The Problem of Christianity*. This earlier exposition, however, is instructive in its own right. First, Royce defines Christianity as "an interpretation of life,—an interpretation that is nothing if not practical, and also nothing if not guided from within by a deep spiritual interest and a genuine religious experience."[85] The question, then, says Royce, is What interpretation of life is vital to Christianity? It must be answered, he believes, in terms of solving both the personal problem of salvation and the problem of the salvation of mankind. It also demands an answer about the spiritual attitude that is essential to the Christian religion.

There are, notes Royce, two basic answers to the question of what is vital to Christianity. One focuses on the gospel of Christ and living according to those teachings, while the other stresses the superhuman nature of Christ and his atoning death. Royce engages in a critical analysis of each of these views. About the first, Royce makes the following important points. First, nobody can doubt that the sayings of Christ, taken as a whole, embody a new and profound teaching. The two essential teachings, in Royce's view, are (1) the Fatherhood of God, which involves the divine love for man, and (2) the assertion of the infinite worth of each individual person. Second, Jesus not only taught this doctrine sincerely, he lived it and won others to this way of life, and he was ready to die for it; when the time came, he did die for it. Third, the Master meant his teaching to be related not only to the individual soul and its salvation, but also to the reform of the whole existing and visible social order. Or, "expressed in our modern terms, the teacher contemplated a social revolution, as well as the before-mentioned universal religious reformation of each individual life."[86] Royce further asserts: "The meek, the poor were to inherit the earth; the mighty were to be cast down; the kingdoms of this world were to pass away; and the divine sovereignty was to take its visible place as the controller of all things."[87] The prophets of our day, such as Cornel West, would resonate with this statement. Royce does, however, caution that interpretation of "the Kingdom of Heaven" is problematic.

Royce feels that the emphasis in Christianity on Jesus and his message is incomplete and inadequate when viewed alone as a religious ideal. More vital, argues Royce, are the doctrines of the incarnation and atonement when they are rightly interpreted. Further, he writes that the truth in these notions must be separated from legends. Royce then identifies these two ideas: the first is that God is a spirit and person, but does not exist in separation from the world as its external creator, that "He expresses himself in the world; and the world is simply his life, as he consciously lives it out. . . . In this entire world God sees himself as lived out."[88] Second, there is triumph over suffering: "Perfect through suffering,—that is the universal, the absolutely necessary law of the higher spiritual life,"[89] and "the most precious and sacred of human relationships, are raised to their highest levels . . . only when we not merely learn in our own personal case to suffer, to sorrow, to endure, and be spiritually strong, but when we learn to do these things together with our own brethren."[90] Here is the religious mission of sorrow discussed in *The Sources* and the emphasis on the communal discussed in *The Problem*. Finally, as for atonement, there are those who tell us what atonement means; they "are the ones who are willing to suffer vicariously."[91]

Royce summarizes this discussion:

> First, God wins perfection through expressing himself in a finite life and triumphing over and through its very finitude. And, secondly, Our sorrow is God's sorrow. God means to express himself by winning us through the very triumph over evil to unity with the perfect life; and therefore our fulfillment, like our existence, is due to the sorrow and the triumph of God himself. These two theses express, I believe, what is vital in Christianity.[92]

In my judgment, Royce has provided a number of insights about religion in general and Christianity in particular, and these will be discussed in the last chapter. But here, one surely can say that for a religious Christian, this should be a stirring and significant statement.

The essay "What Is Vital in Christianity?" sets out themes for both *The Sources* and *The Problem;* however, before turning to these works, we should consider the additional insights on the nature of religion contained in the encyclopedia article "Monotheism."[93] After briefly reviewing monotheism as a doctrine in contrast to polytheism and pantheism, Royce makes the following claim: "[F]rom the historical point of view, three different ways of viewing the divine being have been of great importance both for religious life and for philosophical doctrine."[94] The three ways to which Royce refers are three forms of monotheism, "which India, Greece, and Israel put before us."[95]

Royce then discusses what, in his view, are the essential features of monotheism as developed in these three cultural contexts. From Israel, we have "the ethical monotheism of the Prophets of Israel," and God is defined in this religious context as "the righteous Ruler of the world, the 'Doer of justice' or as the 'one whose law is holy' or 'who secures the triumph of the right.'"[96] Turning to Greece and to Hellenistic monotheism: God is defined as the "source, or the explanation, or the correlate, or the order, or the reasonableness of the world."[97] The third type of monotheism is labeled Hindu pantheism. Royce notes that this understanding had many different historical origins and appeared, in fact, as part of the Neoplatonic philosophy and the philosophy of Spinoza. This type of monotheism not only insists upon the sole reality of God, but also asserts the unreality of the world.[98]

More relevant to our previous discussion, Royce argues that the "whole history of Christian monotheism depends upon an explicit effort to make a synthesis of the ethical monotheism of Israel and the Hellenic form of monotheism."[99] This effort, however, says Royce, has proven especially difficult. The Hellenic tradition with its intellectualistic emphasis on the Logos was in favor of defining the unity of the divine being and the world as the essential feature of monotheism, whereas ethical monotheism dwells upon the contrast between the righteous Ruler and the sinful world, and between divine grace and fallen man. Royce concludes: "Therefore, behind many of the conflicts between the so-called pantheism in Christian tradition and the doctrines of 'divine transcendence' and 'divine personality,' there has lain the conflict between intellectualism and voluntarism, between an interpretation of the world in terms of order and an interpretation of the world in terms of the conflict between good and evil, righteousness and unrighteousness."[100] In my judgment, this is an insightful observation on the history of Christianity.

This history is made even more complex, says Royce, by the influence of the Indic type of God. This concept influenced mysticism and, of course, Neoplatonic philosophy, which, in turn, influenced Christian philosophy and theology. Augustine is a prime example of this influence. Further, within Christianity, the mystics have often pointed to the failure to resolve the conflict between moral and intellectual interests. Royce writes: "The mystics . . . have always held that the results of the intellect are negative and lead to no definite idea of God which can be defended against the skeptics, while . . . to follow the law of righteousness, whether or not with the aid of divine grace, does not lead, at least in the present life, to the highest type of knowledge of God."[101] Then Royce, with his respect for the experiential in religion, writes: "Without this third type of monotheism, and without this negative criticism of the work of the intellect, and this direct appeal to immediate experience, Christian doctrine, in fact, would not have reached some of its most characteristic forms and expressions, and the philosophy of Christendom would have failed to put on record some of its most fascinating speculations."[102]

Royce then reviews the history of the so-called proofs for God's existence—generally an expression of the Hellenistic influence in Christianity—and says that there is some basis in the claim that these efforts to grasp the divine nature via the intellect lead to results remote "from the vital experience upon which religious monotheism, and in particular, Christian monotheism must rest, if such . . . is permanently to retain the confidence of a man who is at once critical and religious."[103]

Royce also reviews Kant's struggle with the intellectualism-voluntarism conflict and notes that the God of Kant is the righteous Ruler and the kingdom of ends is a universe of free moral agents. This realm, for Kant, stands in contrast to the ideal realm of holiness or moral perfection, which can never be known by men through either mystical vision or logical demonstration. For Kant, God is defined in terms of will; the righteous man wills that God exists.[104] These struggles remain, says Royce. He predicts that the question "Is God personal?" will become more explicit as the modern thought becomes more aware of what constitutes a person.

Finally, it is not surprising that Royce argues that whatever answers to the questions about the nature of the world that are developed—is it real, rational, ethical?—we must not put exclusive emphasis on any one characteristic. For, "as we have seen, the problem of monotheism requires a synthesis of all the three ideas of God"; thus any attempt to address these three questions must be an answer that does adequate justice to the three ideas and the three problems.[105] As we well know, Royce's own efforts were aimed at achieving this synthesis and providing an answer to these three questions. Thus, he sought in his conceptions of God to give an account of the nature of reality that would satisfy the moral insight, the theoretic insight, and the religious insight. And the three conceptions of being addressed in *The World and the Individual* embody aspects of the three ideas of God and address the three questions.

The Sources of Religious Insight

Now we turn to *The Sources of Religious Insight*. This work is, in my judgment, a truly classic phenomenological exploration of the nature of religion and of religious experience. Although it is a parallel to *The Varieties of Religious Experience* by William James,[106] it transcends that work in a number of ways. First, it explores religious experience common to much of mankind rather than the special, genius cases that are the subject of James's work. Second, it studies both individual and communal religious experience. James defines religious experience in purely individualistic terms; it is, for James, "the experience of individuals who regard themselves as 'alone with the divine.'"[107] To this Royce responds: "Individual Experience, therefore, must abide with us to the very end of our quest, as one principal and fundamental source of insight. But it is one aspect only of Religious Experience."[108] James also was convinced that communal religious experience was always conventional and without passion. Royce believed, as we shall see, that ordinary social experiences could channel as well as obstruct religious insight. Further, in *The Problem of Christianity* it is the community that is the vehicle of atonement and restoration for the individual. Third, *The Sources* is solidly based in the empirical and experiential. Royce writes: "The issue will be one regarding the facts of living experience."[109] James's work is considered a classic in the psychology of religion, yet James seeks to explain man's religious need in terms of an experience that "wells up from the subliminal self, from the soundless depths of our own subconscious."[110] Royce, on the other hand, asserts that "the principal religious motives are indeed perfectly natural human motives."[111]

In a previously unpublished, unfinished manuscript, "Religious Experience and Religious Truth," Royce writes: "Religious experience, like any other sort of human experience, has its natural history." In this piece, Royce argues that religious experience, like all experience, "is the result of two general characteristics of our nature, viz., our sensitiveness, and our docility."[112] Docility is, we recall, a power that relates to preserving experience, to reacting to the past and to taking the past up into the present in order to provide meaning. Sensitiveness concerns selective attention, interests, the familiar. Royce provides the following description:

> Somebody whose experience is in question is a being both sensitive and docile. Because he is sensitive in a certain way, his fortunes have aroused in him sensations and feelings. These, so far as they are to enter into his more organized experience, he interprets in a certain way. His interpretation, viewed with respect to its mere natural history, is a result of his habits, and so, of course, is a result of his social traditions, of his past life, of all that has happened to him, and of all his former efforts to find his way in the maze of life. And of course his interpretation, like any other human interpretation, is also the result of an active process. There is no such thing as a passive reception or idea. Every bit of insight is a construction . . . a creation of the person who is to get it. Nobody observes anything without putting himself, with all his own nature and habits into the facts. . . . To perceive facts is to adopt one's own life to one's world, and one's world to one's own needs.[113]

Finally, Royce asserts: "Any man's religious experience, then, is, as a natural process, an incident in the history of his sensitive life, of his personal interpretation of the world, and of his more or less creative effort to fulfill his needs, and to respond in his own way to the universe."[114] Religious experience, then, for Royce, is natural and profoundly personal and social—it is the experience of a human self in the history of his own life, set in the material, historical, social, and cultural context of that individual history and life.

A fourth way in which Royce's *Sources* transcends James's *Varieties* is that Royce deals with the "paradox of revelation," which is also the "paradox of religious insight." This paradox concerns the troubling question for all individuals and communities who must deal with claims to religious experience, and particularly with claims to religious truth that comes from a religious experience. How do I know this is a true revelation? What conditions assure that one validly hears the divine voice and it is not all an illusion or delusion? The question is how is it possible for a being "so weak as to need saving, should still hope, in his fallible experience, to get into touch with anything divine?"[115] One wonders indeed how James's individualistic approach could provide any criteria for testing the validity of voices from something beyond. This question is especially relevant today in an age where many claim to be acting by command of the divine.

Royce begins his exploration by asserting that the essential postulate of religion, of whatever religion, is *"that man needs to be saved."*[116] Then he proceeds to demonstrate the validity of his postulate by reviewing the essentials of Buddhism, the writings of Plato in *The Republic,* and various literary sources. He believes that these examples show that the search for salvation belongs to no "one type of piety or of poetry or of philosophy."[117]

Royce then provides two defining characteristics of this postulate. He writes:

> The first is the idea that there is some end or aim of human life which is more important than all other aims, so that, by comparison with this aim all else is secondary and subsidiary, and perhaps relatively unimportant, or even vain and empty. The other idea is this: That man as he now is, or as he naturally is, is in great danger of missing his highest aim as to render his whole life a senseless failure by virtue of thus coming short of his true good.[118]

Thus religious insight means *"insight into the need and into the way of salvation."*[119]

The next major question is, What are the sources of insight? Royce will consider seven sources, beginning with the human self viewed first as uniquely individual and then as social: these are the basic and most elementary. However, Royce will find individual life and social life insufficient to meet the religious need for salvation. He then turns to five other sources. These are all dependent on the first two sources but will develop, strengthen, correct, and transform these in some way. The five are reason as a synthesizing power; the will or the volitional; loyalty; the religious mission of sorrow; and the unified community of the spirit. My focus will be on the basic sources, with some attention to the religious mission of sorrow and with only brief reference to the others. Before turning to the individual as a source of religious insight, I note that in referring to reason and will as sources of religious insight Royce is addressing the conflict—noted in the article "Monotheism"—between the intellectual and the ethical interpretations coming from Greece and Israel. The synthesis occurs in loyalty, which combines both the unifying of reason and the commitment of will; it also addresses the passion of the mystic.

In turning to the individual alone with his problem of salvation and with his efforts to know the divine that can save, Royce asserts that the individual can be in touch with a genuine source of insight, one of value, although also a source with limits. There are, says Royce, three objects that individual experience, as a source of religious insight, can reveal: The ideal, the need, and the deliverer. The ideal is, of course, the standard in terms of which the individual estimates the sense and value of his personal life. The need for salvation is that degree to which he falls short of attaining his ideal and is sundered from this ideal by evil fortune, his own paralysis of will, or his inward baseness. The deliverer is that presence, that power, that light, that truth, that great companion who helps the individual and saves him from his need.[120]

As humans, we are creatures of wavering and conflicting motives, and although we strongly desire a unity that makes life meaningful, we cannot find this unity on our own: we always miss our mark. Further, we have only glimpses of what would fulfill us, what would meet our need: "a life infinitely richer than our own." As James argues, we want to get in touch with something that will give us a new dimension to our lives. We want something more. Further, for Royce, our need and desire are crucial. Royce writes: "Unless you have inwardly felt the need of salvation and learned to hunger and thirst after spiritual unity and self-possession, all the rest of religious insight is to you a sealed book."[121] Paul Tillich, too, often argued that there must be a seeking for and response to the ultimate.

But we are not alone in this world, and we have no grounds for assuming our need is any more valuable than that of our neighbor. Indeed, my neighbor's reality is prior to mine, as Royce argued throughout his philosophical career. He writes: "So long as man views his fellow man *merely* as fellow-man, he only complicates his problem, for both he and his fellows equally need salvation. Their plight is common; their very need of salvation chains them in the prison of human sorrow."[122] Thus we must turn to the social and to shared human life to attain a broader religious insight. Royce writes that "no one who remains content with his merely individual experience of the presence of the divine and of his deliverer, has won the whole of any true insight. For as a fact, we are all members one of another; and I can have no insight into the way of my salvation unless I thereby learn of the way of salvation for all my brethren. And there is no unity of the spirit unless all men are privileged to enter it whenever they see it and know it and love it."[123] Here again is Royce's emphasis on the social expansion of the human self and the equal worth of each human self, which he previously discussed in "Tests of Right and Wrong."

Indeed, Royce argues that one of the principal sources of our need for salvation is our narrowness of view about things and especially about the meaning of our own purposes and motives. The social world, as Royce has constantly argued, broadens our outlook; an individual corrects his own narrowness by trying to share his fellow's point of view. Social responsibilities can set limits to our fickleness; social discipline can keep us from indulging all our caprices; human companionship may steady our vision. The social world may bring us in touch with our public, great self, wherein we may find our "soul and its interest writ large."[124] Social experience is a source of religious insight, and the insight it can bring is knowledge of "salvation through the fostering of human brotherhood."[125]

A most insightful excursion into religious insight is Royce's discussion of the experience of moral suffering, of the deep sense of guilt accompanied by the belief that one is an outcast from human sympathy and is hopelessly alone. He illustrates this with two literary examples: the title character in "The Ancient Mariner" and Raskolnikov in *Crime and Punishment*. The curse of the Ancient Mariner is to be alone with his guilt on a wide-wide sea. His escape from the horrors of his despair begins with the first stirring of love in his heart toward all living beings. This poem, says Royce, has its great value as a picture of "the loneliness of guilt and of the escape through loving union with one's kind."[126] Turning to *Crime and Punishment*, Royce writes: "Raskolnikov, the hero, after his thoughtfully conceived crime, and after his laborious effort at self-justification, finds himself prey of a simply overwhelming sense that he walks alone amongst men, and that, in the crowded streets of the city, he is as one dead amongst specters. There is nowhere, I think, a more persuasive picture of the loneliness of great guilt."[127] The central conception in these two literary pieces is of salvation as reconciliation with both the social and the divine orders, an escape from the wilderness of lonely guilt to the realm where men can understand one another.

This brings us directly to the "religious mission of sorrow." Sorrows are defined by Royce as evils that we can assimilate. These become part of a "constructive process" that involves growth rather than destruction, a passage to a new life. We take these sorrows up into our plan of life, give them new meaning as they become part of a new whole. This was Royce's emphasis in his essays on the problem of evil as well as in *Religious Aspect* and *The Spirit*. In this book, Royce illustrates his ideas through a story based on an actual incident. A young man, Oliver Pickersgill, falls in love with Ruth, the daughter of Peter Lannithorne, who is serving a six-year term in the penitentiary for embezzlement. Given the family history and the sorrow within that family, Oliver is concerned that his marriage to Ruth would only bring new sorrow and tragedy to the person he loves. Thus he seeks advice. He turns first to Ruth's mother, who, having suffered the bitterness of a marriage gone wrong, does not want her daughters to marry. But she tells Oliver to consult her husband, no criminal at heart, and see if he wants his daughter to take up the burden of a possible new tragedy. Consulting his father, Oliver is advised that the proposed marriage will only lead to misery. Yet he, too, advises Oliver to visit the convict and see what advice such a man, who has brought on the original sorrow, has about the proposed marriage.

Oliver does visit the man in jail. Peter admits to Oliver full responsibility for his crime and makes clear that he also believes justice has been served by his being in jail. Here, of course, is the repentant sinner discussed by Royce in his essay "The Knowledge of Good and Evil." Peter Lannithorne, however, believes that Ruth's mother and Oliver's father have the wrong point of view. They want security, the one thing a human being cannot have. Peter tells Oliver that he has learned that *"You are safe only when you can stand everything that can happen to you"* and that *"Courage is security."*[128] He tells Oliver he and Ruth must take their chance in life; they have a right to trust the future. This, says Royce, is insight. It shows you

> [t]he possibility, not of annulling an evil, or of ceasing to regret it, but of showing spiritual power, first, through idealizing your grief, by seeing even through this grief the depth of the significance of our relations as individuals to one another, to our social order, and to the whole of life; secondly, through enduring your fortune; and thirdly, through conquering, by the might of the spirit, those goods which can only be won through such sorrow.[129]

The stage is now set for *The Problem of Christianity.*

The Problem of Christianity

This book is a culmination of Royce's effort to address the question of a conception of the Ultimate and of the nature of reality that is adequate to human experience and that addresses theoretic, moral, and religious insights, discussed in this chapter. Christianity is viewed as a philosophy of life, and the question Royce asks is "In what sense, if any, can the modern man consistently be, in creed, a Christian?"[130] The phrase "modern man" refers to all contemporary persons entrusted to develop and transmit to future generations the most cherished elements of wisdom of the human race. In focusing on creed, however, Royce is clear that he is not concerned here with dogma or with particular theological beliefs.[131] Rather, he seeks the essentially vital and living ideas that will find expression in communal practices and religious-moral living and that will speak to all humanity. Finally, Royce will focus on living religious experience as expressed in the early Pauline Christian communities. Royce writes: "Historically speaking, the Christian Church first discovered the Christian ideas. The founder of Christianity, so far as we know what his teachings are, seems not to have defined them adequately."[132] Further, he observes: "They first came to a relatively full statement through the religious life of the Pauline Churches; and the Pauline epistles contain their first, although still not quite complete formulation."[133]

As indicated earlier in our discussion of the essay "What Is Vital in Christianity?" Royce refuses to found the essence of Christianity on questions of the founder's person or the details of his life, and he does not see Christianity as a religion of the Master. Rather, for Royce, the essence of Christianity is its stress on the saving community. Royce writes: "The thesis of this book is that the essence of Christianity, as the Apostle Paul stated that essence, depends upon regarding the being which the early Christian Church believed itself to represent, and the being which I call . . . the 'Beloved Community,' as the true source, through loyalty, of the salvation of man." Royce further claims: "This doctrine I hold to be both empirically verifiable within the limits of our own experience, and metaphysically defensible as an expression of the life and the spiritual significance of the whole universe."[134]

It is indeed the community that allows us to understand more fully the teachings of the Master. Of Jesus' teaching, Royce found two ideas especially crucial—his preaching of love and the Kingdom of Heaven. Both were mysterious and in need of interpretation. Thus, love is a mystery, for although we know we are to love God and our neighbor, the question is *how*. How can I be practically useful in meeting my neighbor's needs? Anyone who has tried to be benevolent or to meet the needs of others knows that there can be a huge crevice between your interpretation of what a person needs and what she believes she needs. It is the interpretation of Jesus' teachings in the letters of Paul that make the difference for Royce. What can make the loving of our neighbor less mysterious and difficult is community, for a community "when united by an active developing purpose is an entity more concrete, and, in fact, less mysterious than any individual man."[135] In community we can come to know each other, to see what each other's needs are. I need not ask "Who is my neighbor?" for my neighbor and I are members of one and the same community.

The essence of Christianity, for Royce, is contained in three ideas. The first of these is that the source and means of salvation is the community of believers. Community is also the basis of the ethic of love taught by Jesus. Royce writes: "This, the first of our essential ideas of Christianity is the idea of a spiritual life in which universal love for all individuals shall be completely blended, practically harmonized, with an absolute loyalty for a real and universal community, God, the neighbor and one church."[136]

The other two essential ideas are the moral burden of the individual and atonement. In discussing the moral burden of the individual, we need to briefly review Royce's understanding of sin. Sin is grounded in two human conditions. The first **is the finitude of our consciousness:** *"Our finitude means, then an actual inattention—a lack of successful interest, at this conscious instant, in more than a very few details of the universe."*[137] This finitude of consciousness is not itself sin, but the condition of sin. Because of our finitude we are called upon to do two things if we wish to be fully human beings: (1) to intensely develop our power of response to the universe around us, to maintain as much openness as possible; and (2) to recognize that full truth and reality are still to be discovered. Our sinfulness thus is twofold. First is the sin of irresponsiveness, which is the deliberate choice to narrow our focus, but in a very specific sense, namely, to choose to forget what we already know. In other words, *"To sin is consciously to choose to forget,* through a narrowing of the field of attention, a thought that one already recognizes."[138] Second, we have the sin of pride, the lack of humility about our limited grasp of truth and reality. Sin, in this sense, is making absolute that which is only finite. This is the "illusion" of selfishness but restated as an inordinate responsiveness to one's own present interests, parallel to the irresponsiveness to the greater world beyond.

Though human nature is finite, it also has an infinite dimension. This is manifested in our very possibility of self-transcendence and aspiration to goals and ideals that are not finite. This is the demand for self-actualization in an ideal, for loyalty to a cause. Thus, the first condition for sin is our finitude, understood in terms of irresponsiveness to the broader world, and inordinate responsiveness to self-interests. Royce writes that "[t]he deeper tragedies of life thus result from this our narrowness of view."[139]

The **second condition for sin** lies in the very solution one seeks to broaden one's view, namely, in **social life.** Social life helps us toward self-transcendence, but in the very process of social cultivation and self-development, the self-will and the individual are brought to fruition. In Royce's view the social order can lead a person to sin in two specific ways. It can encourage him to give in to the collective will and become a "they," a part of the crowd, rather than a unique self. One can refuse to take responsibility for one's own existence, to be a self. Royce thus expresses his notion of guilt in terms of self-loss: "Now the sense of guilt, if deep and pervasive and passionate, involves at least a dim recognition that there is some central aim of life and that one has come hopelessly short of that aim . . . the true sense of guilt in its greatest manifestation involves a confession that the whole self is somehow tainted, the whole life, for the time being, wrecked."[140] However, in addition to loss of self and refusal to be a self, one may fall into another sin fostered by socialization, namely egoism—a belief that salvation can be achieved by the individual alone. This is the sin of pride, a withdrawal into the world of self-sufficiency. This error also results in a deep sense of guilt, the "expe-

rience of guilt, anxiety, and inner conflict which results from the painful awareness of deeply rooted egoism."[141]

To be saved, an individual cannot help himself by any word or deed of his own.
The only escape, contends Royce, is loyalty. In loyalty the individual achieves
transcendence and a unity; he achieves his unique goal, which he genuinely
chooses and loves, and this goal is the social will of the community. Individual
and social will unite. However, this unification must not be social conformity and
a blending of wills. Royce writes: "Even if the individual needs his social world as
a means of grace and a gateway to salvation, the social order, in turn, needs individuals that are worth saving and can never be saved itself unless it expresses
itself through the deeds and inner lives of souls deeply conscious of the dignity
of selfhood, of the infinite worth of unique and intensely conscious life."[142] The
community which saves must be one which truly loves the individual, which
values his uniqueness, and one in which the individual truly loves and values
the community and each of its members. Such a community cannot be created
by any merely social will, but only by an act of love, of grace on the part of an individual, and, in the case of Christianity, by the act of Jesus Christ. Some potent
and loyal individual, acting as a leader, must declare that for him the community
is real. In such a leader, and in his spirit, the community will begin its own life, if
the leader has the power to create what he loves. Royce writes:

> We know how Paul conceives the beginning of the new life wherein Christian salva-
> tion is to be found. This beginning he refers to the work of Christ. . . . He both knew
> and loved his community before it existed on earth. . . . On earth he called into this
> community its first members. He suffered and died that it might have life. Through
> his death and in his life the community lives. *He is now identical with the spirit of this
> community.*[143]

Thus, for Royce, we achieve what he calls the realm of grace, the realm of pow-
ers and gifts that save, by thus originating and sustaining and informing the loyal
life. The realm contains three essentially necessary constituent members.

> First, the ideally lovable community of many individuals in one spiritual bond; sec-
> ondly, the spirit of the community, which is present both as the human individual
> whose power originated and whose example, whose life and death, have led and
> still guide the community, and as the united spiritual activity of the whole commu-
> nity; thirdly, charity itself, the love of the community by all its members, and of the
> members of the community.[144]

This is the community of grace, the saving community, and the beloved community. Salvation lies in loyalty and love to the beloved community. However, Royce

was very aware of the depth of human failure and sin, and so he identifies another type of sin, the most tragic of all. It is the sin of betrayal or treason, which occurs after the individual discovers a loyalty that gains his inner commitment, a loyalty that allows him to overcome the sins of conformity and loss of self, the conflicts of conformity and self-will. This sin occurs when, after finding a cause, he betrays it and cuts himself off from the community of loyalty, the community of grace. The traitor is one who has had an ideal and has loved it with all his heart, soul, mind, and strength, but now has been deliberately false to his cause. Such a sin of betrayal or treason places the traitor in "the hell of the irrevocable." Hell is the awareness on the part of the sinner and the community that the deed of betrayal has been done and cannot be undone; although it may be transformed in its meaning and changed in its consequence, it cannot be erased. Such is the temporal nature of human action. Royce writes:

> The hell of the irrevocable; all of us know what it is to come to the border of it when we contemplate our own past mistakes or mischance. But we can enter it and dwell in it when the fact "This deed is irrevocable," is combined with the further fact, "This deed is one that unless I call treason my good and moral suicide my life, I cannot forgive myself for doing.[145]

The guilt of this free act of betrayal is as enduring as time. This is the "moral burden of the individual."

This act of treason can be overcome only by an act of atonement. This is the third essential Christian idea. In explicating his idea, Royce rejects two traditional doctrines of atonement, the penal and the moral. The penal theory fails because it ignores the individual personality of the sinner. To say someone else has been substituted to pay for one's sins is not to reconcile the sinner to himself or to God. The moral theory urges the sinner to repent, which he has already done, and, indeed, this repentance is at the heart of his moral existence in the hell of the irrevocable.

To overcome this deepest of sins, this treason, the sinner must be reconciled both to himself and to the community. And, for Royce, it is not just a matter of love and forgiveness; it is true that love must be restored, but it will be the love for the member who *has been a traitor,* and the tragedy of the treason will permanently form part in and of this love.[146] The treason can be overcome only by the community or by a steadfast loyal servant of the community who is the incarnation of the very spirit of the community itself. Royce writes:

> This faithful and suffering servant of the community may answer and confound treason by a work whose type I shall next venture to describe in my own way. Thus:

first, this creative work shall include a deed, or various deeds, for which only this treason furnishes the opportunity. Not treason in general, but this individual treason shall give the occasion and supply the condition of the creative deed which I am in ideal describing. Without just that treason, this new deed (so I am supposing) could not have been done at all. And hereupon the new deed, as I suppose, is so ingeniously devised, so concretely practical in the good which it accomplishes, that, when you look down upon the human world after the new creative deed has been done, you say first, "This deed was made possible by the treason"; and secondly, *"The world as transformed by this creative deed, is better than it would have been had all else remained the same, but had that deed of treason not been done at all."* That is, the new creative deed has made the new world better than it was before the blow of treason fell.[147]

Several significant aspects of Royce's analysis of sin and atonement need emphasis here. First, he recognizes sin, conversion, and salvation as ongoing processes and not single events. Second, salvation is both personal and communal, and both personal and communal alliances must be continually renewed. Third, sin is both personal and communal in two more senses. Its consequences affect both the individual sinner and other individuals as well. To personally repent and achieve salvation is not enough. There must be healing of the community; the sinner is loved but only as a traitor. Others must move out in love and initiate forgiveness and atoning acts. And these acts must be specific and concretely relevant to the situation. If a life is the act of betrayal, an act of truth and openness must occur that increases the sense of trust in the community and makes the sense of individual and communal obligation higher and stronger.

Sin is both personal and communal in still another sense. There can be communal sin in that a community may portray itself as the ultimate goal, worthy of the ultimate loyalty. It betrays the goal of loyalty to loyalty and engages in the sin of making absolute what is finite. Communal sin needs atonement. It, too, can come through the individual or the community. The individual member must somehow atone in the world of communities by being critical of his own community and seeking to bring about a higher level of loyalty. Presumably, another community can lead the sinful community to a higher level of meaning and loyalty by a creative act of atonement and transformation. Royce does not develop this latter idea, but it is an implication of his views and will be explored somewhat in the next chapter.

Thus, the three central ideas of Christianity are community, the moral burden of the individual, and atonement. This true crux of the matter, however, is the beloved community. It is the highest exemplification of graced community. Grace transforms persons into new creations; in this beloved community, members will become instruments of good to each other and vessels of grace to each other, atoning and transforming. Indeed, the beloved community is engaged in a temporal yet endless task of uniting individuals in love and understanding, in unfolding the mystery of one's neighbors to each member. It is engaged in the work of the spirit. Royce writes: "The essential message of Christianity has been the word that the sense of life, the very being of the time-process itself, consists in the progressive realization of the Universal Community in and through the longings, the vicissitudes, the tragedies and triumphs of this process of the temporal world."[148]

5

Developing Genuine Individuals and Communities

Royce's reflections on concrete problems of the human community provide a framework for a new approach to social and political issues. First, Royce fully engages the central issue of individualism versus collectivism, the individual versus the demands of social order. Like Nietzsche, Royce honored the individual, noble, courageous self who could transcend narrow interests, mediocrity, and the powerful draw of social conformity in order to live as "captain of one's own soul,"[1] possessed of one's unique moral value in the face of the chaos, the hardships, and the struggles that such dedication entailed. Royce asserts that one sin for a human self is self-loss, becoming part of the crowd, a "they" instead of an "I"; however, Royce is equally concerned about community. Thus, near the end of his life, he noted that his task as a teacher was to teach "that we are saved through community."[2] Parallel to the sin of "self-loss there is the sin of self-sufficiency," of the individual who "goes it alone" and believes that genuine selfhood can be achieved in this manner. Royce notes that Nietzsche's great limitation was his failure to see that real power for the genuine self lies with the "true life of cooperating individuals," and he did not deal with "the great problem of reconciling the unique individual with the world order."[3] Further, Nietzsche did not appreciate enough the richness and core of wisdom that could be obtained from one's personal and cultural past. The aspect of the individual-social concern is summarized well in the words of George Herbert Mead, a student of Royce: "We wanted full intellectual freedom, and yet, the conservation of values for which had stood Church, State, Science, and Art."[4] For Royce, individuality and community, individual and social interests are inextricably bound together; each is uniquely valuable, and each arises out of their mutual interaction in a creative, ongoing, and infinite process. This individual-social conflict and interaction is a theme that flows throughout each of the works and issues discussed in this chapter.

Second, Royce asserted that communities are, in their own right, "persons," with histories, future goals, and temporal continuity, and thus originators of actions that can be judged on their social and moral merits. This view allows judgments to be made upon the goals and loyalties and actions of communities, whether they are corporations, cities, or even nations. It was from this conviction as well as from his concern for loyalty and sorrow at betrayal of the human community that Royce wrote a scathing condemnation of Germany and the war in the last years of his life. Contrary to popular opinion, these statements were not the emotional outbursts of a tired and disappointed idealist, but thoughtful reflections based on his developed philosophical views. In the same vein, Royce argues for an international community that honors the uniqueness of each nation and for provinces that seek their own identity, but that, at the same time, honor the identities of other provinces. Communities, as persons, must develop unique goals and seek to live in harmony with other communities with different goals, but also with the common goal of broadening the human community.

Third, Royce provides us with a set of conditions or criteria for achieving consciousness as a genuine community. These, in turn, provide us with a valuable set of tools for assessing communities, including parasitic, dysfunctional, and immoral ones. Since these conditions are for developing the genuine, beloved community, they also set goals for existing communities. Indeed, Royce utilized these conditions indirectly in his history of California, although his explicit statement of them occurred in his later philosophy, and they play a role in his statements on Germany and the war as well. In concert with his conditions for developing community consciousness, Royce also provides us the principle of loyalty to loyalty as a standard for assessing communities' loyalty: there are loyalties that are immoral and damaging.

Finally, Royce, through his extensive work on interpretation and mediation, provides a solid basis for creating community out of conflict, whether it is at the level of the family, state, or nation, or in work to build a global community. Indeed, interpretation has built into it ethical demands, and it plays a central role in Royce's philosophy; it is a key for understanding self, community, and the universe itself. Royce's plan for an international insurance, believed by many to be eccentric, is based on the interpretive process and thus offers a unique methodology for community building. Royce believed that it would provide, on the international level, a way to bypass the diplomatic and treaty route, and to allow deliberative dialogues among autonomous international agents acting together in communities of interpretation, thus making "the community of mankind visible."[5] At the heart of Royce's insurance scheme, in addition to its essentially unifying and reconciling characteristics, is the "mutual" aspect of insurance, which asks a person, in seeking a "beneficiary," to transcend self-interest and narrow perspective and to link to the social order in varying ways.

With this framework in mind, this chapter will turn first to an explication and discussion of Royce's conditions for community and his doctrine of interpretation—a community-creating process and essential to self and community. The principle of loyalty to loyalty will also be discussed, in parallel to the conditions of community. This will allow an analysis of functional and dysfunctional communities and harmful and disloyal loyalties. In three essays, "The Duties of the Americans in the Present War,"[6] "The Destruction of the Lusitania,"[7] and "The First Anniversary of the Sinking of the Lusitania,"[8] Royce directly discusses disloyalty and community betrayal and applies the principles of community and loyalty.

Next we focus on Royce's exploration of the balancing of individuality and social order. This is done first in the context of Royce's visit to Australia and his reflections on how this colony exemplifies in the concrete the attempt to balance loyalty of the individual to the social order while also maintaining genuine individuality. He draws some interesting parallels between this problem as addressed in Australia and in California, which also allows discussion of "An Episode of Early California Life: The Squatters' Riot of 1850 in Sacramento."[9] Continuing the parallels between Australia and California, we look at the essay "On Certain Limitations of the Thoughtful Public in America." Then we turn to Royce's exposition of the notion of a "wise provincialism." Finally, we will discuss Royce's application of his notion about provincialism in several essays on higher education: "Present Ideas of American University Life,"[10] "The Carnegie Foundation for the Advancement of Teaching and the Case of Middlebury College,"[11] and "The Freedom of Teaching."[12]

The fourth section of the chapter analyzes Royce's essay "Race Questions and Prejudices."[13] I believe this essay has been misunderstood; in an attempt to clear up some of this misunderstanding, I interpret the essay in terms of a critical examination by Royce of various approaches to the race problem, including scientific and cultural approaches. It is my judgment that in discussing his experiences with the race problem in Jamaica, Royce intends an exploration of a possible solution but also a satire and criticism of our Southern solution. This approach to the essay may also shed light on the question, In what senses was Royce a "racist?"

The last section of the chapter will focus on Royce's view of "dangerous dyads" and the need for mediation and interpretation. Our first discussion will focus on the family and Royce's extensive analysis of family dyads, and especially on a mother-daughter conflict. In his 1916 Course on Ethics,[14] the latter conflict provides a brilliant illustration of the process of interpretation. This process and the task of mediation are then explored on the international level through Royce's two books *War and Insurance*[15] and *The Hope of the Great Community*.[16] These ideas, I believe, are relevant in dealing with conflict resolution in our time. These chapter explorations should leave little doubt that Royce contributes to social/political philosophy and that he was very much a "public philosopher."

Genuine Communities, Loyalties, and Moral Betrayal

In his *The Problem of Christianity,* Royce focuses on the conditions needed for the development of community consciousness and on the question whether these communities are supportive or parasitic, moral or immoral; he also provides some conditions for what he believes are "genuine, supportive and saving" communities, that is, those communities that foster genuine, moral selves.[17] In discussing conditions of community, we are also establishing conditions for adequate self-development and for addressing the problem Nietzsche did not address, namely, reconciling the unique individual and the social order. It should be clear that for Royce the social and the community is always prior to the individual self; indeed, this is the context in which selves develop. The community, the social world, provides the context for self-interpretation, for self-planning, and for moral action. Moreover, as we learned in the previous chapter, it is the community that saves the individual traitor.

For Royce, "the detached individual is essentially a lost being."[18] The individual self is always at war within; not only are there numerous conflicting desires, but as the self interacts in the social world a conflict develops between self-will and the social laws and customs of tradition. Both Christianity and Buddhism see the detached individual as a lost being, one who cannot save himself. Buddhism seeks the salvation of the detached individual through an act of resignation whereby all desires are abandoned, while Christianity sees salvation through willing service to the community.[19] Thus, for Royce, to establish the conditions of community is to establish those conditions that will save detached and separated individuals. Indeed, he would argue that such individuals have not achieved genuine individuality or the freedom they crave.

What then are the conditions for developing communities that do create unique individuals who have the freedom to be "captains of their own souls?" First, Royce asserts, "[a] true community is essentially a product of a time-process."[20] A community has a past and will have a future. It has a more or less conscious history, real or ideal, and this history is a part of its very essence. To maintain community consciousness it must foster and maintain memory of key events, significant objects, important actions, and goals, values, and ideals. This is true, of course, also for the individual self. Royce writes: "My present carries farther the plan of my past."[21] Again, an essential part of that past is the social and communal, and without the communal context the self could not achieve unification or find a plan or become a moral individual. Even our conscious perception is dependent on past experience. "Our present conscious perception of any object which impresses our sense organs is a sort of *brief abstract and epitome of our previous experience in connection with such objects. . . . We see in our world, in general, what we come prepared to see.*"[22]

Both the community and the self, then, must be grounded in a past that becomes the material for moving forward in the future. Indeed, as we shall see, moving forward for humankind and its communities, even in a revolutionary sense, is thoroughly grounded in and on the past. In terms of the self, connecting with the past seems simple, although, Royce asserts, "most of our memories of long-past events are systematically, although very unequally, falsified by habit."[23] In terms of the community, however, says Royce, the question arises: How can many different selves possess identically the same past as their own personally interesting past? Royce, as is his usual practice, turns to a concrete illustration for an answer. Consider the individual Maori in New Zealand who says, "I came over in the canoe Tai-Nui." This is his way of identifying with his ancestors and the history of travel to New Zealand in a "legendary canoe." Now any two or three or however many members of a tribe whose legendary ancestors came over in Tai-Nui possess, from their own point of view, identically the same past, in just this respect.[24] These Maori say, "We are of the same canoe," which means "We are of the same community."

Not only is the community dependent on its past, it is also a temporal being moving toward the future. Thus, just as a group of selves may accept the same past fact or event as a part of the individual self, so each one of many present selves may accept the same future event, which all of them hope or expect, as part of his or her personal future. Royce writes: "Thus, during a war, all of the patriots of one of the contending nations may regard the termination of the war, and the desired victory of their country, so that each one says, 'I shall rejoice in the expected surrender of that stronghold of the enemy. That surrender will be my triumph.'"[25] Thus, for Royce, the first two conditions for any community are that they be a community of memory and a community of hope. These two conditions must be present for any community of whatever type to exist.

Likewise, a self must also be a community of memory and hope. Royce writes: "In brief, my idea of myself is an interpretation of my past,—linked also with an interpretation of my hopes and intentions as to my future."[26] Community and self, for Royce, are products in time, and essential to their temporal flow and temporal continuity is a process of interpretation. Interpretation, for Royce, is a distinctive form of mental activity, a third form of knowledge, in addition to perception and cognition. Interpretation is triadic in character, involving a mediator between two minds. Thus, I am mediating the mind and thought of Royce, accessible through a set of signs contained in his work, to the mind of my reader. Three items are brought into determinate relationship by this interpretation: (1) I, the interpreter, who must have some understanding both of Royce and also of my audience; (2) the object, Royce's thought; and (3) a mind to whom the interpretation is addressed. The relationship is non-symmetrical, that is, unevenly arranged with respect to all three of the terms. If the order of the relationship were reversed, it would change the process. Further, those involved in the process would take on different roles, such as that of the interpreter. In real situations of mediation, having different persons play the role of interpreter increases the possibility of broader understanding of the situation.[27]

Interpretation is a temporal process; each of the terms of the relation corresponds to three dimensions of time: past, present, and future. Thus, I am presently interpreting to you what Royce wrote in the past for your future interpretation. The process of interpretation is irreversible, partial, and ideally infinite. Once I have spoken, what I have said cannot be revoked. But what I have said is not the final word, for there will be future interpretations of Royce, unless, for arbitrary reasons, the process of interpretation is interrupted or permanently stopped.

Interpretation creates a community among selves, including within self and between past self, present self, and future self. Thus, in order to interpret Royce to you, I had to take my past ideas of Royce, compare them with my present ideas, and then achieve a new understanding to convey to you. In achieving a new view, a new union of my ideas, I have thus transcended my past self and connected to my future self. I now transcend self again as I seek to connect with you and to connect Royce, via my interpretation, to your thoughts. Reaching beyond the limitations of one's own perspective and consciousness, as we have seen, is crucial for self and also for communities.

Further, interpretation involves an act of will, an act of loyalty, and an element of risk. I had to choose to re-immerse myself in Royce's thought, and I committed myself to be loyal to whatever truth I found therein. I had to put beside my ideas those of Royce so that they might interact. Moreover, I risked having my ideas changed. In addition, in conveying Royce's thought to you now, I risked being told I am wrong, and then the community of interpretation must rectify my error. By attending to my interpretation of Royce, you chose to enter into the community of Royce's interpreters, and you may risk having your ideas changed. If my attempt at interpretation is successful, a new meaning will come forth and a new unity of conscious will be achieved. I will have united your mind with Royce's in a shared understanding.

The crucial elements in interpretation then, are (1) respect and regard for selves as "dynamos of ideas," (2) will, and (3) reciprocity and mutuality. The will to interpret, in turn, involves (a) a sense of discontent and dissatisfaction both with partial meanings—a narrowness of one's own view of things—and with estrangement from others as carriers of meanings and ideas, and (b) an aim to unite selves in a unity of interpretation. There must be willingness to play one's part in the interpretive process. The listener to whom the interpretation is addressed must be kindly and sympathetic. What is gained from interpretation is self-knowledge, because we co-discover who we are and what our ideas and goals should be by contrasting them with the ideas and ideals of another. We also gain community because our isolation has been transcended, a new vision and an experiential conspectus achieved.

Interpretation is essential to building community, and it is the process whereby communities develop their meaningful pasts and produce meaningful projections for the future. It is not surprising, then, that Royce's third condition for the development of community is the imperative for members to engage in the interpretive process. It is in this process that each participating self, each member, can and does consciously extend its individual life in an ideal fashion, so as to regard some remote past or future events and deeds as part of the self's own life. Each self is an interpreting being and incorporates these deeds and events into its self-identification, and thus becomes a member of a community that needs historical traditions and long-range hopes. The self interprets itself in terms of the communal past and future. Self needs community and community needs the self. Thus, Royce provides a new definition of community, namely, "the community is a being that attempts to accomplish something in time and through the deeds of its members. . . . It involves the idea of deeds done and ends sought or attained. . . . In so far as these personalities [members] possess a life that is for each of them his own, while it is, in some of its events, common to them all, they form a community."[28] Thus, community is a temporal being; it has a past and will have a future.

As temporal, a community is the bringing forth of an embodied ideal. A community is a plan of action.

A fourth condition necessary for the existence of a community is that a number of distinct selves engage in mutual communication and interpretation among themselves. Communication and interpretation of shared events and deeds is an essential part of the selves' common life; they indeed create the common life. Since the interpretive process involves respect for others, mutuality, and reciprocity, deeper communal relations evolve among the members. A community also needs unification, and this occurs as every member identifies with a single meaningful event, object, or symbol. Thus, the fifth condition for community is that "the ideally extended past and future selves of the members include at least some events which are, for all these selves, identical."[29] Royce uses the example of St. Paul's Corinthian community to illustrate this and the other two conditions as well. This community shared the same past, the Resurrection event of Jesus, and they shared the hope of their own resurrection. Further, their interpretation of this event was the same, namely, its "saving" significance. Community requires one "tie" that clearly binds members in an identical event or object with the same meaning; there must be an unquestionable consciousness of unity. The community involves a commitment of true selves to a higher goal and ideal that they share. However, for Royce, this unity is always also a unity with variety. He asserts that the fact of a clear unity does not "annul the variety of the individual members."[30]

This shared meaning and unity is, however, not sufficient. A community must also possess common deeds and arouse a common love. There must be conscious participation in cooperative deeds, but in such a manner that the cooperating member says: "This activity which we perform together, this work of ours, its past, its future, its sequence, its order, its sense,—all these enter into my life, and are the life of my own self writ large."[31] There must be conscious understanding of the nature of my own deeds and those of my fellows, and especially the belief that "without this combination, this order, this interpretation of the co-working selves, just this deed could not be accomplished by the community."[32] Without this act of cooperation, of interacting, the community cannot accomplish its aim. Further, there must be mutual appreciation of the efforts of every member as part of accomplishing the mutually shared aim. Thus, in a jazz combo, only by each member playing his part and his instrument can a musical composition be performed. Each member of the community must encourage, stimulate, correct, and enjoy each other's acts, just as do members of a fine combo or orchestra.

The final condition for consciousness of genuine community is each member's loyal love of the community. Each self identifies his own life with the ongoing life of the community, sharing the goals of the community as his own goals. Loyal dedication of each self to the community leads each of the members to love his successful cooperation and the contribution of each self. There is mutual acceptance of each self as a fellow member of the community. All members of the community are respected, accepted, and loved by the other members. This overcomes separateness and allows each self to include in its life the lives of its fellows. However, love of members for each other must be transcended in a higher love: the love of the common deeds of the community. Thus, in a family or a friendship, it is the unity of action and goals that is the higher love, and it is that love that sustains the love members have for each other. Royce summarizes his discussion of the conditions of community as follows:

> And so, first, each of us learns to say: "This beloved past and future life, by virtue of the ideal extension, is my own life." Then, finding that our fellows have and love this past and future in common with us, we learn further to say: "In this respect we are all one loving and beloved community." Then we take a further step and say: "Since we are all members of this community, therefore, despite our differences, and our mutual sunderings of inner life, each of us can, and will, ideally extend his present self so as to include the present life and deeds of his fellow."[33]

We now turn to a discussion of loyalty as a further element of community building and action.

Loyalty and the Principle of Loyalty to Loyalty

Although we have discussed loyalty in our chapter on ethics, in this context we view loyalty as a force for uniting selves and building community. If one is a loyal servant of a cause, there are possible fellow servants. Loyalty tends to unite persons in one service. Further, as in the love for community, the loyalty is to the tie, to the union of the lovers, to their love, which is more than both of them viewed as distinct individuals.[34] The focal point of loyalty is a relation-based entity that transcends the individuals who constitute it. Further, the relationship stays with them; like the condition of community, the crucial aspect of the relationship enters into the sense of identity of each individual, into their biography.

Loyalty is an important aspect of the historical self. It is a defining set of familial, institutional, and national relationships. Loyalty involves a sense of shared histories. By the mere fact of my biography, I incur obligations toward others. Loyalties circumscribe communal circles, all members of which take others within the circle to be objects of concern. One stands by these friends, or this nation. Further, since my loyalty is part of my self-identity, in acting on their behalf, I reveal that identity. Indeed, one also reveals one's true identity in acting against one's obligations to the circle circumscribed by the loyalty.

Thus, as with community, there can be betrayal of one's loyalty. A betrayal of cause is first against self because the cause is an essential part of one's personal identity. Second, the betrayal is against fellow servants of the cause, who have placed trust in the relationship and in the loyalty pledge. The sense of community is profoundly injured.

A key test for disloyal communities is the principle of loyalty to loyalty. This principle commands us to seek to broaden loyalty and community, to connect us to other communities in fellowship, and to expand one's own perspective. It means respecting the loyalties of other communities unless they violate the principle of loyalty. If there is violation, we need to seek in some way to change this community. How then can communities be disloyal?

First, communities can commit the sin of pride and self-sufficiency. A community may portray itself as the ultimate goal, worthy of the ultimate loyalty. This is a betrayal of the principle of loyalty to loyalty, to the call to transcend narrow perspectives and to build broader communities. This community makes the finite absolute and stops arbitrarily the search for higher causes and broader community. Such a community and cause is in error, and the demand of the loyal person is to seek to correct this error. Second, a community may demand a loyalty to a cause or loyalty that is ultimately anti-community. These communities prey on other communities and tear down relationships rather than building them. Royce writes: "A robber band, a family engaged in a murderous feud, a pirate crew, a savage tribe, a Highland robber clan of old days. . . . Men have loved such causes devotedly, have shared them for a lifetime. Yet most of us would easily agree in thinking such causes unworthy of anybody's loyalty."[35]

This describes a disloyal community. What, then, is a dysfunctional community? The first two conditions for genuine community described earlier, namely, that there be a community of memory and a community of hope, apply to all communities, whether dysfunctional and immoral or functional and moral. I observe, however, that a central failing today for many of our communities comes about with these two conditions. For example, a remembered history is no longer the case in many families or communities—consider the failures in the ghetto areas of our cities and communities. Many ethnic groups do an excellent job of maintaining historical ties to their culture as well as within their families; others fail miserably in this regard. As for hope and future, in many areas in our country there seems no hope. A poignant example of a desperate attempt to maintain both history and hope is the tragedy in New Orleans after Hurricane Katrina. It remains to be seen if the attempts will be at all successful to reestablish community in many areas of that city and perhaps in the city as a whole.

Turning to the remaining conditions for maintaining a community consciousness, we find, first, dysfunction in failure to identify self with the community. The members of the community do not see its events and deeds as part of one's life. Or, second, the members fail to communicate and to engage in interpretation in order to create common meaning. Third, they do not have a shared significant event or deed. Fourth, they do not share in cooperative deeds, knowing that, without this cooperation, the aim or deed of the community will not be accomplished. Further, there is not mutual respect and acceptance. Finally, there is not loyal love to the community itself and especially to the common aim or cause or goal of that community. What one would have, essentially, is a collection of separate individuals pursuing their own aims and working under the same umbrella only for convenience, for a salary, for prestige, or for other motives. Unfortunately, many of our social institutions today fit this description, such as our families, churches, universities, and even friendships. And much of our social and political theory, in my judgment, fails because it views groups as collections of atomistic individuals and communal relations as established by external contract for purposes of self-preservation and the pursuit of self-interests.

Destruction of loyalties and communities is evil, and such destruction, says Royce, should be strongly and justly opposed.

Germany, *Lusitania,* and Betrayal

With these ideas in mind, we turn now to Royce's writings on the war. It is my contention that these essays are focused on betrayal of the human community and on an evil loyalty that violates the principle of loyalty to loyalty. In "The Duties of the Americans in the Present War," Royce establishes a clear contrast between Belgium, a nation that remained loyal to its international duty and sacrificed for the future of human brotherhood, and Germany, which rejected its international duty and betrayed the human community. About Belgium, Royce writes: "[I]n this war, there is constantly before our eyes the painfully tragic and sublime vision of one nation, through all its undeserved and seemingly overwhelming agonies, [which] has remained unmistakably true to its duty—that is, to its international duty, to its honors, its treaties, to the cause, to the freedom, and to the future union of mankind."[36] In Royce's view, the people of Belgium should be seen as fellow servants of the cause who have maintained their loyalty pledge to the circle of concern, the human brotherhood, whereas Germany has betrayed the trust others had in the human relationship. Thus, Germany has betrayed the loyalty pledge, and the sense of community is profoundly injured.

In the case of Germany, we also find an attitude of self-assertion. Germany rejects any moral obligation or international duty because of what it holds as its higher cause, namely, itself as a state. Royce notes that Germany has asserted that "for its own subjects, the State is the supreme moral authority, and that there is no moral authority which ranks superior to the will of the State."[37] This attitude by Germany is a betrayal of the principle of loyalty to loyalty; it commits the sin of self-pride and elevates its cause above all others.

In addition to the case of Belgium, Royce refers to the sinking of the ship *Ancona* by Austria while her passengers were still in danger of drowning. Austria is an ally of Germany, notes Royce, and her submarine policy is *"made in Germany."* President Wilson had addressed a note to Austria stating that "the officially reported act of the submarine commander was in principle barbarous and abhorrent to all civilized nations."[38] The Austrian reply, argues Royce, was that of Cain, who stated that "he was not his brother's keeper" and then asked "what law of God or man he was supposed to have broken?"[39] In terms of one's loyalty to the human brotherhood, one is his brother's keeper, and the law of man, the trust of others in principles of human decency and respect for persons, especially the vulnerable, has been broken.

Further, in the spirit of his discussion of treason in *The Problem of Christianity*, Royce argues that "deliberate national deeds cannot be undone, nor can their official justifications be lightly condoned by reason of later diplomatic trifling, and by reason of speciously well-written notes of apology and withdrawal."[40] These are acts that cannot be undone or forgiven. This brings us directly to the *Lusitania* case.

In his essay "The Destruction of the Lusitania," Royce asserts that it is not hate that motivates him, even over the bodies of those slain on the *Lusitania*, but "longing and sorrow for stricken humanity." This case has given us, says Royce, a "deeply unified and national indignation, coupled with a strong sense of our duty towards all humanity."[41] Again, the act is seen as a betrayal of humanity. This is even more clearly stated in the address Royce gave at the memorial for the first anniversary of the sinking of the *Lusitania*. There are those, notes Royce, who make light of this tragedy, arguing that those who went down with this ship met a fate "properly suited to their folly in taking passage on her despite the warnings." Further, Von Jagow, the German diplomat, argues that the intent of the ship, in carrying arms, was to "kill some of our brave soldiers."[42]

On the contrary, argues Royce, many of these passengers were being loyal to the call of duty. Calling on a communiqué from a relative of one lost on the

Lusitania, Royce shares this statement. "Whatever the other passengers were doing, these men had accepted professional tasks no one of which had anything to do with the war. They were going to meet their engagements. . . . Is that not the sort of professional courage and loyalty that we want to have the young men of the future exemplify?"[43] Royce cites two further cases, a young bride fulfilling her obligations to visit family in England and a Scottish mother taking her babies to their old home.

These persons, says Royce, were presumably doing their duties. But, in addition, they were asserting a basic right of humanity to the dignity and protection they should receive from humanity. They were traveling on a peaceful passenger steamer, and even if the steamer did have in her cargo some ammunition, an order was given to torpedo the ship without warning and without an opportunity for the passengers, especially women and children, to get away. This dignity and privilege of humanity Germany betrayed. It broke trust, and the human community was deeply wounded. Royce's remarks on this occasion raise serious doubts about political theories and policies that blithely discuss the necessity of collateral damage in the case of war. This will be discussed in more detail in our last chapter.

Finally, for Royce, there has also been another betrayal of the human community, a betrayal of the community of the dead and the obligation all humanity has to honor their memory and to renew the community's own life by the restoration of their presence into that life in a newer and deeper meaning. Royce writes:

> We honor our dead of the *Lusitania* because we know that their works do follow them, and we honor these works. Whoever, knowing the facts, scorns this our reverence, declares himself cut off in spirit from the community of mankind, and can be restored to that community only after he changes his mind.
>
> . . . It is their [Germany's] contempt for our piety in case of our dead that constitutes in this instance of the *Lusitania,* their own sin against the Holy Ghost, a sin officially committed by their Government from the moment when the submarine policy was authorized.[44]

Again, there has been betrayal of the community of humanity, of the circle of concern, of the historical past that should be honored, shared, and taken up into new meaning for the community. Instead, the attitude has been that of ridicule and excuse. Treason has been committed against the community, yet atonement is difficult since Germany acknowledges no sin.

Thus, rather than an emotional response to this affair, Royce offers a very reasoned, though obviously deeply sorrowful, reflection based solidly in his philosophy of loyalty and philosophy of community. Germany has violated the principle of loyalty to loyalty by elevating her cause above all others, and particularly the cause of humanity. Further, she has betrayed the community of humankind and its ideals of dignity and protection of human selves who are living their lives and doing their duty. Finally, there is Germany's attitude to the whole matter; she is an unrepentant traitor, and thus the community and a suffering servant are unable to carry out an act of atonement. Royce calls on Germany to change her mind and to "repent." Later, in his writings on international insurance, Royce does address ways to rebuild the sense of human community.

Before leaving this topic, however, I wish to address the question of inconsistency in Royce's view. In advocating that we assist our loyal brethren, the allies, in any manner possible, does Royce violate his own principles and philosophy of community? Can an advocate for respect of others' loyalties and the building of a "beloved community" support non-peaceful methods to resolve a conflict? Is this inconsistent with loyalty and with his call for a "beloved community"? About loyalty, Royce writes: "Enlightened loyalty, as we have now learned, means harm to no man's loyalty. It is at war only with disloyalty, and its warfare, *unless necessity constrains,* is only a spiritual warfare."[45] I believe it is reasonable to assert that Germany's act was a clear act of disloyalty and that, given its attitude of self-sufficient superiority, necessity required other than "spiritual means" in warring against such disloyalty.

As for the "beloved community," my treasured colleague Dwayne Tunstall argues that in his advocacy for measured violence in the case of Germany, Royce is advocating against his own notion of the beloved community, which, says Tunstall, "is built only by *agapic* acts."[46] This assertion of inconsistency depends on the assumption that *agape* is by nature nonviolent. My own studies of various interpretations of *agape,* including that of Anders Nygren,[47] lead me to disagree with this assumption; however, this is not the context for presenting such an argument. In addition, Tunstall emphasizes *agape,* but Royce did not use the concept of "love" in his discussion of Christianity. He speaks of love as mysterious and argues that Paul has made this notion more concrete with the development of the notion of the "spirit" of the community. Royce's preferred word was "loyalty." Again, this is not the context for extended discussion of this issue. The best response I can make to the charge of inconsistency is Royce's own words: "Christianity is a religion of love rather than of vengeance, not because it is a religion of non-resistance, for, since the Apostle Paul, it never has been a religion of non-resistance."[48] Finally, Royce, on another occasion, writes:

> [Y]ou know now why I should view militarism as a decidedly blind, although often very sincere and intense, form of loyalty,—a form which will vanish from the earth

whenever men come to an enlightened sense of what loyalty to loyalty implies. But one has to use, for the best, such types of loyalty as now prosper among men; and the good side of militarism is indeed the devotion that goes with it, even as the bad side of militarism is due to its implied suspicion that the loyalty of the foreigners to their country's cause is somehow in essential opposition to our own loyalty. This suspicion is false. It breeds war and is essentially stupid.[49]

Royce was no friend of militarism, but, again, the issues with Germany are the betrayal of the trust of humanity and the failure to admit any betrayal or sin, which prevents atonement from occurring. And, finally, I suggest again that Royce turns to the question of atonement for Germany's act by turning to the question of healing nations and bringing them together via a scheme of international insurance. He also argues for "hope for the great community," an issue that will be discussed in the last section of the chapter. Now, we move on to other aspects of loyalty and community.

The Unique Individual as Loyal to the Social Order

Loyalty is a way that unique selves can be both "captains of their souls" and yet also loyal to their social context and community. Royce writes: "My philosophy of loyalty . . . is an endeavor to harmonize individual right with social duty, private judgment with a willingness to accept a certain sort of external authority, the personal consciousness with the voice of our wiser moral traditions."[50]

As Royce was a philosopher who sought to develop his philosophical views in dialogue with experience, his own experience as well as human experience in general, it is not surprising that philosophical reflections would develop out of his various sea voyages and visits to other countries. This was the case with his visit to Australia. In 1888, after publishing *The Religious Aspect of Philosophy*, his history of California, and his novel, as well as a number of articles, Royce found himself in a state of exhaustion. Seeking respite and cure, he undertook a three-month cruise to Melbourne, Australia, spent two months in Australia and New Zealand, and returned to Harvard for the autumn term of 1888. Royce was no mere tourist, but a highly sensitive observer of the natural beauty and life in these two countries. Also, he traveled in Australia with Alfred Deakin, later to become their prime minister, and in New Zealand he enjoyed intellectual discussions with Sir Saul Samuel, another influential political figure. In New Zealand, Royce also became acquainted with the Maoris, learned their legends, and was impressed with their communal memory (part of which was discussed in the previous section: the story of their adventuresome journey to New Zealand in a set of canoes). Royce drew heavily on his experiences in Australia to reflect on the nature of community and particularly the question again of maintaining independent, unique selfhood yet remaining in a constructive relationship to the demands of basic social ties. These reflections were published, upon his return, in a two-part article, "Reflections after a Wandering Life in Australia"[51] and "Impressions of Australia."[52] The community of Royce scholars is grateful to Frank Oppenheim, S.J., for bringing these reflections to our attention and for providing insights about Royce's intellectual development during this journey.[53]

This episode in Royce's life is significant for our context because here we find Royce giving full expression to a sociopolitical view, which is already latent in his writings on California; also, as suggested by Oppenheim, he is developing his philosophy of loyalty out of the context of this experience.[54] In addition, Royce explores a phenomenology of the experience of the alien or strange, and reflects on the importance of geography and climate in a community's development, a topic he also developed in an article on the Pacific Coast.[55] Our focus will be Royce's political observations and especially his analysis of Australia's development of political forms, which arose in circumstances similar to those of California but which take on very different contours from those in the Pacific Coast state.

In fact, Royce begins his reflections by noting certain analogies between the U.S. and Australia. Both countries learned to reclaim the wilderness, and particularly the desert. There was also the developing of mineral resources, especially gold. Royce writes: "In Australia, as with us, the story of exploration goes hand in hand with the story of conquest and of general progress on various frontiers."[56] However, Australia developed a type of frontiersmen quite different from our own. Royce met a concrete embodiment of a "bushman," a frontiersman from Australia, on his return trip to California. This older man was a survivor of the early ill-fated exploring parties and was for many years an independent editor. He was, says Royce, all "fire and ferocity," strongly critical of dominant and full-of-self personalities, the shams of the aristocracy and the greed of the rich, but at the same time he was "courageously idealistic" and had a deep love for strong government. Royce sees him as a "sharply defined, loyal and yet self-reliant character."[57]

In our country, observes Royce, there is a decidedly individualistic temper that results in an often cultivated flippancy "for the sake of not seeming too submissive to order and social bondage." With this attitude, we even rebel against our own progress, denouncing our creatures, the corporations and labor unions, as monopolies and public enemies. We do not see that it is "we ourselves whose combined will is expressed in these great organizations."[58] The attitude of the labor unions in Australia is, indeed, quite different from that in America. Deakin tells Royce that there have been few labor problems: "[O]ur laborers have learned that their own trades' unions must exist, not merely for the sake of establishing fair dealing on a fair basis . . . but have begun to establish the principle that laborers organize to protect the social welfare rather than to gain their merely selfish ends. The aim with us is everywhere popular sovereignty under a strict organization."[59]

Indeed, Royce finds that the most remarkable thing about both Australia and New Zealand is their political maturity and the rapid growth of state organizations. He observes: "Here are pure democracies with what an American must unhesitatingly call strongly socialistic tendencies."[60] Australians regularly accept state ownership of the railroads and expect government to provide services or intervene on their behalf. Moreover, Royce finds an illuminating contrast between so-called American socialists and their counterparts in Australia. Royce writes: "[O]ur state socialists are generally philanthropists rather than men of business, and desire more to take care of the subject's soul and stomach than to carry his goods to market."[61] For the Australian, the purpose of the state is commercial and not philanthropic. This observation, I believe, can provide much insight for contemporary politics in America.

The interventions of the state in Australian are also different. In 1855, four years after the discovery of gold in Australia, squatters, worried about loss of laborers to the mines, petitioned the government to stop all mining. Royce finds this event to provide not only an illustration of Australians' attitude toward governmental roles but also an interesting contrast to an event in California, namely, the Squatters' Riot in Sacramento in 1850. In the Squatters' Riot the emphasis was on "rights," on the right to own land, while in Australia the concern was protection of one industry against another. The desire was to protect agricultural interests, so crucial to Australia's general welfare, as opposed to the desire of individuals to find their fortune. The emphasis was again on concrete commercial matters and not on abstract political issues. Indeed, in Royce's view, one of the problems in the Squatters' Riot was "wrong-headed abstractness."[62] Royce's reflections on the Californian episode were published in 1885, three years before his visit to Australia. But the contrasts between the Californian and Australian incidents do shed light on Royce's social-political views. A discussion of the Squatters' Riot episode will follow shortly.

Royce notes three other interesting contrasts between America and Australia. First, because general elections are always possible, there is a great interest among the Australian people in politics and elections, and politicians hone a personal sensitivity to the needs of the public, which results in the development of a sympathy between the people and their legislators. In America, by contrast, Royce observes, politics is viewed as dull, and the people are thankful to be let alone; apathy is the predominant mode. How contemporary all this sounds for America. Second, the newspapers in Australia provide a balanced amount of news and is-sues, and they are almost encyclopedic. In America, says Royce, the news tends more to flame mob spirit and deal with the trivial. Again these observations on the American press sound all too contemporary. Royce himself was so impressed with Australian newspapers that he maintained a subscription to them when he returned to Boston.

A third contrast between Australia and America concerns public sport. Royce was very much interested in the role "sport" plays in building loyalty and self, and he discusses this in his *Philosophy of Loyalty* as well as in other articles.[63] Sports, in Royce's view, can build social connection and notions of fair play and of loyalty. Sports also allow the self to develop motor and other skills that can contribute to acts of loyal and moral action. Royce asserts that we need all aspects of self to serve a loyal cause and to carry our moral actions. Further, because of the dedica-tion, discipline, and training involved in developing one's physical skills, "good physical training also contributes to a sound will," and "the training of physical strength and skill is one important preparation for a moral life."[64] Royce notes the prominence of public sports in Australia; most communities have a team and sup-port it enthusiastically. And the sport is truly "public." In Australia, it is the young people of the community who engage in the sport and carry the contest, whereas in America, the most popular athletes are professionals. Royce writes: "The ath-letic rivalries between clubs, towns, and colonies do not lead, as with us, to a mere buying and selling of a few prominent professional athletes to represent the con-testing associations and communities."[65] Again, there are insights here for con-temporary America.

Royce notes another contrast between America and Australia, and it concerns the attitude toward nature. Royce remarks on the "gardens" present in Austra-lia and New Zealand and notes: "[N]ature is not torn to pieces, as so often is the case in the neighborhood of our Western villages, but is rather overgrown with a wealth of new vegetation."[66] Royce, as we noted earlier, believed in a close con-nection between the climate and geography of a region and the culture and com-munal attitudes that develop in that region. Further, he had a deep respect for nature, believing in a close affinity between human consciousness and the un-communicative consciousness of the natural world—a deep continuity within nature. In his *The World and the Individual,* he offers three hypotheses about na-ture: (1) "[t]he vast contrast which we have been taught to make between ma-terial and conscious processes really depends merely upon the accidents of the human point of view"; (2) "we have no right whatever to speak of really unconscious Nature, but only of uncommunicative Nature"; and (3) "in the case of Nature in general . . . we are dealing with phenomenal signs of a vast conscious process, whose relation to Time varies vastly."[67] Royce's work provides an excellent foundation for developing an ecological view and for supporting more reasonable public policies on the many problems besetting the world because of our human disregard for the natural world. His views on nature, along with his discussions of evolution, also provide a fresh view of many contemporary discussions of mind, body, and brain and of naturalized ethics, politics, and philosophy. Further, having personally traveled extensively in Australia and New Zealand and having spent considerable time there, I find his descriptions of the natural beauty of these countries breathtaking and amazingly insightful. I urge others to read these descriptions, and especially those of the Wentworth Valley. About scenery there, Royce writes: "What is going on here is too large to be made out. It tames you . . . this childish fright and joy of yours is what more pious and reflective people call a sense of the sublime."[68]

All of Royce's observations provide material for developing a reflective view of social and political issues. Further, all are relevant to life in America today. Thus, Royce finds in Australia a live example of the struggle between the individual and the social order, in circumstances similar to those described in his history of California, but unlike Californians, the Australians have somehow balanced a sense of personal freedom with their serious recognition of social order. In sum, Royce observes: "The colonist has often drunk hard, like our frontiersman, has often gambled, has lived his wild life; and yet, after scarcely a generation of organized freedom, the colonies show a degree of conservatism, of public spirit, of social discipline, of cheerful conformity to the general will of the community, which decidedly puts to shame, I think, such a region as our own California."[69]

Community Life in America:
Land Rights and a Thoughtful Public

In his reflections on Australia, Royce sets out more precisely his ideas on social and public issues, ideas already present in his history of California and in his novel on California. Indeed, three years before his visit to the Pacific lands, Royce did discuss political issues, specifically those of concern in the Squatters' Riot in Sacramento in 1850. Royce makes his purposes quite clear as he writes:

> The present paper, in dealing with a single incident of the early struggle, is led to study, however, not so much the special problem as to the best form of land ownership, as the still more universal question of the conflict between abstract ideas and

social authority, at a moment when the order of a new society, and the eternal conflict between the private and the Universal Selves had to be settled, for the time, by
men of energy, if idealistic temper, and of very fallible intelligence, just as we to-day
have, as men and as citizens, to solve our own analogous problems.[70]

In discussing this episode, we need to establish several facts. First, much of the
land in California originally came to ownership through land titles of Mexican
origin, and by the treaty of 1848 between Mexico and the United States the general validity of all such titles was guaranteed. However, many of the settlers
to California during the gold rush came with the notion of land ownership as
"squatter's rights," a system of temporary land ownership, determined by actual
occupancy and use of the land itself, the limits of such occupancy to be subject
to local regulation by miners' meetings. This issue of land ownership was further
complicated by the fact that the lands of the gold region were generally untouched
by the original land grants, and the national government had yet to survey these
lands or establish any rule of ownership for them.

The second fact that is crucial to understanding Royce's sociopolitical observations on this incident is that a certain moral idealism was overlain on the whole
affair. Several of the newspapers of the time and an association of squatters called
the Settler's Association portrayed the issue as a matter of good versus evil, of
manifest destiny and of inalienable rights. The squatters viewed the Mexican
land grants as un-American, a creation of base people, and argued that conquest
should make "American ideas" paramount in the country. Royce describes the
view as follows: "Providence, you see, and manifest destiny were understood
in those days to be on our side, and absolutely opposed to the base Mexican."[71]
Finally, the issues become even more abstractly portrayed with the arrival of
Dr. Charles Robinson on the scene. He enters into the struggle with a letter to the
paper in which he argues for the abstract rights of Man and claims that "[i]t is the
mission of the squatters to introduce the divine justice into California: no absurd
justice that depends upon erroneous line of latitude, and establishments at New
Helvetia, and other like blundering of details of dark Spanish days, but the justice
that can be expressed in grand abstract formulae, and that will hear no less arbi-
ter than the United States Court . . . and is quite independent of local courts and
processes."[72] With these ideas in hand, Robinson urged the squatters to demand
their God-given rights and to ignore any claims that Sutter or anyone might have
based on foreign (in this case, Mexican) land grants. Sutter's Mill was a sawmill
owned by nineteenth-century pioneer John Sutter. It was located in Coloma,
California, at the bank of the American River. This was where gold was first discovered in California.

The courts and the mayor of Sacramento attempted to find resolution, although Royce believes they acted much too hesitantly and unclearly in the matter. Unfortunately, the affair ended in a violent encounter in which two squatters and one member of the citizen group were killed; the mayor was severely wounded, as was Doctor Robinson. A second affair, outside the city, resulted in the death of another squatter and his wife and the sheriff of the town. After these incidents, the war ended: the public saw the squatters as lawless aggressors, although no one spoke ill of the dead. Royce writes: "[T]here was a decided sense, also of common guilt. The community had sinned, and suffered."[73]

Royce draws several lessons from this episode, and they present a nice contrast to his discussion of the Australian version of settling social disputes. First, he notes that this episode demonstrates both the weakness and the strengths of the Sacramento people, who in their weakness let the crisis develop, but in strength found resolution. Second, he argues that the episode shows the difference between healthy and diseased states of social activity. Third, he demonstrates the prejudice of the Americans toward the Mexicans, showing further the injustice in our treatment of them and their rights and needs. Fourth, he points out the dangers of a wrongheaded idealism. Royce writes that "patient loyalty to the actual social order is the great reformer's first duty . . . [that this loyalty] is the best service that a man can render to the Ideal; that he is the best idealist who casts away as both unreal and unideal the vain private imaginings of his own weak brain."[74]

These reflections reveal several aspects of Royce's own thought. First, causes, as he argues in *The Philosophy of Loyalty,* are not abstract, but need to be concrete in a manner that enables clear moral and social action by individuals. The very abstract idealism preached by Robinson inflamed the situation rather than providing moral leadership for responsible social action. Second, loyalty demands that advocacy for a cause be sensitive to the loyalties of others and particularly to the social order and context in which the change is sought. Fourth, loyalty must be critical and not blind, seeking action that is reflective and community building. And finally, actions for one's cause must be decisive; one's work for community must not be hesitant. Above all, action must be sought that, in the end, will benefit the total community. The miners seem to have been driven more by individualistic, self-interested concerns than by a desire to build a community in which all, whether foreign or American, could live and flourish.

The Australian frontiersman is, as Royce argued, self-reliant and individualistic, but also "idealistic." Royce is using the term "idealist" here not in the sense of a person holding a particular philosophical or theological view, but rather as "a man or woman who is consciously and predominantly guided, in the purposes and in the great choices of life, by large ideals, such as admit of no merely material embodiment, and such as contemplate no merely private and personal satisfaction."[75] The Australian's idealism is manifested in a belief in the value of the social order and social community, and, although the individual may be critical of many of the community's actions, there is readiness to act loyally on behalf of that community.

Royce turns directly to the problems with American "idealism" in "The Limitations of Public Thought in America." Royce is concerned in this essay with what he sees as an ineffectual and weak, perhaps even "dangerous," public. There seems to be no "public voice" in America, but rather many "publics," many competing self-interests. People in American too easily fall prey to members of the public who believe they act in the public interest or for "high ideals," but who really are acting for their own, limited, "blind" version of the general good. In America, argues Royce, our greatest national danger lies in an extravagant love of "ideally fascinating enterprises," whose practical results are highly suspect. He writes: "Whoever desires the reputation of the founder of a new sect has merely to insist upon his plan for reforming society and saving souls,—has merely to announce repeatedly to the public the high valuation that he sets upon his own ideas concerning nobler topics in order to win a respectful hearing."[76] Such a man was Dr. Charles Robinson. Also, unfortunately, says Royce, these so-called idealists always find people who blindly follow appealing ideals.

Essentially, in this essay, Royce is arguing for a more critical, reflective public. He observes several tendencies in our current American life that seem to go against this hope. First, many seem to believe that great reforms will be possible merely though good resolutions. Not all ideals can be properly formulated, and, more importantly, one needs to know the goal of that formulation and whether in fact it can be put to practical use in a specific area. Further, in addition, one must be more thoughtful about how ideals may be given articulate expression and then must subject these expressions to the equally thoughtful criticism and comments of others. No one in the squatter situation played the role of the critic. The press, thought Royce, should have undertaken this role as it did in Australia.

Royce argued all his life that criticism and interchange of ideas were crucial to clear and effective thinking, and he sought this always for his own thought. Yet, Royce also recognizes that argument and reason can be taken to an extreme, that debate and argumentation can become ends in themselves. Further, too much trust in reason alone without its proper interaction with feeling and practical action often ends in trusting to mere formulas, to seeking the all-solving word. Finally, there is a tendency in America to forget the individual limitations in thought and act and to believe that an expertise in one field endows one with expertise in many fields. Royce summarizes his advice on being a thoughtful member of the public as follows:

> Be thoughtful, reason out some of your ideals for yourself. Know something and know that something well. Have the region where you have a right to mistrust your instincts, to be keenly and mercilessly critical, to question, to doubt, and to formulate, and then devotedly to maintain and to teach . . . let that region be the little clearing in your life's forest,—the place where you see, and comprehend, and are at home. . . . In that region be indeed the creature of hard-won insight, of clear consciousness, of definite thinking about what it is yours to know. . . . In that region believe only when you know why you believe. But remember, life is vast, and your clearing is very small.[77]

All of these reflections on the public in America are relevant to our situation today, and even more so perhaps than in Royce's time.

Provincialism and Reflective Citizenship

Royce realized that advice to individual citizens on reflective citizenship was not enough. One must provide enabling social conditions for individuals who will become thoughtful, creative, critical members of the public. The enabling must begin with the individual in his immediate social context—family, neighborhood, village, and province. We will discuss "family" in another section, but now we turn to what Royce calls "wise provincialism."

What, then, is a province? Royce writes: "[A] province shall mean any one part of a national domain, which is, geographically and socially, sufficiently unified to have a true consciousness of its own unity, to feel a pride in its own ideals and customs, and to possess a sense of its distinction from other parts of the country."[78] Further, Royce asserts that the development of a "wholesome provincialism" is a social imperative for the world. To have a wholesome provincialism is, for Royce, as one might surmise, to operate as a genuine community, enabling its members to be genuine individuals and to engage in creative actions. These provinces will operate as small communities where there is communication among unique individuals who learn to share a common past and future, where the members of the province seek together to perform common deeds and to encourage the growth of each member of the province (group, community). A province, it should be clear, can be any small community that possesses "a set of customs and ideals and a love and pride which leads the inhabitants of the province to cherish as their own these traditions, beliefs, and aspirations."[79] In addition to building this local loyalty, the province, as any community of loyalty, must also be guided by the principle of loyalty to loyalty. It must create broader community. Above all the wholesome province must combat false sectionalism, a condition in which the interests of the province are held above those of other provinces and of humanity as a whole. Royce, of course, knew well the dangers of false sectionalism, having been a child of the Civil War era.

Royce holds that wholesome provincialism would fight off or avoid three evils. The first is "homelessness," a condition increased by the freedom of social mobility but also by the inability of individuals and communities to provide for creative assimilation. Such a form of assimilation cultivates individual differences rather than inculcating a uniformity of belief and behavior. For those seeking assimilation into the community, this involves consciously situating themselves within the new community, bringing at the same time their unique personal talents, interests, and perspectives. This infusion of unique individuality and creativity invigorates and enriches a community. Thus, thus new members with all their diversity should be welcomed. To fail in creative assimilation leads to apathy for individuals and a tendency to dulling habit and viewpoint. Creative assimilation then is an important condition for fostering individual and community creativity. Further, this assimilation must not be seen as only an act of the newcomer or stranger. Rather, the community must have qualities that will attract a newcomer to become part of its life. The community must share its history and its plans for the future in such a way that "every stranger who enters it shall at once feel the dignity of its past, and the unique privilege that is offered to him when he is permitted to belong to its company of citizens."[80]

Wholesome provincialism combats a second evil, namely, the "leveling tendency." Royce's description of this is poignantly relevant to our world today. He writes:

> [B]ecause of the ease of communication amongst distant places, because of the spread of popular education, and because of the consolidation and centralization of industries and social authorities, we tend all over the nation, and in some degree, even throughout the civilized world, to read the same daily news, to share the same external fashions, to discourage individuality, and to approach a dead level of harassed mediocrity.[81]

Royce declares that the result of this leveling is the tendency to crush the individual. To be creative as an individual one must seek both to love and support one's province and also to enrich it by seeking outside contact with other individuals and communities. A wholesome province should create the conditions for developing and enriching individuality as well as community life in the province. The history and future a community develops should be unique and in contrast to that of other communities. In my own California community there is a very rich and unique Basque community that has maintained its own language, customs, cuisine, art, and music that it transmits to the younger and future generations. At the same time, this community is situated within the larger community, also contributing in many ways to that history and future.

The leveling tendency was brought home to me in a very direct manner several years ago when I was teaching a course entitled "Building Bridges and Telling Stories." One aspect of the course was to invite prominent community members of varying backgrounds and histories to tell their stories—to share unique aspects of their family histories. Another assignment for the class was for class members to tell their own stories. One student, of Anglo background, came to me and said, "I have no story." I urged that student to consult her grandparents and others in the family. Her presentation to the class was most interesting and included a "family quilt," with many layers of meaning. All of us have "roots," and we need to be in touch with them and to share them with our communities. Enrichment of all will follow, even from discordant and disruptive stories. Of course, with broken and troubled families so prominent today, capturing a sense of story may be more difficult.

The third evil that wholesome provincialism addresses is "mob spirit." This spirit is fostered by the other two evils, which result in general apathy and lack of individuality. Royce describes the mob spirit as a state of high emotions, which, when unchecked, result in a "State of irrationality," described by Royce as "sympathization without thought." In such times, Royce argues, "the social group may be, and generally is, more stupid than any of its members."[82] Social groups that are wiser than their members tend to be characterized, says Royce, by an emphasis upon the contrasts between various individuals. This emphasis on individual difference is crucial to a genuine community, which Royce sees always as a "unity with variety." Further, such a creative individual benefits the community, for it is she who can generate a multiplicity of viable potential strategies for serving a cause or a project or solving a problem, thereby enhancing both individual and communal opportunity for effective action. Royce writes: "[T]he effectiveness of human action at the level of community will be enhanced by a pluralism of ideas and strategies which can be realized only through the cultivation of individual differences."[83]

Further, individual variety leads to exchange of ideas, as well as to contrast and criticism, which test ideas and make them clearer. These are exactly the skills that Royce argued were needed for a "thoughtful public." Stuart Gerry Brown has argued that the values represented in Royce's wholesome provincialism are individual freedom and democracy. Summarizing his assessment of Royce's social theory, Brown writes:

The dearest social values are the liberty and dignity of the individual man and the democratic method of arriving at social decisions. In order to preserve and enhance these values, we must re-emphasize, re-dignify, and re-vitalize the smaller units of society which are known as provinces, for within the provincial life individual variety will most surely flourish. A democratic nation requires a variety of provinces just as a democratic province requires a variety of individuals; a world order which is at once free and democratic will require a variety of nations.[84]

In a set of three essays on higher education in America we find Royce applying his ideas on provincialism and the building of a thoughtful public in America. The primary idea in two of these essays is the role of higher education in fostering creative, critical thinkers who, in turn, can work to make their communities positive forces for reflective citizenship. In an essay on "The Freedom of Teaching," Royce argues that the main role of a teacher is "to make his pupils as embryo investigators to be made into mature investigators as far as possible."[85] He writes: "Mind is activity. Dead statements remain dead till a student is taught to discover them afresh for himself. . . . Mind is a bundle of interests in things. Investigation is the effort to satisfy the interests."[86] The argument for freedom of teaching then follows. If a teacher is to accomplish his task, he must himself be an investigator, but the air of investigation is freedom; thus, the teacher must be free in his teaching—he must be an example of untrammeled investigation.[87]

The second essay addresses a report from Columbia College entitled "Changes in the Collegiate Curriculum."[88] The proposal argues for a university curriculum that combines the scholarly method with scientific investigation. Unfortunately, in the arguments concerning the report, Royce sees false abstraction taking hold, namely in the supposed conflict between "the moral and intellectual discipline of the mind" and "practical and progressive knowledge." Royce writes: "The favorite abstract statement of the partisans of the 'new' method was that they, for their part, were minded to study 'things,' not 'words.'"[89] Royce's humorous response is worth quoting in some detail. He writes:

It is curious to observe how fond educational theories have often been of such false abstractions. Herein, to be sure, they only follow the fashion of many political theories. Just as "freedom," or "balance of trade," or "money," have often come to be talked of as if all these were names of things that could exist alone among themselves, and could be estimated without reference to other social facts, or to anything else in the universe, so in educational matters, men love purely abstract catch words, and love judgments founded upon such terms. Which would you rather study, "words" or "things?" Which would you rather possess, "money" or "credit?" Do you prefer the "law," or would you be more content with "freedom" instead? All such questions remind me of an illustration . . . if the soul of some still indefinite animal, not yet embodied here on earth, were to be asked, in some pre-existent state, "When you come to be incarnated on earth, which of the two organs would you prefer to have in your body, a great toe, or a tail?"[90]

This article and this discussion would be most relevant to our discussions today about the value of humanities versus the sciences or liberal education versus career education. Royce is amazingly contemporary.

In addressing this supposed controversy, Royce argues that scholars of any field seek to understand the truth as embodied in word and things, thought and object, insight and apprehension. One wants to be both a critical thinker and a doer of the word. Above all, the ideal example of the truly academic person, says Royce, is one who can criticize and be criticized. He writes: "Only the academic life can teach a nation the true freedom of enlightened controversy."[91] Here Royce connects higher education directly with the need to develop a thoughtful public.

The final article is a direct defense of provincialism in education. It is, in effect, a letter addressed to the Carnegie Foundation for the Advancement of Teaching concerning a proposed action by the state of Vermont against Middlebury College on the grounds that this institution was not following the aims and purposes of higher education in that state. Royce does not address the specific issues because he says they are local to Middlebury. Rather, he is concerned about standardization in higher education; he sees the "principle" proposed by the Carnegie Foundation as "opposed" to a "wise provincialism in education." For our purposes, the following summary is sufficient:

> I hope then, that we shall always bear in mind that one of the topics which this association must frequently consider in its future work, is the relation of the Carnegie Foundation for the Advancement of Teaching to the provincial, to the institutional, to the individual interest of those highly distinct, and contrasting regions, colleges and universities, upon whose very variety and freedom, the higher life of our country always depends.[92]

Again, these reflections by Royce seem very relevant to the situation in higher education in contemporary America.

The Problem of Race and Reform

Royce, as should be clear, was always advocating for the building and broadening of community. As we have seen, he is highly critical of the California squatters for their prejudicial attitude toward the Spanish Californians. In his history of California and especially in the chapter on "The Struggle for Order," Royce identifies as one of the negative tendencies against establishing order in early California the often unrecognized aversion to "anything foreign" and the propensity to charge to the foreigners themselves "whatever trouble was due to our brutal ill-treatment of them."[93] He describes in some detail the laws developed specifically against foreigners. One famous set of resolutions had a committee of three Americans in each camp "decide what foreigners were 'respectable' and to exclude all others by a sort of executive order."[94] Foreigners as a class, especially Sonorans and Southern Americans, were excluded from the mines by mob violence, including hangings. Royce, in fact, describes a particularly outrageous act, namely, the "hanging of a woman, whose death, under the circumstances, was plainly due, not merely to her known guilt, but quite as much as she was not an American."[95] She was, in fact, Spanish-American. Royce insightfully argues that these actions injured society in at least two senses. First, the popular conscience was debased by the physical brutality of the acts and lulled into believing that justice was vindicated by such actions. Second, the crimes were those of the community as such. Royce writes: "[T]he outrages committed by foreigners were after all, however numerous, the crimes of individuals. Ours were crimes of a community, consisting largely of honest but cruelly bigoted men, who encouraged the ruffians of their own nation to ill-treat the wanderers of another."[96]

Indeed, Royce was not afraid to acknowledge even worse crimes committed by the community as a result of the permissive attitude to the appalling behavior of individuals against a race considered "not civilized," namely, the American Indian. He writes: "[W]e indeed did not treat them [the foreigners] as some nations have done, we did not massacre them wholesale. . . . [T]hat treatment we reserved for the defenseless Digger Indians, whose villages certain among our miners used on occasion to regard as targets for rifle-practice, or to destroy wholesale with fire, outrage, and murder, as if they had been so many wasps nests in our garden at home."[97]

In his 1906 "Race Questions and Prejudices,"[98] Royce tackles the question of race relations. Royce addresses race questions by looking to various kinds of experience: the work of science, the experiences of other nations, and the work of anthropology and sociology. In my judgment, he finds none of these answers satisfactory, though he seeks pieces of insight in them all.

Royce begins his discussion by noting that the numerous questions and prejudices that are aroused by the contact between various races of humans have always been important factors in history. Today, however, numerous means of communication, increased migrations, and the imperial ambitions of nations have brought people together in more frequent and closer contact. The problem begins with our human tendency to view other selves primarily in an external fashion, as well as our natural instinct to view the strange as frightening or incomprehensible. Thus, in his reflections on Australia, Royce writes: "Distance in one sense is almost annihilated nowadays; but we annihilate it for the mind much more readily than for the heart, which is a stubborn barbarian in us, loving what is near and dear to it."[99] In *Race Questions, Provincialism and Other American Problems*, Royce notes that this earliest social problem of humanity, namely, learning to deal with life in the presence of alien races, is "the problem of dealing with men who seem to us somehow very widely different from ourselves, in physical constitution, in temperament, in all their deeper nature, so that we are tempted to think of them as natural strangers to our souls, while nevertheless we find that they are stubbornly there in our world, and that they are men as much determined to live as we are, and as men who, in turn, find us as incomprehensible as we find them."[100] Above all, argues Royce, we must learn to live with these persons in the same social order.

Given this problem in all its manifestations, where then can we find advice? The first answer, says Royce, is science. Royce, however, provides scathing criticism of any essentialist understanding of race as a "natural kind," or as an established scientific concept. Indeed, Royce clearly affirms a non-essentialist view of race. He writes: "In estimating, in dealing with races, in defining what their supposedly unchangeable characteristics are, in planning what to do with them, we are all prone to confuse the accidental with the essential. We are likely to take for an essential race characteristic what is a transient incident or a product of special social conditions."[101] Not only does Royce see "race" as a social/historical phenomenon, he also chastises those who would "marshal all the resources of their sciences to prove their own race-prejudices are infallible."[102] With a wonderful note of sarcasm, Royce observes that he begins to wonder "whether a science which mainly devotes itself to proving that we ourselves are the salt of the earth, is after all so exact as it aims to be."[103] Royce concludes that race problems are not problems caused by anything essential to the existence of the nature of the races themselves. Royce asserts that our notions of race are "illusions," and he notes: "We all have illusions and we hug them. Let us not sanctify them in the name of science."[104] Science, then, for Royce, provides no guidance to us in dealing with these questions of race.

He then turns to his own experiences of racial issues as exemplified in or by two different cultures: Japan and Jamaica. He recalls his childhood textbooks and their descriptions of the land of Japan, a "weird land" where foreigners were excluded, where perverse things were possible, where criminals were boiled in oil and Christian missionaries martyred. "Whatever the Japanese were, they were plainly men of the wrong race."[105] But then Japan opened its doors and came out into the world, and we Westerners viewed them as imitating all our Western customs. They became in our eyes "a plastic race of wonderful little children."[106] He argues that our Western view of these people as "imitative children" is much belied by their accomplishments and actions and that these views clearly demonstrate the fallibility of our racial judgments. His own experiences with Japanese students taught him two things: (1) that they had "a vast background of opinions and custom that I could not fathom"[107] and (2) that "[t]hey learned well, but plainly they meant to use this learning for their own purposes."[108] Royce next narrates, with tongue in cheek, this story. A Christian lady declared to the Japanese student: "[W]hat a boon our missionaries have brought you in introducing Christianity into your land." The student answered, "You are right. They have completed the variety of religions in Japan."[109] Royce draws the following lesson from these experiences: "[P]erhaps the Japanese are not of the right race; but we now admit so long as we judged them merely by their race, and by mere appearances, we were judging them ignorantly, and falsely. This, I say, has been to me a most interesting lesson in the fallibility of some of our race judgments."[110]

Royce now moves to the Negro question in the South. The question seems to be, How can the white man and the Negro, once forced, as they are in the South, to live side by side, best learn to live with a minimum of friction, with a maximum of cooperation? Royce says that his Southern friends contend that this "end can only be attained by a firm and by a very constant and explicit insistence upon keeping the negro in his proper place, as a social inferior."[111] Royce sarcastically observes that these pedagogical methods seem to awake much lively and intense irritation, and irritation does not seem positive. Is it, then, that this irritation, this increase of race hatred, is a necessary and inevitable evil for the transition to peace? In this context, Royce introduces his experiences in Jamaica.

Royce's approach here is similar to the one he used in his comparison of Australia and America on key social issues. In this case, the comparison is between the American South and Jamaica. Royce approached Jamaica in a manner similar to Australia. He visited a number of places in Jamaica, talked to a wide variety of people, read the literature, and made numerous observations of the daily life of the nation. At the time there were more than six hundred thousand blacks and only about fifteen thousand whites in the population. Royce observes several times that life in Jamaica is not ideal; rather, it is a concrete example of a community that has dealt with a similar problem. Are there answers here for America?

Royce focuses on two basic contrasts. The first is between "pedagogies," namely, the methods used to instruct people in citizenship, in "loyalty" to the social order. In the South, the pedagogy is "negro domination," teaching the Negro "their place." In Jamaica the pedagogy is to provide good social order—good civil service, good health service, good roads, and fair and open courts—and at the same time, to include the Negro as participants in these administrative functions, including serving as policemen. The second contrast concerns attitude. In both Jamaica and the South there is a belief in the superiority of the white person. In Jamaica, unlike the South, the Englishman has, says Royce, "a great way of being superior without very often publicly saying he is superior."[112] He adds, "Superiority is best shown by good deeds and by few boasts."[113]

Royce addresses his Southern friends, saying they complain about safety but have not yet made the Negro part of their policing efforts. Look at Jamaica and other places where there are Negroes and Whites living together and see the differences. Learn from these lessons. Summing up his experiences with both countries, Royce writes: "In estimating, in dealing with races, in defining what their supposedly unchanging characteristics are, in planning what to do with them, we are all prone to confuse the accidental with the essential. . . . We are disposed to view as a fatal and overwhelming race-problem what is a perfectly curable accident of our present form of administration."[114]

Royce now turns to the area of anthropology to seek some answers to race questions. He notes immediately the difficulty with the term "race." He points to the racial antipathies between Russian and Poles, the French and the Germans, writing, "Thus, almost any national or political or religious barrier, if it is old enough, may lead to a consciousness of difference of race."[115] Second, he turns to a "history of the human mind," that is, manifestations of human behavior in history.

Among so-called primitive men, wherever they appear, we find common traits such as superstition, cannibalism and human sacrifice, destructiveness, resistance to change, sloth, and cruelty. These, says Royce, are "simply the common evil, traits of primitive humanity, traits to which our own ancestors were very long ago prey, traits against which civilized man has still constantly to fight. Any frenzied mob of civilized men may relapse in an hour to a level of very base savagery."[116] These primitive thoughts, however, says Royce, are not the outcome of racial difference; they appear in the customs, legends, and superstitions of all races.

Now Royce considers the view that humans can be classified by the trait "capable of civilization." Yet Royce does not believe this to be a viable test. First, this test has not been fairly applied. There have been vast differences of circumstances among men that might explain differences. The Germanic peoples, says Royce, were given extraordinary opportunity to learn about civilization. We need, says Royce, to give all races "some equal opportunity to show of what sort of manhood they are capable."[117] Sarcastically Royce speculates what might have happened to the Germans if they had been civilized by our "modern devices—unlimited supplies of rum, of rifles, and machine guns," and keeping the few survivors in place by "showing them how cultivated races can look down upon savage folk."[118] Royce writes: "Well, in that case, the further history of civilization might have gone without the aid of Germanic peoples."[119]

Nor does Royce believe we can talk about the origin of civilization. Probably physical environment played a role, but no one race has the honor of beginning the process. He writes: "Neither Chinese nor Egyptian, neither Caucasian nor Mongol, was the sole originator of civilization. . . . Chinese civilization, and, in recent times, Japanese civilization have shown us that one need not be a Caucasian in order to originate a higher type of wisdom."[120] In conclusion, Royce argues that our so-called race problems are merely the problems caused by our antipathies. These antipathies exist toward all sorts of beings and often are quite capricious. The danger comes, says Royce, when human beings are trained to give names to these and to see them as sacred. These result in racial hatred, religious hatred, class hatred, and so on. The social training raises these antipathies to a level of the sacred and to the level of the revelation of truth. In other words, these antipathies have received social standing.

Royce asserts that he has, in this essay, dealt not with social justice, but with illusions. He concludes that he is a member of the human race, a race that "very badly needs race elevation. In this need of my race, I personally and very deeply share. And it is in this spirit only that I am able to approach our problem."[121] What, then, shall we say about Royce as a "racist"? I believe that Royce makes every effort to avoid racism. He may well be too sanguine about solving problems by providing good social order, and he uses the terminology of his time such as the word "civilization," yet, my view is that he is quite progressive for his time on the matter of race and race relations. I also believe he leaves us some insights on race and race antipathies. Whether these views are progressive for our time, I will leave to others to judge.

Building Community: Interpretation and Mediation

It is clear that a central theme of Royce's philosophy, as well as his whole life, was to build bridges, whether between various scholarly disciplines or different races, and to build communities, especially communities of loyalty that could foster fulfilled, unique, moral persons. One difficult problem for community building, as we have seen, is the detached individual. This is a problem for the province that must welcome strangers and encourage them to "creative assimilation." It is the problem of any nation, such as Australia was to become, to balance loyalty to social order with unique individuality. Connection with community is essential to individual health and to the community. Building loyalty and connection, respect and mutuality is, of course, at the heart of race problems. Bringing the detached individual into community, while maintaining his uniqueness, is a major problem.

There is, however, another barrier to community, and that is what Royce calls "dangerous pairs." In his *War and Insurance* Royce declares: "*[T]he dyadic, the dual, the bilateral relations of men and women, of each man to his neighbor, are relations fraught with social danger. A pair of men is what I may call an essentially dangerous community.*"[122] How, then, do we address this problem? The answer is through loyalty and interpretation. Loyalty, says Royce, always involves relations that concern more than two people. This is because the loyalty of the two is always to a higher being, a cause, their union, a community.

The process whereby community is achieved is interpretation. The creative action of loyal individuals and communities is to engage in the work of an interpreter. An interpreter is one who seeks to build common understanding and community among individuals and communities. As discussed earlier, an interpretation is a triadic relationship among three agents: an interpreter and two other entities, whether they are ideas, individuals, or communities. Often the two parties in an interpretive (mediating) relationship are what Royce calls "dangerous pairs." A relationship becomes a dangerous-pair relationship because the two individuals or groups approach each other as adversaries. They have, or perceive that they have, mutually clashing interests, various and mutually estranged motives and activities, and seemingly incompatible ideas or views. Each individual or group has its own interpretation of the facts of the matter, and each is convinced that theirs is the only valid understanding of the situation. The parties essentially see their relationships as a zero-sum game: only one side can win. The interpreter, as a loyal and humble servant of building community, seeks to alter the relationship between the dangerous pairs, allowing a sense of communal relationship to develop. The interpreter represents or interprets "the plans, or purposes, or ideas of one of his two fellows to the other of these two in such wise that the member of the community who I call the interpreter works to the end that these three shall cooperate as if they were one."[123]

Now, the relationship between the parties is no longer a zero-sum game but becomes one of a deliberative conversation in which mutually estranged parties, with the help of the interpreter, work to arrive at a kind of consensus, though not necessarily a substantive agreement between the dangerous pair. What has been created is a conversational context where the parties no longer seek to trump one another but seek to achieve a mutual understanding of their disagreements as well as their overlapping areas of common understanding. Further, a community is created in which the dignity of each individual or group is confirmed. Interpretation, we recall, involves respect of each individual, for each view. The interpreter exhibits the virtue of humility, recognizing that to interpret one must become an attentive and sympathetic listener, not letting one's own view of the situation get in the way. One must be able to listen to and appreciate each view, interest, and motive of each of the individuals.

To understand more fully interpretation and how it works to build relationships and overcome dyadic, dangerous relationships, we turn to Royce's comments upon a specific case of dyadic conflict between a mother and daughter, an actual case but also one given by Royce as a midyear exam question for his 1915–1916 Extension Course in Ethics. His comments are entitled "Principles of the Art of Loyalty."[124] Very briefly, the mother and daughter have lived together for a number of years. The daughter was raised to a strict social code, is not aggressive, and is generally under the domination of the mother. The widowed mother has become a trusted servant of a large corporation. Now, however, the daughter is suspicious that her mother is cleverly and secretly defrauding her employers. The daughter remains silent, and the relationship between mother and daughter grows tense; there are concealments, lies, and mutual suspicions. Royce's questions about the case and his comments are highly insightful, and a reading of these would be beneficial to anyone who is interested in ethical case analysis or is engaged in interpretive mediation.

In this context, we briefly mention some principles and general insights. First, Royce asserts that no one has any right to pretend to an infallible judgment, either about this case or about any similarly reported, and fragmentarily presented, life problem. In other words, all interpreters must humbly be aware of the fallibility of all their interpretations. Second, Royce argues that these estrangements of dangerous pairs may, in many cases, be healed through the presence, the inventiveness, and the interpretations of some mediating third person or group. Third, Royce clearly states that there is no one formula that can be applied mechanically to any case. Fourth, he emphasizes sensitivity to the situation: "[Y]ou cannot apply my formula about the triad of interpretation as a remedy for the troubles of a Dangerous Pair, unless you have some knowledge of the case in question which enables you to state definitely what interpreter may properly be sought, and what interpretation may rightly be hoped for."[125]

Royce readily admits that in many cases estrangements will be healed by Mother Wit, by deeper loyalty, or by patience and growth in wisdom. He writes: "When my next door neighbor and I quarrel, we very often cannot wisely send for the mediator, a least so long as neither of us had determined on consulting a lawyer. We very generally have to learn to wait a little, to consider whether or not and how to build a fence between our lots, or to keep our quarrelsome children apart, or perhaps to endure the annoyance until they grow up."[126] Yet, estrangements need healing.

More importantly, the world, argues Royce, needs healing. "*[I]f the world's peace is to be furthered, such progress must take the form of creating and sustaining certain definable communities of interpretation.*"[127] Concerned for world peace and for rebuilding after the war, Royce proposes a scheme for building and making visible the community of humankind. This is a method of building international consensus based on his doctrine of interpretation, and it involves the insurance community. Royce had considered three other communities displaying triadic relationships that could, possibly, enhance the possibility of developing communities of interpretation—communities intent on bringing together the nations of the world. These were the judicial community and the communities of banking and commercial ventures in general. Royce dismissed each as inadequate to the task. He dismissed the judicial community because of its adversarial nature and the communities of banking and commercial activity because they might well involve each of the three parties in a conflict of self-interests.

The insurance community is a viable candidate because it exemplifies the religious admonition: "Bear ye one another's burdens." Risk, of course, says Royce, is part of life. Humans take risks all the time. But when a person takes a risk someone else has to bear the consequences. It may be his friend, his creditor, or his heirs. Set this risk taking in dyadic relations and you set the stage for creating embittered debtors and creditors, for making people penniless, and for inspiring hate. Now the community of insurance, says Royce, brings the man who takes the risk into a true and active union of interest with his possible beneficiary. B insures the beneficiary C against any loss due to the risk that A takes. Further, the insurance community asks the risk taker to think beyond his or her own self-interest. Royce proposes that an international insurance community be established that could take on the risk of common calamities that befall all humankind, such as earthquakes, migratory pestilence, recurrent famines and crop failures, and marine disasters. The international board would be set up in such a way that it was beyond politics and beyond problems of loss because of defeat in war.

Royce is convinced that this community of insurance could insure its members progressively against the destructive calamities of war. Rules could be set up that prohibited those nations committing the first act of war from receiving insurance compensation. Victors could demand indemnity from all those defeated and then could actively establish the international insurance company with this

indemnity. From that point on, the insurance company could deal with other calamities. Royce's *War and Insurance*, though viewed by some as eccentric at best,
is a practical plan for instituting an international insurance organization, a plan
based upon the realities of the First World War and the possibilities of having to
make financial settlements at the peace table. Royce's suggestion that repara-
tions be put into an international insurance fund to be used to underwrite an organization for the mutual insurance of nations was, again, a plan to enable the
development of nations and the rebuilding of communities. If Royce's plan had
been activated, perhaps democracy might have had a chance to survive in central
Europe.[128]

Such a plan today could conceivably be a plan for social action. Insurance is a
common idea among nations of the world, existing in various types of political
and economic arrangements. Properly constituted, an international insurance
organization, staffed by experts and suitably capitalized, might well assist the
world in dealing with such tragedies as crop failure, damage caused by various
natural disasters, and perhaps even health crises. Whatever the validity of his insurance scheme, Royce certainly saw in it a hope for building a great community
for the world.

Royce envisioned a global community as emerging by "uniting the already
existing communities of mankind into higher communities."[129] The unity envisioned by Royce, however, is once again the aesthetic unity within variety. It is a
unity that will respect the "internal motives for loyalty" and "modes of expression" of the loyalty exhibited in each community; it will be a "plurality of morally
autonomous" communities. Jose-Antonio Orosco, in a fine article on Royce and
the creation of a global community, argues that Royce would warn against any
notions of "cosmopolitanism" that would urge people to eschew their national
identities and consider themselves only as "citizens of the world."[130] Royce would
view such a notion of global community as too abstract, as too utopian, and as an
understanding of relationships that is "too thin." A truly international community as envisioned by Royce would find a way to respect the liberty of individual
nations. Royce writes:

> Therefore, while the great community of the future will unquestionably be in-
> ternational by virtue of the ties which will bind its various nationalities together, it
> will find no place for that sort of internationalism which despises the individual va-
> riety of nations, and which tries to substitute for the services of those who at present
> seek merely to conquer mankind, the equally worthless desire of those who hope to
> see us in future as "men without a country." . . . There can be no true international
> life unless the nations remain to possess it.[131]

To achieve such a unity with plurality would involve much creative interpretation and dialogue. This interpretation would begin, so to speak, at home. We have to seek to live with our neighbors, and we need to do our best to discover common bases of mutual understanding, common desires, common arts, and common loves. As loyal individuals we need to "[s]eek, through whatever common ties now bind you to bring to consciousness what may heal this estrangement."[132]

I believe that Royce's work on interpretation and mediation provides a solid basis for creating community out of conflict and thus for working to build a global community. Such a global community, as Orosco has so eloquently argued,[133] will not develop out of political institutions, but rather will be the result of "deliberative dialogues among autonomous international agents acting together" in communities of interpretation. There are now international corporations and other international groups working on common issues such as human rights or health care; these could be the basis for building broader communities of interpretation. A Catholic priest, Father Alex Reid, is essentially using the process of interpretation in actual conflicts in the world. He has been successful in Ireland, and he is now working with the Basque. His primary method he calls "dialogue," which allows each party to defend "their own political cake," but also to listen to others "telling their story." A key step in Ireland was bringing the Sinn Féin to the table. Father Reid spoke of the dialogue as developing a dynamic toward a "common good." This view is, I think, very Roycean.

Royce's views on interpretation and mediation also lay the foundation for a new social and political philosophy. In this vein, Shibley Telhami argues for "the need to build bridges of mutual understanding," particularly between the United States and the people in Arab and Muslim countries. He calls this a "compassionate approach that builds coalitions and considers the vital interests and wishes of other states and peoples around the globe."[134] Such a method, he believes, would allow a chance to build moral consistency among various parties about the illegitimacy of terrorist tactics while empowering influential segments of the various Arab and Muslim societies to wage their own struggles for change. It would also reinforce notions of openness and democracy that have been a part of America's greatness.

Finally, Royce saw his notion of "communities of interpretation" as promoting those values integral to the stability of a democratic community.[135] Among these values is the principle of equality. Royce views the community of interpretation as fundamentally egalitarian. No one of the three parties has the power to coerce another into accepting a viewpoint, and once the dialogue has begun different members of the community of interpretation will have to assume the role of interpreter as preliminary interpretations and schemes for cooperation are offered. Further, the process of interpretation is open-ended, and thus particular interpretations are always open to reconsideration. In addition, in concert with democratic ideals, the interpretive process provides a model of deliberative decision making, and it promotes dispositions of fairness, open-mindedness and a willingness to alter positions when reason or evidence demands.[136]

Royce, I believe, provides us a number of insights for building a viable new social and political philosophy for our day.

6

The Thought of Josiah Royce

A Treasure of Riches for Contemporary
Philosophical and Public Issues

Royce provides many insights for contemporary thought and life. The amazing depth of his interests and experience yields a rich treasure that is key to dealing with public issues such as race, diversity, immigration problems, religious understanding and diversity, conflict and community building, self-development and self-alienation, and the rebuilding and/or redefining of "family." Royce's work also has much to contribute to contemporary philosophical issues. He offers a fresh perspective not only on the naturalized ethics debate, but on refining a concept of "naturalism." In the area of self, mind, and body, Royce's philosophical approach is rich and fruitful, and speaks against the many forms of reductionism prevalent today. His approach also creates a different view of the debates between ethical realism and ethical idealism and of concerns about skepticism. His deep familiarity with life experiences, literature, and history, as well as his rich understanding of ethics, religion, science, mathematics, logic, epistemology, and metaphysics, grounds a philosophical worldview that has much to offer contemporary efforts at philosophical overview. Further, Royce's understanding of philosophy as a discipline offers a model for countering the strongly perceived irrelevance of philosophical endeavors for world problems and for living.

The chapter begins with Royce as a model philosopher. Royce saw philosophy as a serious, critical reflection on life and the world we live in: thus, philosophy is compelled to provide insight for the living of life. Royce believed all human knowledge limited and fallible, and so philosophy was not a quest for certainty. Further, Royce was not interested in the hyper-specialization that is so often the case in philosophy today. Rather, he was deeply versed in a number of disciplines, and he worked as a bridge builder to bring scholars from various disciplines together to share perspectives and engage in critical, yet sympathetic discussion. Reflections on Royce as a philosopher, as a teacher of philosophy, and as a public philosopher will allow us to address the concerns that philosophy, as it became a "profession," lost touch with its mission and has, therefore, failed to attain its full potential. James Campbell describes the situation well when he writes: "Academic philosophy, in America, despite its admitted technical and institutional advances, has never attained its full potential because its striving after professionalized existence has continued to damage its roots in the life of the broader society, roots from which any institutionalized social practice must draw its challenges and sustenance."[1]

The second section of the chapter will deal with Royce as a psychologist and with his views on the self. As a psychologist, Royce can be seen as ahead of his time on many psychological issues, predating insights credited to William James, Sigmund Freud, and George Herbert Mead. Although Royce's views are relevant to many areas of the human psyche, this section will focus on three issues: the nature of memory and the role of autobiography in self-identity; the central role of imitation in self-development; and the significance of play in the life of a human self. To these issues and others, Royce offers a perspective on a holistic view of the self as a complex phenomenon that cannot be reduced to any one of its aspects, whether physiological or psychological, sociological, or spiritual. Further, Royce views all of these factors interacting in a variety of ways to form the psyche of a human being. Here, Royce supplies us with a much-needed view that counters the reductionism of various kinds that runs rampant in contemporary thought.

Turning to Royce's views on ethics, we find a different perspective on the contemporary debates between ethical realism and ethical idealism, on skepticism and on the "moral attitude." Much of contemporary philosophy works in the context of evolutionary theory. As we know, Royce addressed evolution and its implications in a number of ways, and he offered serious criticism of "evolutionary ethics." This critique is relevant today, when "naturalized ethics" is quite the "in thing" in philosophy; it also has relevance for contemporary debates on the free-will problem.

The fourth section of this chapter will deal with religion. Royce's views on religion have much contemporary relevance. He had a deep understanding of both religion and science, and his views on these could contribute much to contemporary debates about the conflict of science and religion. Royce's exploration of sin, guilt, atonement, and grace also has much to add to contemporary religious concerns.

The final section focuses on the relevance of Royce's views on social and political issues. His profound understanding of individuality as being constituted by exclusive interest and embedded in social and communal relations offers a much-needed alternative to the economic, self-interested, solipsistic individual so praised and defended today. A look at Royce's ideas can add much to the debate about the nature of democracy, whether as a system of institutions, as a system of ideas, or as a way of life. Royce's view of "dangerous dyads" and the need for mediation, which is developed in his *War and Insurance* and *The Hope of the Great Community,* are relevant to conflict resolution in our time.

The Philosopher as Wanderer, Scholar, Teacher, and Critical-Clarifying Voice

In 1981, John E. Smith, in his Eastern Division presidential address, pointed to three sins of the contemporary professional system of philosophy—the pursuit of certainty, the fetish of preparation, and the idolization of science. He argued that these errors have diverted philosophy from its main task "of relating the inescapable abstractions of thought to each other and to our primary experience of the world." These so-called sins, he asserts, have also turned philosophy to purely technical matters bearing "no direct relation to the perplexities confronting human beings in a precarious world."[2] Brand Blanshard, a member of an APA committee charged with examining the state of philosophy in 1945, noted that philosophers were perceived as isolated in ivory towers, "engrossed with solemn trifles."[3] Finally, John Dewey complained that philosophy had relegated the practical problems of contemporary life to a place subordinate to an "alleged problem of knowledge." For him, philosophy was a search for wisdom, and "[w]isdom differs from knowledge in being the application of what is known to intelligent conduct of the affairs of human life."[4]

Josiah Royce was, of course, in at the beginning of the effort to professionalize philosophy and to establish a prominent place for it as a respected academic discipline within the curriculum of the university.[5] He was a founding member of the American Philosophical Association and one of its presidents; he was a very successful chair of the department of philosophy at Harvard and, in fact, built it into a full-fledged department. Yet, Royce, if alive today, would believe that philosophy has betrayed its mission. He and Dewey agree on philosophy's central task, namely, wisdom for the living of life. We recall Royce's statement about this task: "You philosophize when you reflect critically upon what you are actually doing in your world. . . . The critical inquiry into what all these things mean and imply is philosophy."[6] Royce was interested in the problem of knowledge that is so central for contemporary philosophers,[7] but for him knowledge was not an end in itself, but was to assist in providing an adequate view of human experience and human life. Like many contemporary philosophers, Royce wrote on mathematics and logic;[8] yet, he also addressed many public issues such as race, war, and academic freedom. He was a "public philosopher."[9]

Further, Royce, like Peirce, Dewey, and James, criticized any quest for certainty. He affirmed the significant role of doubt, genuine doubt, not Cartesian hypothetical doubt, in the formation of beliefs.[10] Royce asserts: "The true born student of philosophy, *while* he studies philosophy, should act only as a philosopher,—freely, fearlessly, unsparingly,—questioning solely for the sake of insight."[11] Royce detested those in philosophy who claimed to have any final view of matters. He writes: "Dogma, as such has no place in philosophy."[12] In his Philosophy 9 Metaphysics course in 1915–1916, Royce discussed three forms of knowledge and argued that all failed to be complete.[13] He asserts: "One who seeks for finality in his views of life or of his fellowmen will not be satisfied so long as he is living in time."[14] Finally, Royce claims "the right to criticize as fearlessly, as thoroughly, and as skeptically as may be, the foundations of conduct and faith."[15]

As we know, Royce would include science in this category. For him, the scientific world of experience is not foundational as perceived today, but represents a modification of primordial experience for the sake of highly specialized interests. He argues that all knowledge of the external world has been and is intimately tied to and dependent upon the social context. For Royce, objectivity is intersubjectivity; belief in one's fellow men is prior to belief in nature. Royce develops these views in a number of places in his corpus but especially in the essay "The External World and the Social Consciousness."[16]

Royce claimed neither too much nor too little for science.[17] He viewed science as a fallible, yet genuinely progressive, epistemic endeavor. Imagination plays a key role in science, but not at the expense of coming into direct contact with an external and stubborn reality. Royce believed that the progress of science largely depends upon the more or less provisional choice of "leading ideas." A leading idea is a hypothesis that is used as a guide or a regulative principle of one's research. About these leading ideas, Royce writes: "Observation does not, at least for the time, either confirm or refute them. But on the other hand, they awaken interest in vast ranges of observation and experiment, and sustain the patience and enthusiasm . . . through long and baffling investigations."[18]

However, Royce equally affirms the role of experiment and experience. He writes: "In any case your special science prospers by reason of the empirical discoveries you make. And your theories, whatever they are, must not run counter to any possible empirical results."[19] Science, for Royce, is an interaction between what is given to us and what we bring to our investigations.

> We report facts; we let the facts speak; but we, as we investigate, in the popular phrase, "talk back" to the facts. We interpret as well as report. Man is not merely made for science, but science is made for man. It expresses his deepest intellectual needs as well as his careful observations. . . . [T]he theories of science are human, as well as objective, internally rational as well as (when that is possible) subject to external tests.[20]

Science is an eminently social enterprise; its so-called facts are the "possessions of the community."[21] Further, for Royce, interpretation, which is the work of science, is an ongoing, indefinite process. He holds that all human knowledge is limited and fallible and that science is a process of open inquiry that should not cease, either from a presumptive boast of final certitude or from the despairing suicide of final skepticism. Royce speaks of the interpreter as a person of humility and hope. Humility before the meagerness of one's knowledge should be the hallmark of the scientific inquirer; it also should be the mark of a good philosopher. To idolize science is to commit idolatry and to betray the necessary open-ended inquiry of philosophy.[22]

Another charge against professional philosophy is that is has devalued the role of the teacher of philosophy. Royce's student and later colleague, George Santayana, in 1894 wrote: "[T]he main concern of our typical young professor is not his pupils at all. It is his science . . . generally speaking, he wishes to be a scholar, and is a teacher only by accident."[23] As we learned in chapter 1, Royce was always concerned about his teaching and his students, and he was that rare philosopher who welcomed questions and criticism,[24] who was concerned to develop the thoughts of his students rather than to produce disciples.[25] He gave a full course on Hegel to a single student, Jacob Loewenberg, and for a former student's son he "lectured to this single student for half an hour with the same fervor and gravity as if he had been talking before the French Academy."[26] Royce pays his own final, strong tribute to the value of teaching in his comments upon his sixtieth-birthday celebration. He states: "The best concrete instance of a life of a community with which I have had the privilege to become well acquainted has been furnished to me by my own Seminary."[27] Royce believed strongly that a philosopher must be a teacher as well as a scholar; only in the interchange between students and colleagues could one advance one's own philosophy, and only in sending new critical and sympathetic minds into the world could human life and experience be enriched by the endeavor of philosophy.

Finally, not only would Royce despair at the idolization of science, but he would be equally appalled at the isolationist stance of many philosophers who seemed to hold that only philosophy has the correct answers. Royce investigated many disciplines, and he sought interactions with other disciplines, inviting scholars from many areas of expertise to his seminary on logic at Harvard. These scholars noted: "His most notable tribute to the teaching of the university was made through his seminary in logic, which became a veritable clearing house of science."[28] Given the complexity of human experience, the depth of serious human problems, and the burgeoning of knowledge, our world needs more, not less, interdisciplinary focus, interchange, and cooperation. A multitude of perspectives can broaden the view, provide more alternative solutions, and enrich meaning.

A View of Self Relevant to Contemporary Issues

Royce was ahead of his time as a psychologist in asserting views on psychological matters that are quite contemporary today. He shares a number of conclusions with contemporary philosophers, psychologists, and neuroscientists, but he does not fall into the trap of overemphasizing scientific matters, whether those of brain science or of evolutionary theory. This position against reductionism makes his insights even more relevant and useful to contemporary philosophical discussions. Further, Royce brings to these contemporary debates a social view of the nature of knowledge, reality, and mind, and his third kind of knowledge, interpretation.

We turn first to the matter of memory. Memory has played a central role in philosophy in constituting personal identity and also in ascribing personal responsibility. Royce assigns a key role to "the irrevocable past deed" in betrayal and in moral responsibility. However, the emphasis is on the deed as known by the community, by those betrayed as well as by the individual betrayer. Thus, individual recall of past events is not a central issue. Further, for Royce, autobiographical narrative is central for the self. The self is viewed as an interpretive process: the self is continually interpreting self by interpreting the past in terms of the present and for the future. One unifies self around a central ideal or cause, and it is in terms of this that interpretation takes place. In other words, there is a theme to one's narrative.

Royce believes that interests and selective attention, habits of thought and action, feelings and values all play an important role in memory. We are constantly interpreting our self in terms of our past and present with an idea to future conduct and thought. For Royce, our current values and interests play an important role in this construction of self. Thus, memory is about narrative self-construction and not about precise and detailed recall of individual events. Royce writes: *"[O]ur memory of past lives takes the form of a memory of typical fashions of behavior, of experience, of feeling."*[29] A person develops certain habits of narration, and the result, says Royce, is that *"most of our memories of long-past events are systematically, although unequally, falsified by habit."*[30] Royce cites, as an example, the remembrances of different people about winter weather in Boston. There are always debates about the severity of past winters compared with present winters, but the facts in weather reports do not verify these judgments. Rather what memories we retain have to do with the *"more significant habits that winter weather formerly developed."*[31] Like perception, memory is influenced by interests and habits of behavior. Royce believes that we see and remember the world as we are prepared to see or remember. We seek consistency of meaning and behavior.

According to Royce, our stance on the world is basically conservative. We seek change with the least expenditure of energy, modifying things only as necessary. Even revolutionaries, says Royce, often seek to return to some ideal past or some "original" values.[32] New habits, values, and ideas come about only in the face of challenge from the present situation as it presents us with data and problems that cannot be easily fitted into our approach to the world. Further, since the self is future-oriented and ideas are plans of action, memory, as a tool in our self-narrative, must always be future-directed. Thus, Royce would argue that memory, in its fundamental sense, is the ability to store useful information and retrieve it in precisely those circumstances and in that form that allow it to be useful to us in the present moment. Memory, then, is selective and future-focused. It is not the storage of unchanging details and events.

Such a view of memory is also expressed by neuroscientist Michael Gazzaniga in a chapter of his latest book entitled "The Brain Produces a Poor Autobiography."[33] Gazzaniga argues that we do not remember every detail about an experience; rather we remember the important details, the gist, of things. He notes that "our autobiographical memories are remembered anew each day, in a way that best fits our current concept of self."[34] Even more, says Gazzaniga, "Memory is not so much a mechanism for remembering the past as a means to prepare us for the future."[35] This understanding fits with Royce's view of the self as future-oriented and memory as a means to direct us toward the future and to future action.

Further, like Royce, Gazzaniga understands experience in terms of narrative.

The conception we have of ourselves is a story we tell ourselves about ourselves; we construct a narrative that "makes sense." Gazzaniga worked with the original split-brain patients, who often had to deal with conflicting information provided them by the split hemispheres in their brains.[36] In all these cases, the experience is interpreted and made meaningful. In fact, Gazzaniga speaks of the left hemisphere, the supposed brain site for language, as the "interpretive" part of the brain.[37] Royce would no doubt ask why the experience is reduced to brain experience; why is it not the interpretive self who constructs meaning with assistance from brain processes?

Royce would pose a similar question about current proposals to alter memory by erasing traumatic memories through pharmacological therapy. Pharmacological therapy has been used to erase traumatic memories, particularly those associated with post-traumatic stress syndrome. The goal is to help those who are paralyzed in action, deeply depressed, and overcome with nightmares that are peopled with debilitating memories. Royce would, of course, ask why the problem is reduced to brain physiology, but also he would ask about the role of these memories in a person's autobiography, their life plan, and/or their self-identity. How important are these events of the past and their emotional overtones to the present person and his or her goals and plans for the future? Is there a sense of personal responsibility involved, a deed that should not be erased? There are many sorrows in life, many deep traumas, and perhaps it is more healing for self and the future to absorb this trauma into one's overall life, thus transmuting its meaning and allowing the person to move on. Royce would also argue that this focus on a specific set of emotions and memories ignores the holistic self and its social context. Thus, for example, a musician, treated with a drug to reduce his anxiety in performance, reported that this had blunted his emotional experience of the performance. One would presume that the emotional aspect of a musical performance is a significant aspect that should not be blunted for either the performer or the audience. To erase specific memories ignores the role these memories play in the total memory, experience, habits, and actions of the self; it also ignores the social setting of the self, past, present, and future. And, finally, to pinpoint certain brain regions, for example, the hippocampus and amygdala, is to ignore the holistic functioning of the brain.[38]

The strongest philosophical advocates today for a reduction of self to neurological functions are Paul and Patricia Churchland.[39] Both the Churchlands focus on the interface between neuroscience and philosophy. They are associated with the school of thought known as eliminative materialism, which argues that folk psychology notions such as belief, free will, and consciousness can be eliminated in explaining human behavior and that "objective phenomena" such as neurons and their interactions are all that will be necessary for such explanations. According to Patricia Churchland, philosophers are increasingly realizing that to understand the mind one must understand the brain.

Royce would certainly not disagree with the assertion that to understand the mind one needs to understand the brain. But he would emphatically disagree with the view that one can eliminate folk psychology, because philosophy, for him, is critical reflection on human experience and life and also because he had a tremendous respect for the "common mind" and its insights. Further, he would view the self in a much more holistic manner—as an object of biological, anatomical, and neurophysiologic understanding; as a social-behavioral object of understanding; as a subject of consciousness, understood via introspection and through phenomenological description; as "expressive, through facial and bodily gestures; as a participant in cooperative activities such as art, language, custom, religion, understood via a study of the *expressive signs of mental life*";[40] the self, for Royce, is also the locus of moral attributes and the source of ethical action and values.

Royce would fault contemporary analyses as too focused on reason or the intellectual faculties and problem solving. Thus, he would seriously question all the computational and cognitive-science approaches to mind and to mental functioning. These approaches leave out any attention to emotion and desire, motivation and volition; they do not seem attuned to the enormous plasticity of brain and the complex interactions of the neuronal system with other systems such as the immunological and hormonal systems.[41] Further, Royce would hold that cognitive models could not account for the selective, unique aspects of a person's brain and mental states due to each individual's different response to the environment. Royce does not see mind as a "thinking machine." Rather, he defines mind as "essentially a being that manifests itself in signs."[42] Further, he asserts: "The very being of signs consists in demanding interpretation. The relations of mind are essentially social; so that a world without at least three minds in it—one to be interpreted, one the interpreter, and the third for whom or to whom the first is interpreted—would be a world without any real minds at all."[43] Conceptual and perceptual theories of mind, in Royce's view, all fail. It is through interpretation as a mode of knowledge that mind must be understood. This relates directly back to the notion of memory as involving interpretation and of self as a process of interpretation.[44]

In addition to eliminative materialism, another prominent view about the nature of mind is emergence theory. Essentially, emergent entities (properties or substances) "arise" out of more fundamental entities and yet are "novel" or "irreducible" with respect to them. Thus, for example, one can believe that mental states emerge as higher-level properties from lower-level physical properties in the brain, usually by means of interaction between an organism and the environment. About the emergent views, Royce would ask the following questions. Is not emergence also a form of reductionism? Second, is such a view not necessitated by an unwarranted assumption, namely, that somehow the mental and physical, mind and body, are radically or semi-radically different kinds of beings? Is this not a Cartesian assumption, hidden now within a supposed naturalism? Do emergence theories enlighten our understanding of human experience or the human self? Do all of these sophisticated theories arise because we idolize science?

We turn now to Royce's views on the importance of imitation for self-development, social development, and moral development. Royce believed that the self of the child grows and forms itself through imitation and through functions that cluster around the imitation of others. The human self, in Royce's view, feeds on social models for many aspects of its own development. These aspects include learning, motor skills, social skills, and role models for life and for ethical action. More importantly, for Royce, in contrasting self with the models and deeds, the self comes to self-consciousness, to a distinction between self and the other. He writes: "What he (the self) learns imitatively, and then reproduces, perhaps in joyous obstinacy, as an act that enables him to display himself over against others—this constitutes the beginning of his self-conscious life."[45]

It should be noted that selective attention and the interests and desires of the organism play a role, for Royce, in imitation. Especially important in this regard is the past, social influence, and my own unique interests. In all of my experience, I focus on what is familiar and thus the importance of past experience. But I also am attracted by what my friends, parents, siblings, and teachers have been interested in, and herein is the social influence. Finally, there is what uniquely attracts the individual. Royce argues for a tendency in the human self to "deliberate idealization of our imitations, to deliberate deviations from the literal." He writes: "One's play is one's own original fashion."[46] Children, says Royce, often mock a model in a way that is more or less consciously untrue to the model and will even engage in a pretend imitation, an exaggeration.[47] There is also, in one's imitating activities, a desire to contrast and to be other than what one finds merely in one's social models.

To understand how contemporary Royce's views are in this regard, we turn to highlights from a recent two-volume work entitled *Perspectives on Imitation*.[48] In the introduction to this work, we find the following assertion: "[R]ecent work across a variety of sciences argues that imitation is a rare ability that is fundamentally linked to characteristically human forms of intelligence, in particular to language, culture, and the ability to understand the minds of others. . . . Imitation is not just an important factor in human development, it also has a pervasive in-fluence throughout adulthood in ways we are just starting to understand."[49] Fur-ther, it is asserted:

> The study of imitation illuminates substantive issues about the links between per-ception and action and between self and the other; the modularity of mind; the re-lationship among various levels of description of minds in society; the relationship between genetic endowment and social environment in forming human minds; the relationships between cultural evolution, in which imitation is arguably the pri-mary copying mechanism, and biological evolution, which gives rise to the capacity for imitation in the first place.[50]

This volume presents a number of studies and articles that lend credence to Royce's own reflections on imitative functions and human development. Indeed, Ap Dijksterhuis, a psychologist at the University of Amsterdam, advocates two ideas that are very much in agreement with Royce's views. The first is that imi-tation heavily permeates social life and does so more or less continuously. The second idea is that imitation functions as the "social glue" that holds human be-ings together.[51] Dijksterhuis's conclusion is that imitation functions as social glue because it "leads us to like each other" and that the needed social behaviors for a community or society develop because "[w]e do all this because we want to be liked."[52] Yet, Royce would find this analysis inadequate: it does not deal with the various conditions needed for a sense of "community," and it does not see that the development of genuine individuals is dependent on supportive communities that are both nurturing and critical.

The glue that holds society together is much more than some kind of need for social approval, although community acceptance and affirmation of individuals is important for Royce.

In volume 2 of *Perspectives on Imitation*, philosopher Jesse Prinz explores the role of imitation in moral development.[53] He first asserts, as would Royce, that our understanding of the moral domain is not exhausted by cognitive knowl-edge; rather, it also involves a range of emotional capacities. He argues that imita-tive learning plays a key role in developing the right range of emotional capacity needed for ordinary moral competence. Prinz also agrees with Royce that human beings often shape moral attitudes and behavior through role models. He provides an interesting analysis of role modeling as a source of both good and bad conduct and discusses a broad range of issues related to emotions and moral competence, including such topics as emotional contagion in infants, emotional responses to violation of moral and conventional rules, and emotional deficits' role in impair-ing and impeding competence in the moral domain. Prinz asserts: "Psychopaths can imitate the behaviors of others to a reasonable degree, but they cannot imitate the emotional states of others, and this has serious implications for competence and conduct."[54]

The discussion of the role of imitation in moral development could be greatly enhanced with a careful, critical, comparative analysis of Royce's and Prinz's views on role modeling, emotions, and imitation. Additional insight on these matters could also be gained from a review of Royce's critical discussion of ethical theories based on pity or sympathy[55] as well as his overview of the idea, expressed by John Fiske, that moral consciousness is developed via a series of widening communities, evolving in four stages, beginning with the community of mother and child.[56] Royce concludes this discussion of John Fiske's philosophy with the following statement: "[T]hus all civilization develops, in a sense, about the bed of the helpless infant. And the sense of duty grows from the same root. In consequence, our idea of duty is primarily an idea of helpfulness to those whom we love. And this accounts for the evolutionary origin of the sympathetic aspect of morality. All ideals of kindliness thus have their source in an unselfish fondness for fellow beings that need help."[57]

Continuing our discussion of imitation, we turn to the contemporary concern with the connection between imitation and mind-reading. Mind-reading is essentially the ability to understand the actions and intentions of others. There are today three different approaches to mind-reading. The rationality approach says that "ordinary people assume that their peers are rational and proceed to impute to them those desires and beliefs that it would be rational of them to have in their circumstances."[58] This theory, supported by Daniel Dennett and Donald Davidson, makes no attempt to connect to imitation. Royce, of course, would argue that this theory falsely assumes a rational self prior to a social self and ignores that self-consciousness develops via contrast between self and others.

A second theory about mind-reading popular today is the theory-theory view, which argues that attributions of mental states to both self and others are guided by a set of psychological assumptions or judgments that are then tested out against evidence provided by other selves. One makes inferences from one's own psychological judgments to those of the other. The mind-reader is like a scientist testing out hypotheses against the evidence. Again, Royce would argue that understanding another's mental states has nothing to do with inference or analogy and further that the cart is again before the horse. One's own self-consciousness develops via contrast with others; I learn who I am as a self by social interaction with others.

The third contemporary mind-reading theory is the simulation theory. This theory holds that we represent the mental activities and processes of others by mentally simulating them, or generating similar activities and processes in ourselves. Simulation is said to be process-driven rather than theory-driven.[59] Simulation theory is seen as a basic challenge against the view that theory (a "folk" psychology) underlies psychological competence. Without this assumption, what had been a major issue in the philosophy of mind would be baseless: namely, the debate between psychological realists, who thought folk psychology a fundamentally sound foundation for cognitive science, and eliminativists, who deemed it a fundamentally flawed theory.

Royce, more than likely, would see the whole debate as fruitless spinning of wheels. His own view again comes from a holistic view of the human self that includes all of its aspects, but especially the social. Further, the debate assumes a postulate that Royce denies, namely, a basic separation between atomistic, individual selves. Such a postulate requires wheel-spinning to find an answer for basic human beliefs such as belief in the reality of other selves and belief in a common connection between selves that allows mind-reading to occur. Royce emphatically rejected analogical argument as a basis to provide evidence for the existence of his neighbor as a conscious being with a mind of his own.[60] The evidence is provided through contrast. Royce writes: "*Contrasts* are the interesting and fascinating proof of intelligence."[61] Thus, says Royce, suppose you read an advertisement in the newspaper and you discover in it an idea. The idea intrudes upon you, and you realize that the idea is not yours; here is an idea that is not your own. You assume, then, that the advertisement has been written by an intelligent being. Further, if someone shouts "Fire!" you see this as an expression of an idea that isn't your idea. Royce asserts: "The signs of another mind are peculiarly direct in this way. Any idea that isn't my own is *ipso facto* an expression of a self not my own," and "If such ideas hang together well enough, they constitute another mind. Another mind is a system of ideas which is intelligible in itself but which certainly isn't mine."[62] I, for one, find this view on other minds unique and illuminating and much more sensible than the convoluted notions promoted today in philosophy of mind.

Again, Royce assumes that we live in a social world and that our own understanding of self and others comes about within that world. Science can contribute by helping us understand the neurological, psychological, and sociological mechanisms that lead to our ability to recognize the contrast between self and other, but one starts from the social world and moves to the individual self and not vice versa.

A third area where Royce's views have relevance concerns children. As we recall, he argued for the importance of play in a child's life. Play provides the necessary context for the imitative activities that will lead to self-development, and it is also the arena for the self's expression of the restless instinct. This instinct, in turn, is linked to selective attention, initiative, new ideas, and individualism. Human restlessness seeks both unity and a sense of uniqueness, of "placing one's own mark on experience." In play, says Royce, we also see "an *insistence upon trying over and over again the playful activity until it wholly satisfies his own ideal,*" and in this perseverance we find "originality," the "*initiative which the child may himself be said to contribute to the organization of his playful functions.*"[63] Further, play is significant for the development of the self's abilities to integrate and for the ability to experience joy and find fulfillment in integrative experience. Play not only brings together sensory, motor, intellectual, and imaginative elements of the self, but it also synthesizes habit and originality.

The importance of play is fast losing meaning in the contemporary world. Or perhaps one should say that "play" is misunderstood. In a new book, *Children at Play: An American History,* historian Howard Chudacoff claims that adults have taken over the notion of play as a free, imaginative activity and have made it into a highly organized process that seeks to fulfill all kinds of adult and social goals, including the goal of looking good on a preschool application.[64] Chudacoff and others are concerned that too many organized activities, including various sports events, music or ballet lessons, and karate and other such lessons, have crowded out free time for children and constricted children's imaginations and social skills. In his *Philosophy of Loyalty,* Royce advocates for athletics as a training ground for loyalty, but cautions that such could also hinder natural groupings of the young as well as the spontaneity of play.

Chudacoff observes that toys have become commercialized and connected with the television and film industry, and thus "a toy comes with a prepackaged back story and ready-made fantasy life," meaning that "some of the freedom is lost, and unstructured play is limited."[65] As for video games, he believes they put a straitjacket on imagination. In a humorous and yet sad footnote, historian Janet Golden, who is writing a book on the history of babies in the twentieth century, points out that when Dr. Seuss's *The Cat in the Hat* was published in 1957 it was considered subversive. Parents objected that it stimulated children to use their imaginations without being under the "watchful eye of a mother."[66] Today, because of obsessions with safety, playground activity is highly supervised, and many playgrounds are empty. It seems that Royce's beliefs about the significance of play are much needed today, and he would say to critics that life is risky and living life fully requires facing risk courageously.

Royce as Ethicist: New Perspectives on Old Issues

Royce was concerned in his early writings with answering the question, What is the real nature and ground of this distinction between right and wrong? In *The Religious Aspect of Philosophy*, Royce reframes the central question in terms of the conflict between the ethical realist and the ethical idealist. The ethical realist seeks to find the basis for the distinction between right and wrong, good and evil, in the real world. The ethical idealist, like the person of the analytic method, is the person who seeks to demonstrate, if possible, an ideal as the true and only ideal, without in any way making it depend upon physical reality. These methods and views are for Royce opposites. He writes: "The judgments: *This is,* and *This is good,* are once for all different; and they have to be reached by widely different methods of investigation."[67]

Moral realism, in today's philosophical parlance, argues that moral claims purport to report facts. This assertion leads realists into the problem of moral disagreement. Some moral realists argue that the disagreements, though widespread, do not go very deep. Rather, these disagreements play out against a background of shared fundamental principles, and the differences of opinion are really disagreement about non-moral facts. These realist arguments have not appeared convincing to many philosophers, and a number of anti-moral-realist positions have developed. Royce, of course, argues that conflict between values is an essential element in moral discourse, and he sees the inner conflict between values as essentially the reason for skepticism and ultimately for the desire for harmony, since the individual really desires both values. Thus, Royce writes: "The moral life is essentially a life of conflict—of the conflict between humane and narrowly selfish impulses, of the conflict between reason and caprice, between order and chaos, yes, and the conflict between these two moral motives themselves, which ideally ought to harmonize, but which in our balance we do harmonize so ill."[68]

Royce's critique of moral realism is his belief that to base an ideal on the real is to betray the distinctive thrust of the moral ought.[69] This criticism is basically the one raised by G. E. Moore, who points out that a naturalist, and presumably a realist, who sees a moral claim as a natural fact requires moral terms to be defined using terms to refer to natural properties such as seeking pleasure, satisfying one's desires, conforming to the rules in society, and promoting the species. About this, says Moore, one can always ask: But is it (this) good? Realists do acknowledge the force of Moore's argument, as they would also presumably acknowledge Royce's arguments in "Tests of Right and Wrong" and *Religious Aspect.*

To overcome the force of the question, But is this good? realists look for something important in moral claims that capture the sense of the moral ought and that presumably non-moral claims do not have. The answer is sought in motivation. One view argues that sincere moral claims are constituted by a proper motivation. This distinguishes moral claims from non-moral claims since such claims never entail anything about motivation. This view, in its various forms, fails in light of situations in which a person is not motivated appropriately by claims she sincerely believes. There is also the problem of tests for sincerity other than behavior.

Royce would deny the whole assumption underlying the contemporary debate, namely, that there is a distinction between moral beliefs and regular beliefs such that regular beliefs are "motivationally inert" and moral beliefs are not. Royce, as we have seen, united will, intellect, and feeling in action. For him, all beliefs are plans for action. Royce's position would also undercut the foolishness of a position like that of A. J. Ayer, who argues that ethical statements were neither analytic nor verifiable and thus must be meaningless.[70] A corollary to this view was the "emotive theory of ethics."[71]

Royce also criticized ethical idealism, claiming that it loses touch with the diversity of the moral world, and he argued that pursuing the ideal in an ideal world alone ends in caprice and ultimately in falling back on an external justification.[72] Royce asks, How shall we decide between these two views: ethical realism and ethical idealism? He writes: "Alas! The decision is the whole labor of founding a moral doctrine. We have not yet seen deeply enough into their opposition. They may both be one-sided. The truth may lie in the middle. But as yet we have no right to dogmatize."[73] Again, if only we in philosophy today proceeded in this manner: the debate between moral realism and moral non-cognitivism (ethical idealism) continues today in a dogmatic fashion and without any awareness of Royce's work on this issue in the 1880s. In fact, a major problem with the whole debate is that it fails to see, as did Royce, the close interrelationships between intellect, will, and feeling and the involvement of all of these in ethical decisions and action.

A strong trend in contemporary ethics is toward some form of naturalized ethics. Royce, as we know, addressed evolution and its implications in a number of ways. He also offered some telling criticisms of evolutionary ethics, criticisms certainly relevant to naturalized ethics. Royce addresses what he later identified as two hindrances to leading an ethical life. He writes: "From our modern point of view, the ethical interpretation of the universe is hindered by two especially serious difficulties . . . the general presuppositions of modern naturalism . . . and our incomplete appreciation of the meaning and essential limitations of the human type of consciousness."[74]

Both of these problems confront us today. A major limitation of man's consciousness is its supposed tendency to "radical selfishness," which tends to narrow his focus to his own interests and thus to limit his view of reality and life. Related to this is a second narrowing of focus represented by the attraction of aggressive individualism. One hardly needs to argue that major ethical concerns today are various expressions of rampant selfishness and individualism, which can be seen in the greed and fraud perpetuated in many areas of institutional life.

"Naturalism," in a variety of forms, is present in contemporary philosophy, and I believe Royce's discussions of this view, including his discussions of evolutionary theory, provide us with new perspectives on some of the issues raised by naturalism. Royce once remarked that naturalism had no awareness of the free and self-determining nature of human beings. I believe that Royce's intention in this comment is to argue that naturalism misinterprets this problem and offers in some cases a very inadequate understanding of "human freedom." In any case, his observations on this issue might shed some light on the current debate on "free will." The debate takes several turns: (1) a re-defining of "free will" to somehow fit a deterministic stance,[75] (2) an attempt to find free will in quantum indeterminism,[76] (3) an attempt to save free will by a transcendental argument for an "irreducible non-Humean self,"[77] and (4) an evolution-based philosophical exposition in which Daniel Dennett seeks enough "elbow room" in a deterministic world where human beings must be seen as "organic robots," but where we can have what he calls a "good enough" notion of free will.[78] Royce would likely ask, "Good enough for what?" Further, a number of philosophers and neuroscientists try hard to find "within the brain" evidence, primarily that of "brain waves and time lapses," for "free will."[79] Royce would have welcomed excursions into science, including neurological, and would have pursued a sympathetic but critical exploration of their conclusions and their implications. But most importantly Royce would have questioned the operating assumption of all of these discussions, namely, the "truth" of a strictly deterministic position, supposedly a truth based on the physical sciences.[80] Royce would label this assertion as a form of dogmatism and without foundation in either the world of science or the experiential world.

Royce argued that it is social motives that led us to postulate a uniform, predictable natural world. Man's basic interest in nature, argues Royce, is to win control over it. Thus, the notion of "the uniformity of nature" is a socially useful notion. It reveals no absolute truth; it can never be fully verified in human experience.[81] The whole free-will debate, in Royce's view, is based on a false view of science, a false premise of strict determinism.

Finally, Royce and James were both convinced that the solution to the problem of free will and determinism was not be found within the confines of psychology; rather it was a matter of moral philosophy. In *The Conception of God* (1897) Royce writes:

> The empirical psychologist . . . knows nothing about freedom, as such, and those who seek for psychological proofs for the freedom of the will comprehend neither psychology nor freedom. Psychology deals not with the moral self, but with the empirical creature called man, viewed merely as he chances to be.[82]
>
> . . . [O]nce the freedom of the moral individual is recognized, it must be understood as a "distinctly limited freedom," since it is highly dependent upon the network of social relations in which every individual finds himself inserted.[83]

Further, Royce's criticisms of evolution seem insightful in light of the latest philosophical fad of "naturalized ethics." Royce notes that there are those who claim that "the doctrine of evolution shows that selfishness must itself become even in our day altruistic if it would be successful." Royce's question is, So what? He asks: "Is this aspect of evolution any more ethical than the other?"[84] He then writes: "[C]ertain defenders of the application of the hypothesis of evolution to questions of fundamental ethics have tried to establish that the truths of evolution teach us that we ought to do right. The whole undertaking resembles the man who should try to show us that the truth of the law of gravitation clearly indicates that we all ought to sit down."[85] Royce further observes that even if the doctrine of evolution shows that one of the forms of "adaptation" is more successful than another, this only tells us that we would be most prudent in adopting this course rather than another in attempting to achieve our aims. Royce concludes his extensive discussion of evolution as follows: "There is no doubt of the reality and of the vast importance of the physical fact of evolution. Its ethical importance, however, has been, we hold, misunderstood. Evolution is for ethics a doctrine not of ends, but of the means that we can use."[86]

That Royce was highly critical of evolutionary ethics does not at all suggest any lack of concern for the relevance of scientific and other factual matters to ethics; the question is, How relevant and how applicable? Royce repeatedly affirmed his belief that ethics must be informed by a factual understanding of the human self and actor. In his review of *The Principles of Psychology* by William James, he writes: "The ethical theorist must take account of the psychological data that will affect the final statement of his doctrine in its application to mankind. . . . The moral law remains a pious wish unless psychology can show how it has entered the mind and heart of man."[87] And Royce would say that moral law also needs to be informed by evolutionary matters. It assists the application of an ethical doctrine to human life by providing information on the prudent choice of means.

Also, it provides us information on the development of the context of ethical action, namely, the world of social life. This was the topic of Royce's lectures on the work of John Fiske, author of *The Outlines of Cosmic Philosophy*.[88] These ideas on the development of moral consciousness certainly should inform a theory of ethics; they do not constitute an ethic.

Also relevant to contemporary ethics are Royce's ideas about the ethical self as a unified self with a plan of action. Royce declares: "A plan in life, pervading and comprehending my experiences, is, I say the *condition sine qua non* of the very existence of myself as this one, whole, connected Ego."[89] The self who achieves this plan, is, for Royce, an ethical self, and thus a "person." A person is the moral individual viewed as aiming toward an ideal. This person is a subject of value, one to whom moral attributes can be given. And these, for Royce, need not be positive. He writes: "[T]he term 'person' . . . can mean only the moral individual, i.e., the individual viewed as meaning or aiming towards an ideal, good or relatively bad, angelic or relatively diabolical, lawful, or relatively anarchical."[90]

Three contemporary philosophers have views very similar to those of Royce. Thus, Charles Taylor reiterates the need for a unified self as central to ethical action. To act ethically, Taylor argues, one must have moral intuitions and must articulate the grounds of these. This presupposes the existence of evaluative frameworks. I must stand somewhere in moral space. My identity, says Taylor, must be partially constituted by my attachment to a community that provides the evaluative framework within which I am able to articulate what is good and valuable.[91] Here we see close connections with Royce's views on self and on loyalty. We also recall Royce's own assertion about doing ethics in the context of an assumed ordinary moral world.

Alasdair MacIntyre argues that to hold one accountable for actions is intelligible only in terms of an ongoing narrative and in terms of its role in the agent's history. To be accountable to past actions, he says, requires unity of character.[92] Finally, Christine Korsgaard argues that ethical theory should determine one's theory on personal identity. She argues that conceiving ourselves as practical agents simply requires us to view our lives as unified. She speaks of three kinds of unity. First is a synchronic unity, which addresses my basic need to eliminate conflict among my various motivational desires in order to act. Second, I must have a unified deliberate standpoint, within which I view myself as a single deliberator and decider, a being over and above my desires, one who weighs them and decides. Third, there is diachronic unity, which is about my unified agency across time. This is essential to my need to pursue any ends and carry out a rational plan of life. I must be a unified agent both at a time and across time.[93] This statement by Korsgaard is an excellent summary of Royce's views and demonstrates his relevancy to contemporary issues. The insights he could add to these views are those contained in his philosophy of loyalty and philosophy of community.

Relevant Insights on Religion

In *Religious Aspect,* Royce defines religion in terms of belief, feelings, and action. This more holistic view of religion and his analyses of religion, in the *Problem of Christianity* and in "Monotheism," provide an excellent prism through which to understand and address the conflicts and events arising from religion in our contemporary times.

I set the stage for our discussion by drawing first on the recent *CNN Presents* series on "God's Warriors,"[94] which presented on Jewish, Christian, and Islamic warriors. In this set of interviews by Christiane Amanpour, CNN chief international correspondent, certain central themes stand out: (1) The scripture is the blueprint to life and living. (2) Our role is to redeem the entire world. (3) Martyrdom is the biggest wish; this is the ultimate sacrifice—to give your soul as a gift to God, the creator, and the country. (4) Modern society has lost its way. Thus, for Jewish warriors, the Torah says that God promised this land (Israel and especially Hebron and the area of the settlements) to the Jewish people, and until the land has been restored God cannot redeem the world.[95] Interestingly enough, Christian Zionists also support these beliefs.[96] Jewish warriors will sacrifice themselves for their vision. They also believe that modern society is amoral and corrupt and that many do not follow the Torah. Thus, one unidentified man said: "The problem of civilization is that it doesn't offer man somewhere to go. He doesn't know his place in the world."[97] For Muslim warriors the Koran is the blueprint for life and living. They believe it shows America to be a moral wasteland, a place that has lost its soul to materialism. The vision for many radical Muslims, including the Sunni, is to establish a caliphate, a global Muslim state, in the Middle East, which, as in the golden age of Islam, will establish harmony and stability. Abdollah Rezaie, director of culture and arts, Bright Future Institute in Iran, speaks of the "Hidden Imam," who will appear and will save the world. Martyrdom is, of course, sought by many young Muslims because it is supposed to guarantee their direct passage to heaven. Christian warriors for God, in emphasizing the scripture as a blueprint, advocate for "Christian morals" and against abortion, gay marriage, secularism, and evolutionism. In fact, many hold that belief in evolution is the cause of many of America's problems. Under the leadership of the late Jerry Falwell, Christian warriors seek to express their views in politics through the ballot box and other means and through media. For all three sets of warriors, religion and politics are closely intertwined.

When we examine this situation via Royce's views on religion, the following seems relevant. First, in discussing Christianity, Royce is emphatic in his respect for Jesus and his teachings, but he argues against taking the gospel or the teachings of the Master as the essence of faith. For one thing, writes Royce, Christ can hardly have regarded his teaching as the whole of his mission; these teachings should be seen as part of a larger religious process. Further, they are mysterious and incomplete. The two essential teachings, for Royce, are the Fatherhood of God, that is, the doctrine of the divine love for individual man, and the consequent teaching of love of one's neighbor. These teachings can be understood, for Royce, only as they are exemplified in the community of the spirit of Christ, the community of interpretation. For Royce, the scripture of any religion can be the blueprint for living only in the sense of calling each individual to the task of building the universal community of interpretation and loyalty.

Second, Royce was well aware how emphasis on right belief can lead to religious persecution and religious wars as the "inevitable means for defending the faith."[98] Royce, however, believes that those who seek genuine religion would seek "an affair of the whole man, not of deeds alone, nor of the intellect alone, but of the entire spiritual attitude,—of emotion and trust,—of devotion and of motive,—of conduct guided by an inner light, and of conviction due to a personal contact with religious truth."[99] What is wanted is a unity of faith and practice, a "reaction of the whole spirit in the presence of an experience of the highest realities of human life and of the universe."[100] The answer is not in "right belief," but in transcendence of self and of one's community in seeking a harmony and a peace that includes all. The vision of the Hidden Imam, a harmony under Islam, with tolerance for other faiths, is on the right track as a claim to inclusiveness and broad scope, but is falsely overlain with the notion of "one true faith."

Further, for Royce, the way to save self and the world is through community and building community. Martyrdom may be necessary to bring about community, but it is not a "saving event" or the salvation sought by the individual or the world. Only the community can bring the unity, cause, and meaning sought by the self. Only in community can genuine individuality and meaning be found. But the community must not betray the self by falling into idolatry and presenting itself as the only true community of saving grace; it is one among many communities of loyalty and interpretation. The true warrior for God is one who seeks unity with plurality, harmony with differences. Pluralism is not inimical to genuine religion; it is a necessary element of any growing, alive religion. It is in contrast and in the interaction of ideas and beliefs that growth takes place. Each of the religious traditions can be enriched by the others, and they can grow together in seeking to bring spiritual nourishment and ethical reform to the world. The goal of all religions should be to bring the "saving message" of the beloved community. The goal is not a political community, but a spiritual way. The political community should be a means to achieving broader community, to provide the order necessary for individual and communal growth. Religion and politics should be related in terms of the politic functioning as a means to a broader end, not as united in a theocratic or theo-political community.

Finally, Royce would agree with the religious warriors that modern civilization is morally bankrupt because of its stress on possessive individualism, market-driven materialism, hedonistic values, and narcissistic identities. In the words of Cornel West, "The market driven media lead many young people to think that life is basically about material toys and social status," and "older folk become jaded, disillusioned, and weary."[101] Ours is a time of great spiritual malnutrition. Many young people, as well as adults, are depressed and self-medicated because they lack the necessary skills to cope with the challenges in life—disappointment, disease, disasters, death, and various evils perpetrated by others. The radical forms of religion have great appeal to the spiritually undernourished and those who crave meaning. Much of traditional religion, as in Royce's day, seems too caught up in formalism or unable to address the tremendous social and spiritual needs of the people. In this situation, Royce's ethico-religious view and his notion of the beloved community seem most relevant.

Turning to one small aspect of the views of the religious warrior, we focus on the Christian warrior who wars against science and against the doctrine of evolution. In this case, Royce's view both supports and criticizes this stance. First, Royce would agree that evolutionary theory, in the hands of some, has itself engaged in idolatry, claiming a single universal view of everything, including an explanation of religion. Royce's views on evolution have already been discussed, and no more needs to be said here. Second, Royce would argue that religion and science are complementary endeavors; each provides an interpretation of reality, and each captures only a portion of that reality. There need not be any war between them.[102] Third, on the creationist issue, Royce emphatically rejects this doctrine as central to Christianity. He envisions God as a spirit and a person. Royce writes: "[H]e is not a being who exists in separation from the world as its external creator. He expresses himself in the world. . . . God expresses himself in the world as an artist expresses himself in the poems and the characters, in the music or in the other artistic creations, that arise within the artist's consciousness and that for him and in him embody his will. . . . In this entire world, God sees himself lived out."[103]

Royce also is critical of the so-called natural theology, which, he says, is an emphasis on the Hellenic type of theism. The so-called philosophical proofs of the divine existence, in Royce's view, make explicit some aspect of the Hellenic interest in the order and reason of the world. About these efforts at proof, Royce writes: "It has been insisted, and not without very genuine basis . . . that all such efforts, through the intellect, to grasp the divine nature lead to results remote from the vital experience upon which religious monotheism and, in particular, Christian monotheism, must rest, if such monotheism is permanently to retain the confidence of a man who is at once critical and religious."[104]

Finally, we assess the relevance of Royce's analysis of the sin of treason and the doctrine of atonement and of his notions of sin, guilt, and salvation in general. His understanding of the sin of treason and atonement conveys much meaning for our contemporary situation, for the following reasons. First, it recognizes fully the claim of Martin Luther, namely, *Simul iustus et peccator*, "I am simultaneously justified and sinner." Though I find my saving cause and community, I can betray it. Conversion and salvation are not single events, but rather never-ending processes. I can fail again and again and still find atonement or salvation. Faith and salvation is not once and for all.

Second, sin is both personal and communal in two senses. First, the consequences affect both the individual sinner and other individuals. To personally repent is not enough. There must be attempts to heal the community; the sinner is loved but only as a traitor, as a doer of the past deed. Others must move in to love and initiate forgiveness and atoning acts, acts specific and relevant to the concrete situation. If a lie is the act of betrayal, an act of truth and openness must occur that increases the sense of trust in the community and makes the sense of individual obligation higher and stronger. Sin is both personal and communal in still another sense. There can be communal sin in that a community can portray itself as the ultimate goal, worthy of ultimate loyalty. It betrays the principle of loyalty to loyalty. Individuals within the community and other communities must speak for this principle and condemn this betrayal, while seeking also atonement and healing.

Indeed, Royce's identification of the essence of Christianity with the "community of salvation" is a return to what many believe to be a lost insight. Sin is "self-betrayal" in not achieving full human development, and it is sin against others. It injures the order of the human world, the relationships that form the foundation of an individual's existence and all common human existence. Further, the emphasis on community brings out two important aspects of religion, particularly of Christianity, namely, the joy of Christian community and the founding of a genuine Christian social ethic. It is a joy to live in community with one's brethren, to celebrate together the rituals of hope and memory. This would seem true for Judaism as well as Islam. And community grounds the ethic of love. It calls us not only to love our brothers and sisters but to be less complacent about the genuineness of communities, merely because they are called "religious." All religions have work to do today to make their communities more inclusive and more loving. Royce writes: "In brief, speaking ethically, you cannot consciously be merely egoistic. For you, as a man, exist only in human relations. Your aims have to be more or less social. . . . The ethical problem is not: Shall I aim to preserve social relations? But: What social relations am I to preserve?"[105] In seeking inclusion, Royce asserts: *"Look forward to the human and visible triumph of no form of the Christian church."*[106] One would assume that this is true for all earthly forms of religious community.

Fostering Genuine Individuals and Genuine Communities

For many today their lives are dominated by meaninglessness and hopelessness. Many face poverty, poor health, discrimination, and other forms of injustice, while even the economically and socially well-off seek escapism from the world through drugs, ceaseless entertainment or exotic amusement, and boring, mindless sex. The amassing of materialistic toys leaves many empty. There is a hunger for something more, a thirst for something deeper. There is also war and conflict in all areas of life and of the world.

In this situation, we need to foster genuine individuals and genuine communities as well as to address the many social issues of poverty, poor health, violations of human rights and dignity, and economic, social, and political imperialism. To these needs Royce can offer some solutions. Turning first to the individual need for meaning and fulfillment, we know that without interaction with others, without social influence, no coherent human self can arise. This means, of course, that one of the key conditions for fostering individual self-development and search for meaning is the presence of enabling social conditions; genuine communities, in Royce's view, must foster genuine individuals, whether these communities are families, provinces, social organizations, or churches. The place to begin is at home in the family. Many families today are dysfunctional, and some purported families aren't really families at all. This may be because adults are pursuing narcissistic goals or working to provide basic sustenance for their families or are themselves in modes of escapism through drugs and other means. The foster care situation in the United States is a sad case in point, with many youngsters floating through the system without care, love, or opportunities to build self-confidence or self-esteem. Many of these youngsters long for "family," but even when they find it are often too damaged psychologically and socially to benefit from this enabling community. Royce did analyze in some detail the family and its dynamic in terms of developing genuine individuals and fostering growth both of family members and of the family as a unit.[107] His work should be reassessed in terms of today's problems and conditions.

There is also the overemphasis on "rights," in terms of negative liberty, or non-interference. This has become an obstacle to building community and solving problems. Rights need to be stressed in their positive aspect as "circumstantial," providing conditions for individual development and exercise of choice. Civil liberties should be seen as enabling conditions for individuals and for communities.[108] With this approach perhaps more advances could be made in fostering human rights and dignity and health care rights for individuals. Royce emphasizes "rights" in the positive aspect, stressing the responsibilities and obligations that go with rights as well as the needed interaction and mutual support between individuals and their communities.

Royce's views on interpretation and mediation also lay the foundation for a new social and political philosophy. Thus, in a very fine essay on power and compassion, Shibley Telhami, author of *The Stakes: America and the Middle East*,[109] argues for the need to build bridges of mutual understanding by establishing dialogue with various stakeholders.[110] He argues that these bridges need particularly to be built between the United States and the people in Arab and Muslim countries. He calls this a "compassionate approach that builds coalitions and considers the vital interests and wishes of other states and peoples around the globe."[111] Such a method, he believes, would allow a chance to build moral consistency among various parties about the illegitimacy of terrorist tactics while empowering influential segments of the various Arab and Muslim societies to wage their own struggles for change. It would also reinforce notions of openness and democracy that have been a part of America's greatness.

Further, Royce saw his notion of "communities of interpretation" as promoting those values integral to the stability of a democratic community.[112] Among these values is the principle of equality. The community of interpretation is viewed by Royce as fundamentally egalitarian. No one of the three parties has the power to coerce another into accepting a viewpoint, and once the dialogue has begun different members of the community of interpretation will have to assume the role of interpreter as preliminary interpretations and schemes for cooperation are offered. Further, the process of interpretation is open-ended, and thus particular interpretations are always open to reconsideration. And, in concert with democratic ideals, the interpretive process provides a model of deliberative decision making, and it promotes dispositions of fairness, open-mindedness, and a willingness to alter positions when reason or evidence demands.[113]

Democracy is not simply a matter of an electoral system, which we know can be subject to corrupt manipulation. Thus, Robert Reich writes: "democracy means much more than the process of free and fair elections. It is a system for accomplishing what can only be achieved by citizens joining together to further the common good."[114] There is no question today that there is widespread disillusionment with politicians and our media watchdogs. However, we cannot continue to focus on the corruptions of the democratic system but must re-emphasize the role played by an enlightened and motivated democratic citizenry. Genuine communities need critical, genuinely committed individuals.

In his recent article "How Capitalism Is Killing Democracy," Robert Reich notes that many so-called democratic countries, including the United States, have been hobbled by allowing corporations and elites buoyed by runaway economic success to undermine the government's capacity to respond to citizens' concerns.[115] Free markets, he acknowledges, have brought unprecedented prosperity to many, but "they have been accompanied by widening inequalities of wealth, heightened job insecurity, and environmental hazards such as global warming."[116] He writes: "no democratic nation is effectively coping with capitalism's negative side effects."[117] People in the United States, he notes, are feeling an inner conflict between the "consumer in us and the citizen in us."[118]

Further, he argues that a major reason that capitalism is weakening democracy is that companies, in their "intensifying competition for global consumers and investors, have invested even greater sums in lobbying, public relations, and even bribes and kickbacks, seeking laws that give them a competitive advantage over their rivals."[119] And, he says, this arms race for political influence "is drowning out the voices of average citizens."[120] And, further, he argues, because governments are not establishing rules and limits, corporations are being entrusted with social responsibility or morality. However, corporate executives are not authorized by anyone to balance profits against public good, and they have no expertise in moral calculations. Corporate charity, notes Reich, is usually done for public relations reasons, and relying on corporations to do this work has a great danger, "that these conspicuous displays of corporate beneficence hoodwink the public into believing corporations have charitable impulses that can be relied on in a pinch."[121]

More importantly, for Reich, all this emphasis on the social duties of corporations distracts the public from democracy's responsibilities to set the rules of the game and thereby protect the common good. It also distracts us from our individual duties as citizens to "trump the consumers in us," to advocate for laws that "make our purchases and investments social choices as well as personal ones."[122] The private benefits of the global market do have social costs. And, "for those of us living in democracies it is imperative to remember that we are also citizens who have it in our power to reduce these social costs. . . . We can accomplish this larger feat only if we take our roles as citizens seriously. The first step, which is often the hardest, is to get our thinking straight."[123]

The major question is, Do we want to live in a world where the bottom line trumps the common good and government takes a back seat to big business? Reich writes: "If the purpose of capitalism is to allow corporations to play the market as aggressively as possible, the challenge for citizens is to stop these economic entities from being the authors of the rules by which we live."[124] Royce would disagree with Reich that corporations should not be viewed as moral beings with social responsibilities; they are a community and function, in his view, as a personal being with duties and obligations. However, he would emphatically agree with Reich in the call to individual citizens and communities other than corporations to not allow these entities to set the values and rules for our lives. Individuals, provinces, communities must accept the mission of Socrates, namely, to live the examined life, to think critically, and to engage in criticism and healthy debate of issues. In his arguments for a strong provincialism, Royce is advocating for strong citizen involvement in public issues and for critical advocacy for a broader community. Further, he would no doubt embrace, as has Cornel West, a prophetic love of justice. One must not lapse into despair at the atrocities and barbarities, the evils of the world. Rather, as Royce counsels, one must fight these with courage and persistence.

We have discussed four areas where Royce's thought is relevant to contemporary social and political issues: bringing purpose and meaning back into individual lives; creating functional, fostering, supportive families; building bridges through interpretation; and renewing and revitalizing democracy through individual and communal action. Other areas have been discussed in the chapter on Royce's social and political thought. A refocus on Royce can aid us in rethinking our role as America and as American citizens in the world today. There is no doubt in my mind that Royce would join social critic and prophet Cornel West in urging us forward "girded by . . . three moral pillars—Socratic questioning, prophetic witness, and tragicomic hope."[125]

Notes

1. Royce as a Frontier Californian and Intellectual Pioneer

1. Josiah Royce, "Joseph Le Conte," *International Monthly* 4 (1901): 324–34.

2. Josiah Royce, "James as a Philosopher," *Boston Evening Transcript*, 29 June 1911, 13; reprinted in *Science* n.s. (1911): 33–35, 34; and under the title "William James and the Philosophy of Life," in Josiah Royce, *William James and Other Essays on the Philosophy of Life* (New York: Macmillan, 1912), 3–45, 6.

3. Josiah Royce, *The Spirit of Modern Philosophy: An Essay in the Form of Lectures* (Boston: Houghton, Mifflin, 1892), 1. (Hereafter cited as *SMP*.)

4. See Josiah Royce, "Loyalty and Insight," *Simmons Quarterly* 1 (1910): 4–21, reprinted in *William James and the Philosophy of Life*, 49–95. In this commencement address Royce is urging the graduates to develop a philosophy of life. References to this piece will be from the William James volume.

5. *William James and the Philosophy of Life*, 6. Royce speaks of James's work as "interpreter of the problems of the American people," and especially cites his *Varieties of Religious Experience* as American in spirit, 18–25. Most interesting to me is Royce's description of the *Varieties* as "the spirit of the frontiersman, of the gold seeker, or the home builder, transferred to the metaphysical and spiritual realm," 22. In my judgment, Royce's two works on religion as well as other of his works are also in this spirit.

6. Ibid., 49.

7. Royce, "Loyalty and Insight," 60. (Hereafter, citations to simply "Royce" indicate Josiah Royce.)

8. Ibid., 95.

9. Josiah Royce, *The Spirit of Modern Philosophy*, reprint (New York: Dover Publications, 1983), 13.

10. Josiah Royce, *The World and the Individual*, 2 vols. (New York: Macmillan,

1900–1901; reprint, New York: Dover Publications, 1959), 2:3. Citations are from the 1959 Dover edition.

11. Douglas Anderson, *Philosophy Americana: Making Philosophy at Home in American Culture* (New York: Fordham University Press, 2006), 34 and 35.

12. Ibid., 34.

13. Royce, *The World and the Individual*, 2:3.

14. Anderson, *Philosophy Americana*, 34–35.

15. Josiah Royce, letter to E. Stanley Hull, February 1898, in *The Letters of Josiah Royce*, ed. John Clendenning (Chicago: University of Chicago Press, 1970), 370–71.

16. Josiah Royce, "The Problem of Job," *New World* 6 (1897): 261–81, reprinted in Josiah Royce, *Studies of Good and Evil* (New York: D. Appleton, 1898), 1–28. (Hereafter cited as *SGE*.) The quotation is from Josiah Royce, *Fugitive Essays* (Freeport, N.Y.: Books for Libraries Press, 1920), 26.

17. Josiah Royce, "Reflections after a Wandering Life in Australasia," part 1, *Atlantic Monthly* 63, no. 379 (May 1889): 675–86; and "Reflections after a Wandering Life in Australasia," part 2, *Atlantic Monthly* 63, no. 380 (June 1889): 813–28; part 1, 677.

18. Josiah Royce, 1900, "The Pacific Coast: a Psychological Study of Influence," *International Monthly* 2: 555–83.

19. See Royce, *The World and the Individual*, 224, 225, and 226.

20. It has been my privilege to read in advance the manuscript of the book on Royce by Randall Auxier, *Time, Will and Purpose: Living Ideas from the Philosophy of Josiah Royce* (LaSalle, Ill.: Open Court, 2008).

21. Ibid., especially chapter 6.

22. See Josiah Royce, "The Cult of the Dead," in *Josiah Royce's Late Writings: A Collection of Unpublished and Scattered Works*, ed. Frank M. Oppenheim (Bristol, England: Thoemmes Press, 2001), 1:34.

23. Robert V. Hine, *Josiah Royce: From Grass Valley to Harvard* (Norman: University of Oklahoma Press, 1992), 203. Royce, in fact, describes the philosopher as a frontiersman. "The philosopher in the world of thought is by destiny a frontiersman. He may seem the mere wanderer . . . but the solitary labor of the seeker for truth shall in the end be submitted, not only to those theoretical tests which philosophy recognizes . . . but also the social and ethical judgment of the practical man. . . . The frontiersman may wander, but he must some day win what shall belong to the united empire of human truth." Royce, *The World and the Individual*, 1899, 2:3.

24. Royce, *The World and the Individual*, 2:3.

25. Sarah Royce, *A Frontier Lady: Recollections of the Gold Rush and Early California*, introduction written by Katharine Royce, ed. Ralph Henry Gabriel (New Haven: Yale University Press, 1932), iii.

26. Richard Etulain, series editor's preface, Hine, *Josiah Royce*, xii.

27. Royce is reported to have regarded the cat as a "fragment of a person"; Hine, *Josiah Royce*, 134.

28. This story is reported in Harry Cotton, *Royce on the Human Self* (Cambridge, Mass.: Harvard University Press, 1954).

29. There is a story about a dinner party at which James criticized Royce all night long and yet Royce remained, throughout the evening, in good humor. Reported in *The Religious Philosophy of Josiah Royce*, ed. with introductory essay by Stuart Gerry Brown (Syracuse, N.Y.: University of Syracuse Press, 1954).

30. In Royce's tribute to James in his essay, "William James and the Philosophy of Life" (in *William James*), Royce writes: "William James was my friend from my youth to the end of his beneficent life. I was once for a brief time his pupil. I long loved to think of myself as his disciple; although perhaps I was always a bad disciple." As we know, Royce did not believe in discipleship, but in learning from one's teachers and in thinking on one's own.

31. Katharine Royce, in Sarah Royce, *A Frontier Lady*, iii.

32. Hine, *Josiah Royce*, 139.

33. Josiah Royce, "The Case of John Bunyan," *Psychological Review* 1 (1894): 22–33, 134–51, 230–40, reprinted in Royce, *SGE*. Citations will be from *SGE*, 29–75.

34. Quoted in Hine, *Josiah Royce*, 1.

35. Royce, *SMP*, 2.

36. Richard W. Etulain, series editor's preface, *A Frontier Lady*, xiii.

37. Hine, *Josiah Royce*, 44.

38. In *Fugitive Essays*, published posthumously in 1920, with an introduction by Dr. J. Loewenberg, 6–7.

39. Royce, "Reflections after a Wandering Life in Australasia," part 1, 675–86; and Josiah Royce, "Impressions of Australia," *Scribner's Magazine* 9 (1891): 75–87.

40. Josiah Royce, *California from the Conquest in 1846 to the Second Vigilance Committee in San Francisco (1856): A Study of American Character* (Boston: Macmillan, 1886).

41. John Clendenning, *The Life and Thought of Josiah Royce*, rev. and exp. ed. (Nashville, Tenn.: Vanderbilt University, 1999), 35.

42. Hine, *Josiah Royce*, 58.

43. Ibid., 75.

44. Kevin Starr, "The Gold Rush and the California Dream," *California History* (Spring 1998): 57–67.

45. Hine, *Josiah Royce*, 120.

46. In a paper presented on 27 May 2007, at Harvard, Cornel West refers to Royce as a prophet and to himself as a spokesperson for "prophetic pragmatism"; "On the Tragic and Tragicomic: The Relevance of Royce," presented at the 25–27 May 2007 conference: "William James and Josiah Royce a Century Later," Harvard University Divinity School.

47. Rollo Walter Brown, *Harvard Yard in the Golden Age* (New York: Current Books, 1948), 60.

48. Royce, "Loyalty and Insight," 60.

49. Ibid., 52–53.

50. Frank M. Oppenheim, *Royce's Mature Ethics* (Notre Dame, Ind.: University of Notre Dame Press, 1993), 163. These ideas will be discussed in the chapter on ethics.

51. Josiah Royce, "The Intention of the Prometheus Bound of Aeschylus: Being an Investigation in the Department of Greek Theology." Thesis, University of Cali-

fornia, Berkeley, 1875. Printed in *Bulletin of the University of California, Berkeley* (June 1875).

52. Ibid., 67, quoted in Clendenning, *The Life and Thought of Josiah Royce*.

53. Josiah Royce, "The Nature of Voluntary Progress," *Berkeley Quarterly* 1 (July 1880): 161–89, reprinted in *Fugitive Essays*, 96–132. The citations will be from *Fugitive Essays*.

54. Scholars who write on Royce have some disagreement about his intellectual development. Frank Oppenheim, S.J., for example, has argued for three "maximal insights," or periods of thought. See Frank M. Oppenheim, "Josiah Royce's Intellectual Development: An Hypothesis," *Idealistic Studies* 6 (1976): 85–102. Although clearly Royce speaks of "novelty" in describing some of his "transitions" in thought, I believe they are new perspectives on continuing ideas that became deepened and refined and broadened as Royce encountered more experiences and the ideas and criticisms of others. Randall Auxier, I believe, holds a similar view. I cite Royce's comments to Mary Whiton Calkins in a letter on 20 March 1916, after the publication of his *The Problem of Christianity*. He writes: "My book . . . records the experience and the reflections which both led over to that book, and have been working in my mind daily more and more, ever since I wrote that book. The reflections in question constitute, for me, not something inconsistent with my former position, but a distinct addition to my former position, a new attainment,—I believe a new growth. I do not believe that you change in any way involving inconsistency, when you reinterpret former ideas," in *Letters of Josiah Royce*, part 5, 1913–16, 645. Of course, Oppenheim does not argue that there is inconsistency, but he does see "maximal insights." Taking Royce's thought seriously, maybe we are all partially correct and there is truth in the unity of our variety. Randy Auxier agrees with my view on this and defends this explicitly in his 2008 book, especially in chapter 1. See Auxier, *Time, Will and Purpose*, especially chapter 6. Dwayne Tunstall takes a similar position in his forthcoming book, *Encountering Josiah Royce's Ethico-Religious Insight*, a manuscript submitted for publication by Fordham Press, 158–59.

55. Jacob Loewenberg, introduction to Royce, *Fugitive Essays*, 11.

56. Josiah Royce, "Shelley and the Revolution," in *Fugitive Essays*, 76.

57. Josiah Royce, "How Beliefs Are Made," *Californian* 5 (1882), reprinted in *Fugitive Essays;* citations are to *Fugitive Essays*, here 362.

58. Royce, "The Nature of Voluntary Progress," 112.

59. Ibid., 116.

60. Ibid., 344. This same theme is treated in *The Religious Aspect of Philosophy*, chapter 8.

61. In his 2008 book, in chapter 4, Randall Auxier has a very enlightening discussion of Royce's pragmatism and its relationship to that of Peirce, James, and Dewey. For the purposes of this book, an extended discussion of this matter is not in order. See also: Frank M. Oppenheim, *Reverence for the Relations of Life: Reimagining Pragmatism via Josiah Royce's Interaction with Peirce, James, and Dewey* (Notre Dame, Ind.: University of Notre Dame Press, 2005).

62. Josiah Royce, "On Purpose in Thought," in *Fugitive Essays*, 219–60.

63. Josiah Royce, "Tests of Right and Wrong," in *Fugitive Essays,* 187–218.

64. Josiah Royce, "Thought Diary," in *Fugitive Essays,* 35, 31. These comments are dated 3 April 1879.

65. Royce, "On Purpose in Thought," 218, 220, and 232.

66. Royce, *Fugitive Essays,* 249.

67. Ibid.

68. Ibid., 259.

69. Josiah Royce, "The External World and the Social Consciousness," *Philosophical Review* 3, no. 5 (1894): 513–45; Josiah Royce, "Self-Consciousness, Social Consciousness and Nature," *Philosophical Review* 4 (1895): 465–85, reprinted in Royce, *SGE,* 198–248.

70. Jacquelyn Ann K. Kegley, "Josiah Royce: Anticipator of European Existentialism and Phenomenology," in *Doctrine and Experience,* ed. Vincent G. Potter (New York: Fordham University Press, 1988), 175–89.

71. Royce, *The World and the Individual,* 2:132–33.

72. Josiah Royce, *The Problem of Christianity,* 2 vols. (New York: Macmillan, 1913; Chicago: Regnery, 1968), 2:iii. Citations are to the 1968 ed.

73. Ibid., 2:64.

74. For an insight into the development of philosophy at Harvard, see a series of reports published by Josiah Royce in *Harvard Graduates Magazine:* 1 (1892–93): 115–226; 2 (1893–94): 238–39; 4 (1895–96): 246–47; 5 (1896–97): 228–32. Royce also discusses various aspects of the workings of the department in his correspondence with William James.

75. Vincent Buranelli, *Josiah Royce* (New Haven, Conn.: Twayne, 1964), 66.

76. Josiah Royce, *The Religious Aspect of Philosophy: A Critique of the Bases of Conduct and of Faith* (Boston: Houghton, Mifflin, 1885).

77. Royce, *California from the Conquest in 1846 to the Second Vigilance Committee in San Francisco.*

78. Josiah Royce, *The Feud of Oakfield Creek: A Novel of California Life* (Boston: Houghton and Mifflin, 1887).

79. For a discussion of this episode, see Josiah Royce, "The Squatter Riot of '50 in Sacramento: Its Causes and Its Significance," *Overland Monthly,* n.s. 6 (1885): 225–46. This was reprinted with a new introduction and entitled "An Episode of Early California Life: The Squatter Riot of 1850 in Sacramento," in *SGE,* 298–348.

80. Hine, *Josiah Royce,* quoting historian Bernard De Voto, 192.

81. Ibid., 193. Hine argues that in Western historiography Royce holds a pivotal place and is a clear precursor of Fredrick Jackson Turner, author of *The Frontier in American History* (Henry Holt, 1920). Turner's original exposition of the "frontier" idea was in a talk, "The Significance of the Frontier in American History," which he first delivered to a gathering of historians in 1893 at Chicago, then the site of the World's Columbian Exposition, an enormous fair to mark the four-hundredth anniversary of Columbus's voyage. Hine argues that Turner drew on Royce's work on provincialism and on community. See Hine, *Josiah Royce,* 190.

82. Josiah Royce, *The Philosophy of Loyalty* (New York: Macmillan, 1908).

83. Royce, *The Problem of Christianity.*

84. Royce, *SMP,* 116.

85. Josiah Royce, "Before and Since Kant," *Berkeley Quarterly* 2 (1881): 136.

86. Richard C. Cabot, "Josiah Royce as a Teacher," *Philosophical Review* 25, no. 3 (May 1916): 466–72, 468.

87. Charles M. Blakewell, 1816, "Novum Itinerarium Mentu in Deum," *Philosophical Review* 25, no. 3, reprinted in Randall E. Auxier, *Papers in Honor of Josiah Royce on His Sixtieth Birthday,* Thoemmes Library of American Philosophy (London: Thoemmes Press, 2000), 32.

88. Royce, *SMP,* 116.

89. Royce, *William James and Other Essays,* viii.

90. Josiah Royce, "Is There a Philosophy of Evolution?" *Unitarian Review* 22, no. 1 (July 1889): 1–12, 97–113.

91. John Jay Chapman, "Portrait of Josiah Royce, the Philosopher," *Outlook* (1919): 372, 377.

92. Ibid., 373. Jacob Loewenberg reports a similar experience of Royce's generosity in sharing his knowledge. Wanting to round out his study at Harvard, Loewenberg sought Royce's advice. Royce suggested that he take his seminar on Hegel. Though there were visitors to the seminar, Loewenberg was the only enrolled student. Royce nevertheless "conducted the class in no way affected by the fact that it contained but a single member." Loewenberg notes that "Under Royce's guidance . . . the study of it [the *Phenomenology*] proved an exciting adventure." Jacob Loewenberg, *Thrice Born: Selected Memories of an Immigrant* (New York: Hobbs, Dorman, 1968).

93. See Josiah Royce, "Is There a Science of Education?" *Educational Review* 1 (1891): 15–25, 121–32; Josiah Royce, "Present Ideals of American University Life," *Scribner's Magazine* 10 (1891): 376–88; Josiah Royce, "The American University Gymnasium: Its Influence on Academic Life," *Alma Mater* 17 (7 February 1900): 135–38. Royce also gave numerous series of lectures on education before teachers in Brooklyn, Philadelphia, and New Orleans.

94. Royce, "Is There a Science of Education?" 25.

95. Jacob Loewenberg, [tribute to Josiah Royce], *Harvard Alumni Bulletin* 51 (29 January 1949): 350–51.

96. "Tribute to Josiah Royce," *Science* n.s. 44 (1 December 1916): 773.

97. Cabot, "Josiah Royce as a Teacher," 466.

98. Ibid., 467. Cabot writes: "he shocked me into perceiving that a man could really welcome difference of opinion as a precious gift."

99. Ibid., 472. Jacob Loewenberg provides a superb illustration of Royce's determination to make his students independent thinkers in describing his doctoral examination in metaphysics with Royce. Loewenberg had thoroughly "boned up" on Royce's ideas, thinking that the safest way to pass the exam was to "play the role of the disciple." However, Royce, with a merry smile and quizzical look, indicated that he was not sure whether Loewenberg should receive the Ph.D. Rather, he said, "You know too much about Royce and not enough about metaphysics. I wonder if, instead

of the PhD, you should receive the degree of R.D. You are certainly qualified to hold the title 'Doctor of Royce.'" Loewenberg, *Thrice Born*, 91.

100. See Josiah Royce, "The Life-Harmony," *Overland Monthly* 15 (1875): 157–64.

101. Woodrow Wilson, letter to Ellen Axson Wilson, 5 February 1884, in *The Papers of Woodrow Wilson*, ed. Arthur S. Link (Princeton, N.J.: Princeton University Press, 1974), vol. 18, 1908–1909, 10. See also Jacob Loewenberg, "Royce's Synthetic Method," *Journal of Philosophy* 53, no. 3, "In Memoriam of Josiah Royce, Born November 20, 1855" (2 February 1956): 63–72.

102. Royce, *William James and Other Essays*, 66–67.

103. Royce, *The World and the Individual*, 1899 ed.

104. Josiah Royce, *The Conception of Immortality* (Boston: Houghton, Mifflin, 1900).

105. Josiah Royce, *The Sources of Religious Insight* (New York: Charles Scribner's Sons, 1912).

106. Royce, *The Problem of Christianity*.

2. The Self

1. Royce, "The Nature of Voluntary Progress," which is an astute critical analysis of the notion of "progress." Josiah Royce, 1889, "Is There a Philosophy of Evolution?" *Unitarian Review* 32, 1–29 and 97–113; Josiah Royce, 1894–95, "Natural Law, Ethics, and Evolution," *International Journal of Ethics*, 489–500; Josiah Royce, 1895, "Self-Consciousness, Social Consciousness and Nature," in *SGE*, 198–248; *SMP*, especially chapter 10, "Nature and Evolution: The Outer World and Its Paradox," and chapter 12, "Physical Law and Freedom: The World of Description and the World of Appreciation." Royce, *The World and the Individual*, especially vol. 2; Josiah Royce, *Herbert Spencer: An Estimate and Review, by Josiah Royce; Together with a Chapter of Personal Reminiscences by James Collier* (New York: Fox, Duffield, 1904).

2. Royce did write extensively on metaphysical and epistemological issues, and, I believe, with great insight. However, these efforts also were experientially and empirically based and ultimately directed to the goal of providing an adequate philosophy of life and grounds for effective ethical, social, and political action. Further, Randall Auxier, in his new book, convincingly makes the case that these metaphysical and epistemological efforts must be seen as a series of working hypotheses designed to address precisely the ethical and practical issues. Auxier speaks of a fictional ontology. Finally, Royce's work on philosophy of science and philosophy of logic is just now receiving recognition as modern and maybe even cutting-edge.

3. Frank M. Oppenheim, the superb Royce scholar that he is, has already begun this exploration. See: Frank M. Oppenheim, "Royce's Community: A Dimension Missing in Freud and James," *Journal of the History of the Behavioral Sciences* 13 (1977): 173–90, 173.

4. Josiah Royce, *Outlines of Psychology: An Elementary Treatise with Some Practical Applications* (New York: Macmillan, 1903), vii.

5. Randall Auxier thoroughly and expertly discusses Royce's views on indi-

viduation in his new book, and any discussion of mine could not enrich that in any manner; see his *Time, Will and Purpose.*

6. Ibid., ch. 2. Auxier also discusses the notion of "person" in some detail in chapters 5, 7, and 8. Dwayne Tunstall also discusses the concept of "person" in his book *Encountering Josiah Royce's Ethico-Religious Insight,* 158–59. All three of us agree that "person" is an ethical concept.

7. Josiah Royce, letter to William James, December 28, 1881, in *Letters of Josiah Royce,* 106–107.

8. Jacquelyn Ann K. Kegley, "Peirce and Royce on the Betrayal of Science: Scientific Fraud and Misconduct," paper read at the annual meeting of the Society for the Advancement of American Philosophy, Columbia, S.C., March 2007.

9. Josiah Royce, "The Practical Value of Philosophy," *Ethical Record* 2 (1889): 9–22, 12 and 9; emphasis in original.

10. In his introduction to the *Outlines,* Royce asserts that psychology as a field is related to our human experience of constantly judging "the ideas, moods and intents of his fellows, by watching not only their faces, but also their whole range of voluntary and involuntary expressive movements." Psychology merely extends the range of its applications and renders more minute the scrutiny. Included in this range, for Royce, is the "cooperative work of many intelligent beings." Among these are works of art, languages, customs, faiths, institutions, national life. See *Outlines,* 14; italics are Royce's.

11. Royce, "Self-Consciousness, Social Consciousness and Nature," *Studies in Good and Evil,* and *The World and the Individual.*

12. Jacquelyn Ann K. Kegley, "Josiah Royce on Self and Community," *Rice University Studies* 66 (1980): 4; Jacquelyn Ann K. Kegley, "Peirce and Royce on Person: New Directions for Ethical Theory," in *Peirce and Value Theory,* ed. Herman Parret (Amsterdam: John Benjamin's Publishing, 1994), 17–26; and Jacquelyn Ann K. Kegley, *Genuine Individuals and Genuine Communities: A Roycean Public Philosophy* (Nashville, Tenn.: Vanderbilt University Press, 1997).

13. Royce, *Outlines of Psychology,* vi.

14. For reports of Royce's experimental activities and conclusions, see Josiah Royce, "The Imitative Functions, and Their Place in Human Nature," *Century Magazine* n.s. 26 (May 1894): 137–45; "The Psychology of Invention," *Psychological Review* 5, no. 2 (1898): 113–44.

15. In addition to the studies cited above in note 3, we find the following: Royce, "The External World and the Social Consciousness," 513–45; "Originality and Consciousness," *Harvard Monthly* 24 (1897): 133–41, reprinted in *SGE,* 249–60; "Can Psychology Be Founded upon the Study of Consciousness Alone, or Is Physiology Needed for the Purpose?" in *Proceedings of the International Congress of Education of the World Columbian Exposition* (New York: National Education Association, 1894), 687–92.

16. See his presidential address to that group: Josiah Royce, "Recent Logical Inquiries and their Psychological Bearings," *Psychological Review* 9 (1902): 105–33, re-

printed in *Royce's Logical Essays: Collected Logical Essays of Josiah Royce,* ed. Daniel S. Robinson (Dubuque, Iowa: William C. Brown, 1951).

17. See *Outlines of Psychology,* 320–25. Royce also made some fruitful parallels between the development of curiosity in the child and the curiosity exhibited in science. In *The Spirit of Modern Philosophy,* he writes: "Science has an element of noble play about it," 7.

18. Josiah Royce, letter to Granville Stanley Hall, February 14, 1898, in *Letters of Josiah Royce,* 366–73. In this letter, Royce writes: "In brief, the situation is that by this time one has learned, from childhood's little world of pretty well-knit social relations, what self-consciousness is and means, namely, plan, assurance, purpose, and social position; while, on the other hand, in the flood of new experiences, one in youth has lost hold of the concrete facts of the childhood self. One cares no more for the old plans. . . . But one has not yet learned what to be instead," 367. It should be noted that at this time in the history of higher education in America psychology and philosophy as disciplines had not yet emerged as separate entities but were housed in the same department, usually philosophy. Thus, at Harvard, Munsterberg and James were primarily considered psychologists, though they were members of the philosophy department. For an excellent discussion of the interrelationships of these two disciplines in this period, see James Campbell, *A Thoughtful Profession: The Early Years of the American Philosophical Association* (Chicago: Open Court, 2006).

19. James Jackson Putnam, *Human Motives* (New York: Little Brown, 1915). For an extensive discussion of the influence of Royce on Putnam as well as Putnam's correspondence with Sigmund Freud, see Josefina Iglesias de Orro, "The Role of Psychological Theories in the Development of Royce's Ethical Concept of the Human Self," a doctoral dissertation submitted to Columbia University in 1988, 313–21.

20. Oppenheim, "Royce's Community," 173.

21. Royce, "The Case of John Bunyan"; and "Some Observations on the Anomalies of Self-Consciousness," *Psychological Review* (1895): 433–57, 574–84, reprinted in *SGE,* 169–97; citations are to *SGE.*

22. Royce, "Anomalies," 175.

23. Oppenheim, "Royce's Community," 175 and 176.

24. Royce, *The Problem of Christianity,* 2:49–98. For excellent discussions of these conditions, see Frank M. Oppenheim, "A Roycean Road to Community," *International Philosophical Quarterly* 10 (1970): 341–77, and "Royce's Community: A Dimension Missing in Freud and James," 177–79.

25. Oppenheim, "Royce's Community," 182.

26. Royce, "Anomalies," *SGE,* 190. Royce refers to the many case studies in the book *Psychopathia Sexualis* (1886) by Richard von Krafft-Ebing, a German psychologist. This is claimed to be the first book to set out a discussion of sexual pathologies.

27. Josiah Royce, "Primitive Ways of Thinking with Special Reference to Negation and Classification," *Open Court* 27 (1913): 577–98. I have explored aspects of Royce's philosophy of science in my paper "Peirce and Royce and the Betrayal of Science"; this was also the topic of my doctoral dissertation at Columbia University.

See: Jacquelyn Ann Kovacevic Kegley, "Josiah Royce's Theory of Knowledge," *Dissertation Abstracts International* 33, no. 1 (1972): 1954.

28. Letter of Peirce to Royce dated January 19, 1902, quoted in Cotton, *Royce on the Human Self*, 300.

29. Oppenheim, "Royce's Community," 177.

30. Ibid.

31. Ibid., 177. The boat example occurs in *The Problem of Christianity*, 2:240–46. The sharing of experiences of objects, i.e., rowing a boat together, is basic to establishing a notion of externality. See Josiah Royce, "Self-Consciousness, Social Consciousness, and Nature," *Philosophical Review* 4 (1895): 465–85; reprinted in *SGE*, 198–248.

32. Royce, *Outlines of Psychology*, viii.

33. Ibid.

34. Ibid.

35. Ibid., 167.

36. Ibid., 182.

37. Ibid., 185–89.

38. Ibid.

39. Ibid., 174.

40. Erwin Strauss, *The Primary World of Senses*, trans. from the German by J. Needleman (London: Free Press of Glencoe, 1963); and Maurice Merleau-Ponty, *La Structure du comportement* (Paris: Presses Universitaires de France, 1942), translated as *The Structure of Behavior*, trans. Alden Fisher (Boston: Beacon Press, 1963).

41. Royce, *Outlines of Psychology*, 318. In quotations from Royce's work, italics are in original unless otherwise noted.

42. Ibid., 298.

43. Ibid., 331. It would be correct, I believe, to note similarities between Royce's views on the relationships between attention and the restless overflow of energy present in the organism and Baldwin's. See James Mark Baldwin, *Mental Development in the Child and in the Race* (New York: Macmillan, 1895), 456. On p. 453 of this work, Baldwin states that the origin of attention is to be found in the principle of excess: "The attention is the mental function corresponding to the habitual motor coordination of the processes of heightened or 'excess' of discharge."

44. Royce, *Outlines of Psychology*, 317.

45. Ibid., 300.

46. Ibid.

47. Ibid., 197.

48. Ibid., 198–99.

49. See Ignas Skrupskelis, "Royce and the Justification of Authority," *Southern Journal of Philosophy* 8, no. 2–3 (1970): 165–70.

50. 57–63. For an excellent discussion of these lectures, and in particular, on Royce's notions, Josiah Royce, 1893, "Topics in Psychology of Interest to Teachers," Lecture 1: "What Is a General Idea?" HARP, Folio 63; on "general ideas," see de Orro, "The Role of Psychological Theories," 81–96.

51. Royce, "What Is a General Idea?" HARP, Folio 63, 26 and 54.

52. Royce, *Outlines of Psychology*, 290.

53. Josiah Royce, Topics, Lecture VI, "Apperception, Attention, and the Theory of an Orderly Acquisition of General Ideas," HARP, Folio 64, 78–79.

54. Royce, "Topics," Lecture II, "General Ideas and the Theory of Habits," HARP, Folio 63, 63–64.

55. Royce, *Outlines of Psychology*, 291.

56. Ibid., 292.

57. Ibid., 194 and 196.

58. Ibid., 180

59. Ibid., 179.

60. Ibid., 180.

61. Royce, "The Nature of Voluntary Progress," 99.

62. Ibid., 101.

63. Ibid., 99.

64. Royce, "Originality and Consciousness," *Harvard Monthly* 24 (1897): 133–42; reprinted as "The Psychology of Invention."

65. Royce, "Originality and Consciousness," 138.

66. Ibid., 140.

67. Ibid., 141.

68. Randall Auxier spells out Royce's "temporalism" in chapter 6 of *Time, Will and Purpose* (see ch. 1, note 20, above).

69. Royce, *The World and the Individual*, 2:293.

70. See Royce, "On Purpose in Thought," 219–60.

71. Royce, "Tests of Right and Wrong," 187–218.

72. Ibid., 200.

73. Ibid., 200–201.

74. Ibid., 202.

75. Ibid.

76. This view of Royce appears to me much-related to the thought of Henri Bergson, although as Royce scholars know, he did have some points of disagreement with Bergson.

77. Thus, we cited the quotation from Royce's Thought Diary of April 3, 1879, when he wrote: "Every man lives in a present, and contemplates a past and future. In this consists his whole life." Quoted by Loewenberg in his introduction to *Fugitive Essays*, 31.

78. Royce, *The World and the Individual*, 2:290.

79. Royce, *The Problem of Christianity*, 2:43.

80. Josiah Royce, 1879(?), "The Will as the Principle of Philosophy," unpublished papers, HARP, Folio 79. In this early essay Royce undertakes a very critical analysis of Descartes's formulation and notes that this view leads to solipsism.

81. Royce, *The World and the Individual*, 2:268.

82. Josiah Royce, "The Twofold Nature of Knowledge: Imitative and Reflective" (1893), ed. Peter Fuss, *Journal of the History of Philosophy* 4 (1966): 326–37, 334.

83. Ibid., 331. In this essay Royce makes an interesting comparison of Hume's view with that of the early thinkers of the Upanishads, particularly Yjnavalkya. He writes: "Hume enters into himself only to observe that he, Hume, precisely in so far as he is the Subject, is not discoverable there. . . . Yjnavalkya points out that since one necessarily sees or hears *another,* i.e. an object, and not the Seer or Hearer, therefore one who is conscious must be conscious only of empirical stuff—must suffer in this bondage," 332.

84. Ibid., 333.

85. Ibid., 327–28.

86. Royce, *Outlines of Psychology,* 83.

87. Ibid.

88. Ibid., 89. Further exploration of Royce's discussion of this unity consisting of multiplicity would be most worthwhile because he continues on to discuss the manner in which the "variety of different elements" occurs, and in so doing focuses on sameness and difference and on a "relation of between." He writes: *"When we observe that one fact differs from another, we also are able to observe that these two facts have, as we say, something in common, or are similar to one another.* Colours differ from odours. But both the colour and the odour of a rose have in common the features that enable a psychologist to recognize that they are both sensations." Here is Royce's concern with thirds at work.

89. Ibid.

90. Ibid.

91. Ibid., 330.

92. Royce, *The World and the Individual,* 2:256.

93. Ibid., 257.

94. Ibid.

95. Ibid.

96. Royce, *Outlines of Psychology,* 58.

97. Ibid., 9–10.

98. Martha J. Farah, "Emerging Ethical Issues in Neuroscience," *Nature Neuroscience* 5, no. 11 (2 November 2002): 1123–29.

99. Royce, *Outlines of Psychology,* 305. For a discussion of contemporary evidence that experience drives and individuates brain growth, see Robert Ornstein and Richard F. Thompson, *The Amazing Brain* (Boston: Houghton Mifflin, 1984), 165–71.

100. Royce, *Outlines of Psychology,* 13.

101. See Walter Glannon, *Bioethics and the Brain* (New York: Oxford University Press, 2007), especially chapter 3, "Neuroimaging."

102. Royce, "Anomalies," *Psychological Review* 2, 433–57 and 574–84, reprinted in *SGE,* 169–197; citations are to *SGE.*

103. Ibid., 170.

104. Ibid.

105. Ibid.

106. John Gray, *Men Are from Mars, Women Are from Venus: The Classic Guide to Understanding the Opposite Sex* (New York: Harper and Row, 2004).

107. Leonard Sax, *Why Gender Matters: What Parents and Teachers Need to Know about the Emerging Science of Sex Differences* (New York: Broadway, 2006). See also Maxine Baca Zinn, Pierette Hondagneu-Sotelo, and Michael A. Messner, eds., *Gender through the Prism of Difference* (New York: Guilford Press, 2005).

108. Royce, *The World and the Individual*, 2:257.

109. Josiah Royce, *The Conception of God* (New York: Macmillan, 1897), 278.

110. Royce, *Outlines of Psychology,* 160.

111. Ibid., 158.

112. Ibid., 161.

113. See Mark Johnson, *Moral Imagination* (Chicago: University of Chicago Press, 1993); and B. Smith, "Analogy in Moral Deliberation: The Role of Imagination and Theory in Ethics," *Journal of Medical Ethics* 28 (2002): 244–48. Smith writes: "In the present paper I try to secure more firmly a novel understanding of why analogy is an essential component in the attempt to justify moral beliefs. I seek to show how analogical argument both encapsulates and exercises the notions of rationality and imagination and that the construction, development, and comparison of analogies fundamentally underpins ethical argument. In so doing, it enables us to adopt imaginative and ethically illuminating perspectives but in a manner that does not relinquish any claims to intellectual rigor." —Abstract, 244.

114. Glannon, *Bioethics and the Brain,* 8.

115. Ibid., 279.

116. Royce, *The World and the Individual,* 2:260. See also Royce, "Anomalies," and *The Conception of God*, reprint, with an introduction by Randall Auxier (Bristol, England: Thoemmes Press, 2000), 278–89.

117. Royce, *The World and the Individual,* 2:261–62.

118. Royce, Lecture 1: "What Is a General Idea?"; Lecture VI, "Apperception, Attention, and the Theory of an Orderly Acquisition of Ideas," 74–75.

119. Josiah Royce, "Preliminary Report on Imitation," *Psychological Review* 2, no. 3 (May 1895): 225.

120. Ibid.

121. Ibid., 265.

122. In *The Conception of God,* Royce has an interesting discussion of "perished ideal selves." He writes: "A man who has any but the most prosaic self-consciousness is likely to remember not infrequently what he might have been if other people had but given him a fair chance, if that lost skill or that noble purpose has proved stable, or if that dear friend had lived. The sailor, regretting his dog's life at sea and fantastically conceiving . . . a career such as would have been worthy of him . . . the unsuccessful mechanic, who barely earns a hard living, but who would have been . . . a great man if his enemy had not stolen his early inventions . . . —these men are self-conscious in so far as they contrast a painfully real with a hopelessly lost ideal self. You never know a man's self-consciousness until you have learned something of this graveyard of perished ideal selves," 284 (2000 ed.).

123. Ibid., 286.

124. Royce, *The World and the Individual,* 2:276.

125. Ibid., 426.

126. Royce, *The Conception of God*, 290 (2000 ed.).

127. Ibid., 292.

128. Ibid., 291.

3. Royce's Ethical Theory

1. Royce, "Tests of Right and Wrong," 186–87.

2. Royce had already addressed this issue in his 1880 essay "The Nature of Voluntary Progress."

3. Peter van Inwagen, *Essay on Free Will* (Oxford, England: Clarendon Press, 1986). Van Inwagen states the position as follows: (a) for every instant of time, there is a proposition that expresses the state of the world at that instant (physical and not theoretical—change in one time involves change at another); and (b) if A and B are any propositions that express the state of the world at some instant, then the conjunction of A with the laws of physics entails B. In *The World and the Individual*, vol. 2, Royce defines the principle of the "uniformity of nature" as *"We conceive every natural event as preceded by a group of events such that whenever that group as a whole recurs, that same consequent must follow."* Royce also criticized Kant for assuming "causality" as fundamental to human consciousness.

4. Royce, *The World and the Individual*, 1899, 2:197.

5. Royce, "Tests of Right and Wrong," 186–87.

6. Ibid., 188 and 189.

7. Royce, *Religious Aspect*, 133–38.

8. Ibid., chapters 2 and 3.

9. Ibid., 57.

10. Josiah Royce to Elizabeth Randolph, November 16, 1910, in *Letters of Josiah Royce*, 547.

11. Oppenheim, *Royce's Mature Ethics.*

12. Royce, "Tests of Right and Wrong," 187.

13. Ibid.

14. Ibid., 190.

15. Ibid., 191.

16. Ibid., 194.

17. Thus, G. E. Moore points out that a naturalist requires moral terms to be defined using terms to refer to natural properties, such as providing pleasure, satisfying one's desires, conforming to the rules in society, and promoting the species. About this, says Moore, one can always ask, but is it (this) good? Royce presents similar arguments, as we shall see, against the moral realist and the evolutionary ethicist. Further, there is much emphasis today on the motivational feature of moral claims. Thus, "motivational internalism" claims that a person counts as sincerely making a moral claim only if she is motivated appropriately. Royce would certainly argue that naturalism cannot provide this "motivational aspect," but again he would deny the whole assumption underlying the contemporary debate, namely, that there

is a distinction between moral beliefs and regular beliefs such that regular beliefs are "motivationally inert" and moral beliefs are not. Royce, as we have seen, united will and intellect and feeling in action and, for him, all beliefs are plans for action. Royce's position would also undercut the foolishness of a position like that of A. J. Ayer. Ayer argues that ethical statements are neither analytic nor verifiable and thus must be meaningless. A corollary to this view is the "emotive theory of ethics."

18. Royce, "Tests of Right and Wrong," 191.

19. Ibid., 197. In terms of contemporary ethics, both Charles Taylor and Alasdair MacIntyre believe moral action must be situated in a moral world. More will be said about this later in this chapter.

20. Ibid.

21. Charles Taylor, *Sources of the Self: The Making of Modern Identity* (Cambridge, Mass.: Harvard University Press, 1989). This connection will be explored in the final chapter.

22. Josiah Royce, letter to Arthur O. Lovejoy, December 30, 1912, in *Letters of Josiah Royce*, 586–87.

23. Royce, "Tests of Right and Wrong," 198. Thus Royce does not hold to an emotive theory of ethical judgment, although feeling in various forms is involved since sensitiveness, docility, and originality appear involved in all acts.

24. Royce asserts: "Without data no knowledge. Whenever there is knowledge there are simple data of consciousness"; "Tests of Right and Wrong," 200.

25. Ibid., 202.

26. Ibid., 264. Royce writes: "It is the fate of life to be restless, capricious, and therefore tragic." As we shall see, restlessness is a central feature of mental life, one important to attention and to mental initiative. (See *Outlines of Psychology,* chapter 7.) In *The Spirit* (262), Royce also writes: "In fact, pessimism, in its deeper sense, is merely an ideal and abstract expression of one very deep and sacred element of the total religious consciousness of humanity."

27. Royce, *Outlines of Psychology,* 180.

28. Royce, *The World and the Individual,* 1899, 2:293.

29. Royce, "Tests of Right and Wrong," 204.

30. Ibid.

31. Ibid. Royce's discussion here is reminiscent of the philosophical position known as the "Ultimate Responsibility" theory, advocated by Robert Kane of the University of Texas. In his book *The Significance of Free Will* (1996), he argues for an indeterministic free-will position grounded not in the idea of alternative possibilities but in the notion of "ultimate responsibility." This theory focuses on "will-setting actions," namely, those in which the "agents set their wills one way or another in the performance of the actions themselves." In these actions, the agent makes the reasons for preferring one of the options prevail by deciding or acting. Pursuit of the relationship of Royce's arguments to Kane's view and the contemporary "free-will" debate, I believe, will be a fruitful endeavor of scholars.

32. Royce, "Tests of Right and Wrong." From a contemporary point of view and especially in light of a number of compatibilist theories of free will, the following

comment by Royce is intriguing: "It matters not now whether we conceive this Will as free or not." This is a comment worth exploration at another time and place.

33. Ibid., 205.

34. Ibid.

35. Ibid., 207.

36. Ibid., 208.

37. Royce was quite critical of utilitarian thought. His discussion of the inadequacy of the division of human feeling into pleasure and pain in *Outlines of Psychology* was noted in chapter 2. For an extensive criticism of utilitarianism and the "Hedonistic Calculus," see Josiah Royce, "Pessimism and Modern Thought," *Berkeley Quarterly* 2 (1881): 292–316. This essay was reprinted in *Fugitive Essays*, 155–86. In this essay, Royce writes: "[A] worth-judgment about human life is the result of an act of mind, somewhat resembling an ordinary practical volition. *This life is good, this life is evil,* these opposing judgments are two opposing attitudes of will. The ultimate decision in the matter is not to result from a mathematical estimate, but from moral insight. . . . [W]e must be clear as to what we are seeking, viz., not a balance sheet of evil and good, but a watch word to determine our principles of action; an everlasting yes or nay, that shall relate to the whole of life." (The citation is from *Fugitive Essays*, 160.)

38. Royce, "The Tests of Right and Wrong," 209.

39. Ibid., 210.

40. Ibid., 213.

41. Ibid., 212.

42. Ibid., 211.

43. Ibid., 214.

44. To my knowledge the link between this essay and *Religious Aspect* has not been noted or at least discussed. This link adds strength to the argument that Royce's philosophy proceeds forward with deepening and variation but not with distinctive gaps.

45. Royce, *Religious Aspect*, 18.

46. Ibid., 23.

47. Peter Fuss, *The Moral Philosophy of Josiah Royce* (Cambridge, Mass.: Harvard University Press, 1965), 5. Fuss states the conflict of *Religious Aspect* as one between the realist, who insists that the objectivity of moral distinctions must be established, and the idealist, who wants to secure the autonomy of the moral agent. I am not sure I agree with this characterization. I believe both seek to establish "objectivity." Further, the idealist may or may not be concerned to secure the autonomy of the moral agent.

48. Royce, *Relgious Aspect*, 30.

49. Cotton, *Royce on the Human Self*, 64.

50. Fuss, *The Moral Philosophy of Josiah Royce*, 5.

51. Royce, *Religious Aspect*, 33.

52. Ibid., 38.

53. Ibid., 42.

54. Ibid., 44.

55. Ibid., 57.

56. Royce, "Anomalies," *SGE,* 192.

57. Ibid., 192–93.

58. Ibid.

59. Josiah Royce, "On Certain Psychological Aspects of Moral Training," *International Journal of Ethics* 3, no. 4 (July 1893): 413–36, 419–20.

60. Ibid., 420.

61. Josiah Royce, "Loyalty and Individuality," Third Pittsburgh Lecture, 1910, HARP, Folio 82, no. 1, 11–12.

62. Royce, "The Imitative Functions and Their Place in Human Nature," 137–45.

63. Royce, *Religious Aspect,* 76.

64. Ibid., 68–70.

65. Ibid., 85.

66. Josiah Royce, "John Fiske: His Work as a Philosopher and Teacher," *Boston Evening Transcript* (13 July 1901): 14–24; reprinted as "John Fiske as Thinker," *Harvard Graduates' Magazine* 10 (1901–1902), 23–33.

67. Josiah Royce, "John Fiske," unpublished lecture, 11 December 1901, HARP 72, no. 1, quoted in Oppenheim, *Royce's Mature Ethics,* 70.

68. I use biological/psychological because our motor consciousness also plays a key role in imitation.

69. Royce, *Religious Aspect,* 134. Again, Royce's argument here bears strong similarities to the arguments of Robert Kane's theory of "ultimate responsibility." See note 31 above.

70. Royce grounds this third condition psychologically and philosophically in the connection between conceiving an act and performing an act. "If two opposing fashions of action are present to our minds, and if mentally we are trying to realize them both, then mentally we are seeking to reproduce them both. Our skeptical hesitation between them expresses our effort to attain mentally both these ends at once. Who can realize a given end save by somehow repeating it in himself?" Ibid., 135–37. For criticism of these two conditions, see Fuss, *The Moral Philosophy of Josiah Royce,* 52–54. As Fuss notes, the further development of Royce's ethical theory provides a better foundation for the third condition. Most importantly, Fuss shows how moral insight is unifying of the different aspects of the self: the affective, the conative, and the cognitive. Fuss writes: "the 'moment of moral insight' carries at once a cognitive, an affective, and a conative thrust: cognitive in that one recognizes one's fellow men and their goals to be as real as oneself and one's goals: affective in that in and through such recognition one learns to appreciate their reality as voluntary agents striving for goals; conative in that one tends, in the face of this recognition and appreciation, to strive toward the others' realization of their goals," 53n42.

71. Royce, *Religious Aspect,* 145.

72. Ibid., 154.

73. Ibid., 155.

74. Ibid., 160–61.

75. Ibid., 162.

76. In this vein, I quote Royce: "The moral life is essentially a life of conflict—of the conflict between humane and narrowly selfish impulses, of the conflict between reason and caprice, between order and chaos, yes, and the conflict between these two moral motives themselves, which ideally ought to harmonize, but which in our balance we do harmonize so ill," "On Certain Psychological Aspects of Moral Training," 423.

77. I share with Peter Fuss his observation on Royce's views on ethical realism. Fuss writes: "Actually, Royce agrees with the realist that determinations of matters of fact are relevant to the problem of moral justification, but disagrees with the realist's conception of how they are relevant." Fuss, *The Moral Philosophy of Josiah Royce*, 45.

78. Royce, *Religious Aspect*, 172.

79. Ibid., 194–95 and 193.

80. Josiah Royce, Lecture I, "The Conflict of Loyalties," *Pittsburgh Lectures on the Doctrine of Loyalty*, 1908, HARP, Folio 82, 13–14. I am heavily indebted to Josefina Iglesias de Orro for her excellent discussion of the manner in which Royce's cognitive and social psychologies flow into the philosophy of loyalty, in her doctoral dissertation, "The Role of Psychological Theories in the Development of Royce's Ethical Concept of the Human Self"; see especially chapters 4, 5, and 7.

81. Josiah Royce, Berkeley Conferences, 4th Conference, 1914, "The Triadic Theory of Knowledge," in *Josiah Royce's Late Writings*, 2:57.

82. Royce, *SMP*, 455.

83. Josiah Royce, *The World and the Individual*, 2:104.

84. Ibid., 72.

85. Josiah Royce, "The Principles of Logic," in *Royce's Logical Essays*, 336–62.

86. Josiah Royce, *The World and the Individual*, 1:460.

87. Josiah Royce, *The Conception of God*, 264.

88. Ibid.

89. See *Letters of Josiah Royce*, 343. In this letter, Royce refers to "exclusive but unconscious instinctive bases of feeling whereby any other case, a rival, gets rejected." Royce here seems to be assigning a dominant role to instinctual feelings in individualization and in each individual moral decision. Again, we note the close interconnection Royce makes between sensitiveness, docility, and originality in his *Psychology*. As he stated at the beginning of *Outlines of Psychology*, he intends no sharp division between intellectual and voluntary processes. I agree with Frank Oppenheim in his comment that here Royce foreshadows the emphasis by Whitehead on the primacy of feelings in the self-constitution of each actual entity.

90. Royce, *Philosophy of Loyalty*, 25.

91. Ibid.

92. Ibid., 31.

93. Ibid., 32.

94. In his Urbana Lectures of 1907, Royce examines various "personality-ideals" or "moral ideals" that have appeared throughout human history:—the hero, the

saint, the rebellious titan, and the loyal suffering servant, drawing from each a particular kind of value. Here are some of the "models for living" that a self can consider. These lectures were edited by Peter Fuss and published in *The Journal of the History of Philosophy* 5 (1967): 60–78 and 269–86.

95. Ibid.

96. Recall that Royce was a great admirer of Nietzsche. Royce admired him not only for his emphasis on individuality but also for his revolt against social conformism and trivialization of life.

97. Royce, *Philosophy of Loyalty*, 78–79.

98. Royce, "Self-Consciousness, Social Consciousness and Nature," in *SGE*, 201.

99. Josiah Royce, 1897, "Social Factors in the Development of the Individual Mind," HARP, Folio 69, lecture 2, 30.

100. Royce, *Philosophy of Loyalty*, 34–35.

101. Ibid., 119.

102. Ibid., 131ff.

103. Ibid.

104. Royce, "Principles of the Art of Loyalty," in *Josiah Royce's Late Writings*, 2:147.

105. Royce, *Philosophy of Loyalty*, 59.

106. Ibid., 19.

107. Royce, "Illustrations of the Philosophy of Loyalty," in *Josiah Royce's Late Writings*, 2:5.

108. Royce, Urbana Lectures, Folio 76, lecture 3, 24.

109. Ibid., 200–201.

110. Royce, *The Problem of Christianity*, 2:245.

111. Ibid., 248.

112. Ibid.

113. Ibid., 249.

114. Kegley, *Genuine Individuals and Genuine Communities*.

115. Royce, *The Problem of Christianity*, 2:249.

116. Ibid., 404–405.

117. Ibid., 340.

4. Religious Insight, the Spirit of Community, and the Reality of Evil

1. Royce, *Religious Aspect*, 4.

2. Sarah Royce, *A Frontier Lady*.

3. Royce, "The Intention of the Prometheus Bound of Aeschylus," 113–37.

4. Josiah Royce, "What Should Be the Attitude of Teachers of Philosophy towards Religion?" *International Journal of Ethics* 13, no. 3 (April 1903): 280–85, 285.

5. Ibid., 280.

6. Ibid., 282.

7. The major works were: Royce, *Religious Aspect; The Conception of God; The Sources of Religious Insight* (New York: C. Scribner's Sons, 1912); and *The Problem of Christianity.* Among the articles were: "George Eliot as a Religious Teacher," *Califor-*

nian 3 (1881): 300–310, reprinted in *Fugitive Essays*, 261–89; "Browning's Theism," *New World* 5 (1896): 401–22; "Immortality," *Hibbert Journal* 5 (1907): 724–44, reprinted in *William James;* "What Is Vital in Christianity?" *Harvard Theological Review* 2 (1901): 408–45, reprinted in *William James;* and "Monotheism," in *Encyclopedia of Religion and Ethics,* ed. James Hastings (New York: Charles Scribner's Sons, 1916), 8:817–21. On the problem of evil, Royce wrote two major pieces: "The Knowledge of Good and Evil," *International Journal of Ethics* 4 (1893): 48–80, reprinted in *SGE,* 89–124; and "The Problem of Job," *New World* 6 (1897): 261–81, reprinted in *SGE,* 1–28.

8. See Daniel Dennett, *Breaking the Spell: Religion as a Natural Phenomenon* (New York: Penguin, 2007); Richard Dawkins, *The God Delusion* (Boston: Houghton, Mifflin, 2006); and Victor J. Stenger, *God: The Failed Hypothesis* (New York: Prometheus, 2007).

9. Frank M. Oppenheim, *Royce's Mature Philosophy of Religion* (Notre Dame, Ind.: University of Notre Dame Press, 1987); *Reverence for the Relations of Life.*

10. I especially recommend Randall Auxier's *Time, Will and Purpose* and Dwayne A. Tunstall's *Encountering Josiah Royce's Ethico-Religious Insight.*

11. The works that will be referred to in this regard are Paul Tillich, *The Courage to Be* (New Haven, Conn.: Yale University Press, 1952); Paul Tillich, *The Dynamics of Faith* (New York: Harper and Bros., 1957); and J. B. Phillips, *Your God Is Too Small* (New York: Touchstone, 1957 and 2004).

12. Josiah Royce, about 1910, "Outline and Text of 'Religious Experience and Religious Truth,'" in *Josiah Royce's Late Writings,* 5:175–85.

13. Royce, *The Problem of Christianity,* 62.

14. Ibid., 66.

15. Royce, *Religious Aspect,* 3–4.

16. George W. Hackman, Charles W. Kegley, and Viljo K. Nikander, *Religion in Modern Life* (New York: Macmillan, 1957), 14.

17. Tillich, *Dynamics of Faith,* 4 and 1.

18. Ibid., 10.

19. Ibid., 105.

20. Royce, *Religious Aspect,* 4.

21. Tillich, *Dynamics of Faith,* 10.

22. Ibid., 15.

23. Josiah Royce, "Doubting and Working," *Californian* 3 (1881): 229–37, reprinted with revisions in *Fugitive Essays,* 322–44, 341; citations are to *Fugitive Essays.*

24. Ibid., 340.

25. Royce, *Religious Aspect,* 13.

26. Tillich, *Dynamics of Faith,* 98.

27. Royce, "George Eliot as a Religious Teacher," 287–88; citations are from *Fugitive Essays.*

28. Tillich, *Dynamics of Faith,* 96.

29. Royce, *Religious Aspect,* 4.

30. Tillich, *Dynamics of Faith,* 90–91.

31. Phillips, *Your God Is Too Small.*

32. Royce, *Religious Aspect*, 213.

33. Ibid., 134.

34. Ibid., 169.

35. Ibid., 160–61.

36. Ibid., 296 and 298.

37. Royce, "How Beliefs Are Made," 345–63.

38. Ibid., 362–63.

39. Royce, *Religious Aspect*, 359.

40. Ibid., 433.

41. Ibid., 434.

42. Ibid., 467.

43. Charles Hartshorne, *The Divine Relativity* (New Haven, Conn.: Yale University Press, 1948).

44. Alfred North Whitehead, *Process and Reality* (New York: Macmillan, 1927–28).

45. Ibid., 471.

46. Royce, *Religious Aspect*, 467.

47. Royce, *SMP*, 13 and 15.

48. Ibid., 23.

49. Ibid., 14.

50. Ibid., 54–55.

51. Royce, "Monotheism," 819.

52. Royce, *SMP*, 99.

53. Ibid., 112.

54. Ibid., 166.

55. Royce, "Monotheism," 821.

56. Royce, *SMP*, 197.

57. Ibid., 214.

58. Ibid., 240.

59. Ibid., 231.

60. Ibid., 311.

61. Ibid., 395.

62. Ibid., 410.

63. See Royce, "Self-Consciousness, Social Consciousness, and Nature."

64. Royce, *SMP*, 410.

65. Ibid., 411. It is interesting to note that Royce provides a footnote to this passage that refers to "The Moral Insight" in *Religious Aspect*, 131ff.

66. Ibid., 17.

67. Josiah Royce, 1897, *The Conception of God*, reprinted with an introduction by Randall Auxier (Bristol, England: Thoemmes Press, 2000), 288.

68. Josiah Royce, *The Conception of God*, 1897, reprinted with an introduction by Randall Auxier (Bristol, England: Thoemmes Press, 2000), 301–302.

69. Randall Auxier, in his new book *Time, Will and Purpose*, gives us an excellent understanding of this notion of the Absolute, as does Dwayne Tunstall in *Encountering Josiah Royce's Ethico-Religious Insight*.

70. Josiah Royce, 1893, "The Knowledge of Good and Evil," *International Journal of Ethics*, 4, 48–80, reprinted in *SGE*, 89–124; the citations are from *SGE*.

71. Royce, *SGE*, 99.

72. Ibid.

73. Ibid., 119.

74. Royce, "The Case of John Bunyan."

75. Josiah Royce, "What Is Vital in Christianity," *Harvard Theological Review* 2 (1909): 408–45, reprinted in *William James and Other Essays on the Philosophy of Life*, 99–183; the citations are from *William James*, here 101.

76. Ibid., 103.

77. Ibid.

78. Ibid., 105–106.

79. Ibid., 107.

80. Ibid., 109.

81. Ibid., 111.

82. Ibid., 116.

83. Ibid., 117.

84. Ibid., 125.

85. Ibid., 130–31.

86. Ibid., 147.

87. Ibid., 148.

88. Ibid., 167 and 169.

89. Ibid., 173.

90. Ibid., 177.

91. Ibid., 179.

92. Ibid., 183.

93. Royce, "Monotheism," 817–21.

94. Ibid., 818.

95. Ibid.

96. Ibid., 818–19.

97. Ibid., 819.

98. Ibid.

99. Ibid.

100. Ibid., 820.

101. Ibid.

102. Ibid.

103. Ibid., 821.

104. Ibid.

105. Ibid.

106. William James, *The Varieties of Religious Experience* (New York: Longmans, Green, 1902, 1916).

107. Royce, *The Sources*, 27.

108. Ibid., 34.

109. Ibid., 38.

110. Ibid., 47.

111. Ibid., 41–42.

112. Royce, "Outline and Text of 'Religious Experience and Religious Truth,'" 176.

113. Ibid., 178.

114. Ibid., 179.

115. Royce, *The Sources*, 25.

116. Ibid., 8–9.

117. Ibid., 15.

118. Ibid., 12.

119. Ibid.

120. Ibid., 28–29.

121. Ibid., 33.

122. Ibid., 65.

123. Ibid., 34.

124. Ibid., 55.

125. Ibid., 58.

126. Ibid., 69.

127. Ibid., 70.

128. Ibid., 250.

129. Ibid., 252.

130. Royce, *The Problem of Christianity*, 62.

131. Royce writes: "These doctrines, then, need no dogmas of any historical church to define them, and no theology, and no technical metaphysical theory, to furnish a foundation for them. In the second place, however, these Christian ideas are based upon deep metaphysical truths whose significance is more than human." *The Problem of Christianity*, 42–43.

132. Ibid., 43.

133. Ibid., 45.

134. Ibid., 94.

135. Ibid., 98.

136. Royce, *The World and the Individual*, 2:59 (Dover edition).

137. Ibid., 2:359.

138. Ibid., 1:48–49.

139. Royce, *Sources of Religious Insight*, 66.

140. Royce, *The World and the Individual*, 2:349.

141. Royce, *Sources of Religious Insight*, 60.

142. Royce, *The Problem of Christianity*, 131.

143. Ibid., 133.

144. Ibid., 162.

145. Ibid., 178.

146. Ibid., 180.

147. Ibid., 387.

148. Ibid.

5. Developing Genuine Individuals and Communities

1. Josiah Royce, "Nietzsche," *Atlantic Monthly* 119 (1917): 321–31, with an introductory note by W. Fergus Kernan, reprinted in *Josiah Royce's Late Writings,* 1:174–87.

2. Josiah Royce, Words of Professor Royce at the Walton Hotel at Philadelphia, 29 December 1915, in Josiah Royce, *The Hope of the Great Community* (New York: Macmillan, 1916), 122–136, 131.

3. Royce, "Nietzsche," 327–28.

4. George Herbert Mead, "Josiah Royce—A Personal Impression," *International Journal of Ethics* 27 (1917): 168.

5. Josiah Royce, "The Possibility of International Insurance," 1916, in *The Hope of the Great Community,* 71–92, 76.

6. Josiah Royce, "Duties of Americans in the Present War," *Boston Evening Transcript* (2 February 1916): 18, reprinted in *The Hope of the Great Community,* 1–13.

7. Josiah Royce, "An American Thinker on the War," *Hibbert Journal* 24 (1915–16): 37–42, reprinted as "The Destruction of the Lusitania," in *The Hope of the Great Community,* 14–24; citations are to *The Hope.*

8. Josiah Royce, "Professor Royce's 'Lusitania Speech,'" *Boston Evening Transcript* (8 May 1916): 13, reprinted as "The First Anniversary of the Lusitania," in *The Hope of the Great Community,* 93–121; citations are to *The Hope.*

9. Josiah Royce, "The Squatter Riot of '50 in Sacramento: Its Causes and Its Significance," *Overland Monthly* n.s. 6 (1885): 225–46, reprinted as "An Episode of Early California Life: The Squatter Riot of 1850 in Sacramento," in *SGE,* 298–347; citations are from *SGE,* 301.

10. Royce, "Present Ideals of American University Life," 376–88.

11. Josiah Royce, "The Carnegie Foundation for the Advancement of Teaching, and the Case for Middlebury College," *School and Society* (1915): 145–150.

12. Josiah Royce, "The Freedom of Teaching," *Overland Monthly* n.s. 2 (1883): 235–40.

13. Josiah Royce, "Race Questions and Prejudices," *International Journal of Ethics* 16 (1906): 265–88, reprinted in Josiah Royce, *Race Questions, Provincialism and Other American Problems* (New York: Macmillan, 1908), 3–56.

14. Josiah Royce, "Extension Course on Ethics," 1915–1916, in *Josiah Royce's Late Writings,* 2:75–171.

15. Josiah Royce, *War and Insurance* (New York: Macmillan, 1914).

16. Josiah Royce, *The Hope of the Great Community* (New York: Macmillan, 1916).

17. Royce, *The Problem of Christianity.*

18. Royce, *The Hope of the Great Community,* 46.

19. Ibid., 46–48.

20. Royce, *The Problem of Christianity,* 2:37.

21. Ibid., 42.

22. Royce, *Outlines of Psychology*, 226, 236; italics in original.

23. Ibid., 238. Royce also argues that "our memory of past lives takes the form of a memory of typical fashions of behavior, of experience, and of feeling, rather than the form of a precise and detailed recall of the exact order of individual events" (ibid., 237). These views on memory are in concert with contemporary views: see Michael S. Gazzaniga, "The Brain Produces a Poor Autobiography," in *The Ethical Brain* (New York: Dana Press, 2005).

24. *The Problem of Christianity*, 2:45.

25. Ibid., 49.

26. Ibid., 42.

27. I have discussed the interpretive process in other contexts, particularly medical ones. See Kegley, *Genuine Individuals and Genuine Communities*, chapter 7; "A New Bioethics Framework for Facilitating Better Decision-Making about Genetic Information," in *Public Health Policy and Ethics*, ed. M. Boylan (The Netherlands: Kluwer Academic Publishers, 2004), 91–101; and "Community, Autonomy, and Managed Care," in *Pragmatic Bioethics*, ed. G. McGee (Nashville, Tenn.: Vanderbilt University Press, 1999 and 2004).

28. *The Problem of Christianity*, 2:64–65.

29. Ibid., 68–69.

30. Ibid., 79.

31. Ibid., 86.

32. Ibid., 88.

33. Ibid., 94.

34. Royce, *The Philosophy of Loyalty*, 20.

35. Ibid., 108–109.

36. Josiah Royce, "The Duties," in *The Hope of the Great Community*, 3.

37. Ibid., 4.

38. Ibid., 8.

39. Ibid., 9.

40. Ibid., 9–10.

41. Royce, "The Destruction of the Lusitania," 18.

42. Royce, "Lusitania Address," 97.

43. Ibid., 104 and 103.

44. Ibid., 100 and 106.

45. Royce, *Philosophy of Loyalty*, 214. Emphasis is mine.

46. Tunstall, *Encountering Josiah Royce's Ethico-Religious Insight*, 158–59.

47. Anders Nygren, *Agape and Eros*, part 2: *The History of the Christian Idea of Love*, trans. Philip S. Watson (London: Society for the Promotion of Christian Knowledge, 1939).

48. Royce, "Lusitania Address," 114.

49. Josiah Royce, *Some Relations of Physical Training to the Present Problems of Moral Education in America* (Boston: Boston Normal School of Gymnastics, 1908), reprinted in *Race Questions*, 229–87. The citation is from *Race Questions*, 263.

50. Royce, "Loyalty and Individuality."

51. Royce, "Reflections after a Wandering Life."

52. Royce, "Impressions of Australia."

53. Frank M. Oppenheim, *Royce's Voyage Down Under: A Journey of the Mind* (Lexington: University Press of Kentucky, 1980).

54. Ibid., xv–xvi.

55. Josiah Royce, "The Pacific Coast, a Psychological Study of Influence," *International Monthly* 2 (1900): 555–83, reprinted in *Race Questions* as "The Pacific Coast, a Psychological Study of the Relations of Climate and Civilization," 169–225, an address prepared for the National Geographical Society in May 1898.

56. Royce, "Reflections after a Wandering Life," 1:677.

57. Ibid., 2:820.

58. Ibid., 2:814.

59. Royce, "Impressions of Australia," 85.

60. Royce, "Reflections after a Wandering Life," 1:681.

61. Ibid., 1:682.

62. Royce, "An Episode of Early California Life."

63. *The Philosophy of Loyalty,* the chapter on Training for Loyalty; Josiah Royce, "Football and Ideals," *Harvard Illustrated Magazine* 10 (1908): 40–47; and Josiah Royce, *Some Relations of Physical Training to the Present Problems of Moral Education in America* (Boston: Boston Normal School of Gymnastics, 1908), reprinted in *Race Questions,* 229–287.

64. Royce, *Some Relations of Physical Training,* 255 and 256.

65. Royce, "Impressions of Australia," 66.

66. Ibid., 78.

67. Royce, *The World and the Individual,* 1959 Dover ed., 224, 225, and 226.

68. Royce, "Impressions of Australia," 83.

69. Ibid.

70. Royce, "An Episode of Early California Life," 301.

71. Ibid., 320.

72. Ibid., 326.

73. Ibid., 346.

74. Ibid., 325–26. To fully understand Royce's concern here, one needs to read Royce's writings on revolution and reform: "The Nature of Voluntary Progress" and "Shelley and the Revolution." Randall Auxier in his new book gives an excellent overview of this in his discussion of Royce's conservatism.

75. Royce, "On Certain Limitations of the Thoughtful Public in America," in *Race Questions,* 112.

76. Ibid., 115–16.

77. Ibid., 158–59.

78. Royce, *Race Questions,* 61.

79. Ibid.

80. Ibid., 72.

81. Josiah Royce, "Provincialism," in *The Basic Writings of Josiah Royce,* ed. John J. McDermott (Chicago: University of Chicago Press, 1908, 1969), 1069.

82. Ibid., 1080.

83. Ibid.

84. Stuart Gerry Brown, "From Provincialism to the Great Community: The Social Philosophy of Josiah Royce," *Ethics* 59, no. 1 (October 1948): 14–34, 19–20.

85. Royce, "The Freedom of Teaching," 238.

86. Ibid., 237–38.

87. I share this delightful commentary on those "boards" that would trample the freedom of teaching. Royce writes: "There was once a board of managers. It may have been in Babylon or in Nineveh, and its minutes may have been kept in cuneiform hieroglyphics; but, if we remember rightly, it was not so ancient a body as that. However, this board, in its own day and generation, was capable of sending a written order to the instructors in its institution, telling them in effect that some of them were too often seen out of their classrooms, that this seemed suspicious, and that it desired them to stay each in his own classroom from nine to five daily, saving when called away on absolutely necessary business. In other words, this board had never conceived the difference between a university instructor and an office clerk, and actually imagined that an instructor was doing his business then and only then, when he was in his classroom," "The Freedom of Teaching," 239. Unfortunately such a scenario still occurs in 2008.

88. Royce, "Present Ideals of American University Life," 376–88.

89. Ibid., 379.

90. Ibid.

91. Ibid., 384.

92. Royce, "The Carnegie Foundation for the Advancement of Teaching," 147.

93. Josiah Royce, "The Struggle for Order: Self-Government, Good-Humor and Violence in the Mines," in *The Basic Writings of Josiah Royce,* 46.

94. Ibid., 107.

95. Ibid., 111.

96. Ibid., 108.

97. Ibid., 108.

98. Royce, "Race Questions and Prejudices," *IJE,* 16 (1905–1906): 265–88. Reprinted in *Race Questions.*

99. Royce, "Reflections after a Wandering Life," 1:676.

100. Royce, *Race Questions,* 4–5.

101. Ibid., 30.

102. Ibid., 9.

103. Ibid.

104. Ibid.

105. Ibid., 11.

106. Ibid., 12.

107. Ibid.

108. Ibid., 13.

109. Ibid.

110. Ibid., 14–15.

111. Ibid., 16.

112. Ibid., 25.

113. Ibid.

114. Ibid., 29–30.

115. Ibid., 31.

116. Ibid., 37.

117. Ibid., 44.

118. Ibid., 42.

119. Ibid., 42–43.

120. Ibid., 45.

121. Ibid., 53.

122. Royce, *War and Insurance,* 30.

123. Royce, *The Hope of the Great Community,* 64.

124. Josiah Royce, "Comments upon the Problem of the Mid-Year Examination" [or "Principles of Loyalty"], in 1915–1916 "Extension Course on Ethics," in *Josiah Royce's Late Writings,* 2:132–74.

125. Ibid., 144.

126. Ibid.

127. *War and Insurance,* 49. Italics are in the text.

128. Brown suggests this, and I agree.

129. Royce, *The Hope of the Great Community,* 79.

130. Jose-Antonio Orosco, "Cosmopolitan Loyalty and the Great Global Community: Royce's Globalization," *Journal of Speculative Philosophy* 17, no. 3 (2003): 204–15, at 205. Orosco discussed the cosmopolitan ideas of Martha Nussbaum in this context.

131. Royce, *The Hope of the Great Community,* 50–51.

132. Royce, "Principles of the Art of Loyalty," 145.

133. See Orosco, "Cosmopolitan Loyalty."

134. Shibley Telhami, "Of Power and Compassion," in *The Philosophical Challenge of September 11,* ed. Tom Rockmore, Joseph Margolis, and Armen Marsobian (London: Blackwell, 2004), 77 and 79.

135. Orosco, "Cosmopolitan Loyalty," 210.

136. Ibid.

6. The Thought of Josiah Royce

1. Campbell, *A Thoughtful Profession,* 290.

2. John E. Smith, "The New Need for a Recovery of Philosophy," in *The Spirit of American Philosophy,* rev. ed. (Albany, N.Y.: SUNY Press, 1981), 223–42. Quoted in Campbell, 290.

3. Brand Blanshard, "Climate of Opinion," in Blanshard, et al., *Philosophy in American Education: Its Tasks and Opportunities* (New York: Harper, 1945). Quoted in Campbell, 288–89.

4. John Dewey, "Problems of Men," in Blanshard et al. Quoted in Campbell, 289.

5. See Royce, "Present Ideals of American University Life" and "The Freedom of Teaching."

6. Royce, *SMP*, 1.

7. See Josiah Royce, 1915–1916, "The Social Nature of Knowledge: The Theory of Interpretation," in *Metaphysics: His Philosophy 9 Course of 1915–1916 as Stenographically Recorded by Ralph W. Brown and Complemented by Notes from Byron E. Underwood*, initial editor William Ernest Hocking, and co-edited by Richard Hocking and Frank Oppenheim (Albany: State University of New York Press, 1998), 44.

8. Josiah Royce, "The Sciences of the Ideal," *Science* n.s. 20 (1904): 449–62; "Kant's Doctrine of the Bases of Mathematics," *Journal of Philosophy, Psychology, and Scientific Methods* 2 (1905): 197–207; "The Relation of the Principles of Logic to the Foundations of Geometry," *Transactions of the American Mathematical Society* 24 (1905): 353–414; "Axiom," in *Encyclopedia of Religion and Ethics*, ed. James Hastings (New York: Charles Scribner's Sons, 1910), 2:279–82; "An Extension of the Algebra of Logic," *Journal of Philosophy, Psychology, and Scientific Methods* 10 (1913): 617–33. See also Robinson, *Royce's Logical Essays*.

9. Kegley, *Genuine Individuals and Genuine Communities*.

10. Royce, "Doubting and Working."

11. Josiah Royce, February 1898 letter to E. Stanley Hull, in *Letters of Josiah Royce*, 370–71.

12. Royce, *William James and Other Essays*, viii.

13. Royce, *Metaphysics*, 44.

14. Ibid.

15. Royce, *Religious Aspect*, 13.

16. Royce, "The External World and the Social Consciousness," and "Self-Consciousness, Social Consciousness and Nature."

17. See also Mary Midgley, *Science as Salvation: A Modern Myth and Its Meaning* (London: Routledge, 1992).

18. Ibid., 266.

19. Josiah Royce, "Introduction to H. Poincaré, *The Foundations of Sciences*," in *Royce's Logical Essays*, 271.

20. Ibid., 279–80.

21. Ibid., 331.

22. George Herbert Mead, another of Royce's students, observed in 1926 that philosophers had been led astray by a false hope of certainty and by their failure to appreciate the tentativeness of scientific practice. Quoted in Campbell, 287.

23. George Santayana, "The Spirit and Ideals of Harvard University," *Educational Review* 7, no. 4 (April 1894): 313–25, 315.

24. Cabot, "Josiah Royce as a Teacher," 467. Cabot writes: "he shocked me into perceiving that a man could really welcome difference of opinion as a precious gift."

25. Ibid., 472.

26. Chapman, "Portrait of Josiah Royce," 377. Jacob Loewenberg reports a similar experience of Royce's generosity in sharing his knowledge. Wanting to round out his study at Harvard, Loewenberg sought Royce's advice. Royce suggested that he take his seminar on Hegel. Though there were visitors to the seminar, Loewenberg was the only enrolled student. Royce nevertheless "conducted the class in no way affected by the fact that it contained but a single member." Loewenberg notes that "Under Royce's guidance . . . the study of it [the *Phenomenology*] proved an exciting adventure." Loewenberg, *Thrice Born,* 72.

27. Josiah Royce, Words of Professor Royce at the Walton Hotel at Philadelphia, 29 December 1915, in Josiah Royce, *The Hope of the Great Community* (New York: Macmillan, 1916), 131.

28. "Tribute to Josiah Royce," 773.

29. Royce, *Outlines of Psychology,* 237.

30. Ibid., 238.

31. Ibid., 240–41.

32. Royce presents these views in his 1880 essay "The Nature of Voluntary Progress."

33. Gazzaniga, *The Ethical Brain,* 120–42.

34. Ibid., 141.

35. Ibid.

36. In the 1960s, in order to prevent the spread of an epileptic seizure across the whole brain, the connecting tissue, *corpus callosum,* between the two hemispheres of the brain was cut. Experiments were done with these "split-brain" patients by Roger Sperry, and later by Michael Gazzaniga. These led to some amazing results. A person with a split brain, when shown an image on his or her left visual field (the left half of what the eye sees) were unable to name what he or she had seen. This is because the speech control center is in the left side of the brain in most people, and the image from the left visual field is sent only to the right side of the brain. Since the two sides of the brain cannot communicate, the patient cannot name what he or she is seeing. The person can, however, pick up the corresponding object (one within the left overall visual field) with their left hand, since that hand is controlled by the right side of their brain. The chicken coop–snow scene example shows discrepancy because different information flows to the two hemispheres, and thus when asked to reconcile, the person (left hemisphere) provides an explanation and makes sense of the data. See Michael S. Gazzaniga, *The Bisected Brain* (New York: Appleton-Century-Crofts, 1970).

37. For a description of one of these split-brain experiments, see Gazzaniga, *The Ethical Brain,* 136–38.

38. See Glannon, *Bioethics and the Brain,* for an overview of these issues. The musician example is discussed on 88. Glannon points out that many different systems interact within the brain and between brain systems and other systems of the body, such as the endocrine and immune systems. Further, neuroscience today agrees that "functions" are distributed throughout the brain.

39. Paul and Patricia Churchland, *On the Contrary* (Cambridge, Mass.: MIT Press,

1998); Patricia Churchland and T. J. Sejnowski, *The Computational Brain* (Cambridge, Mass.: MIT Press, 1992); Paul Churchland, *The Engine of Reason, The Seat of the Soul: A Philosophical Journey into the Brain* (Cambridge, Mass.: MIT Press, 1995).

40. In his introduction to the *Outlines,* Royce asserts that psychology as a field is related to our human experience of constantly judging "the ideas, moods and intents of his fellows, by watching not only their faces, but also their whole range of voluntary and involuntary expressive movements." Psychology merely extends the range of its applications and renders more minute the scrutiny. Included in this range, for Royce, is the "cooperative work of many intelligent beings." Among these are works of art, languages, customs, faiths, institutions, national life. See *Outlines of Psychology,* 14.

41. See Joseph LeDoux, *The Emotional Brain* (New York: Simon and Schuster, 1996); Joseph LeDoux, *The Synaptic Self: How Our Brains Become Who We Are* (New York: Viking, 2002); and Steven Rose, *The Twenty-First Century Brain: Explaining, Mending, and Manipulating the Mind* (London: Cape, 2006).

42. Josiah Royce, "Mind," in *Encyclopedia of Religion and Ethics,* 8:649–57, reprinted in *Royce's Logical Essays,* 174.

43. Ibid.

44. An interesting aside to this emphasis by Royce on interpretation is the speculation by a contemporary professor of neuropsychology, Charles Frith, that there needs to be a hermeneutics of neuroscience—an investigation into the ways in which theories can be variously interpreted. Further, Frith's main thesis in his new book is that "our brains create an illusion both of the world we inhabit and of our sense of personal autonomy while moving about in it—'a fantasy that coincides with reality.'" Sian Ede, review of *Making Up the Mind: How the Brain Creates Our Mental World* by Chris Frith, *Nature* 448, no. 30 (August 2007): 995. See Chris Frith, *Making Up the Mind: How the Brain Creates Our Mental World* (New York: Blackwell, 2007).

45. Royce, *The World and the Individual,* 2:261–62.

46. Royce, "Preliminary Report on Imitation," 225.

47. Ibid.

48. Susan Hurley and Nick Chater, eds., *Perspectives on Imitation: From Neuroscience to Social Science,* 2 vols. (Cambridge, Mass.: MIT Press, 2005).

49. Ibid., 2:1.

50. Ibid., 2:48.

51. Ap Dijksterhuis, "Why We Are Social Animals: The High Road to Imitation as Social Glue," in Hurley and Chater, 2:209–20, 220.

52. Ibid.

53. Jesse J. Prinz, "Imitation and Moral Development," in Hurley and Chater, 2:266–82.

54. Ibid., 2:282.

55. See chapter 3.

56. *Religious Aspect,* chapter 4, 60–106.

57. Royce, "John Fiske," quoted in Oppenheim, *Royce's Mature Ethics,* 70. See also Royce, "John Fiske: His Work as Philosopher and Teacher," 14–24.

58. Alvin I. Goldman, "Imitation, Mind Reading and Simulation," in Hurley and Chater, 2:79–93, 79.

59. Alvin Goldman, "Interpretation Psychologized," *Mind and Language* 4 (1989): 161–85.

60. Royce, *Metaphysics,* 14.

61. Ibid.

62. Ibid., 16.

63. Royce, *Outlines of Psychology,* 322–323. Italics are Royce's.

64. Howard P. Chudacoff, *Children at Play: An American History* (New York: New York University Press, 2007). Reported by Patricia Cohen in *New York Times,* 14 August 2007.

65. Ibid.

66. Ibid., *New York Times* article.

67. Royce, *Religious Aspect,* 23.

68. Royce, "On Certain Psychological Aspects of Moral Training," 423.

69. *Religious Aspect,* 23. Royce presents a similar argument against naturalist ethics.

70. A. J. Ayer, "A Critique of Ethics," in *Language, Truth, and Logic* (London: Gollanza, 1946), 102–14.

71. Although Ayer is often credited with this theory, it was already present in C. K. Ogden and I. A. Richards, *The Meaning of Meaning* (New York: Harcourt, Brace and Jovanovich, 1923).

72. Fuss, *The Moral Philosophy of Josiah Royce,* 5. Fuss states the conflict of *Religious Aspect* as one between the realist, who insists that the objectivity of moral distinctions must be established, and the idealist, who wants to secure the autonomy of the moral agent. I am not sure I agree with this characterization. I believe both seek to establish "objectivity." Further, the idealist may or may not be concerned to secure the autonomy of the moral agent.

73. Ibid., 30.

74. Royce, *SGE,* ix.

75. For an overview of these debates, see Robert Kane, ed., *The Oxford Handbook of Free Will* (New York: Oxford University Press, 2004).

76. Ibid. See especially Henrik Walter, "Neurophilosophy of Free Will"; Robert C. Bishop, "Chaos, Indeterminism, and Free Will"; and David Hodgson, "Quantum Physics, Indeterminism and Free Will."

77. John R. Searle, *Freedom and Neurobiology: Reflections on Free Will, Language and Political Power* (New York: Columbia University Press, 2007), 56.

78. Daniel Dennett, *Elbow Room: Varieties of Free Will Worth Wanting* (Cambridge, Mass.: Harvard University Press, 1997).

79. One example is the work of Benjamin Libet, "Do We Have Free Will?" *Journal of Consciousness Studies* 6, no. 8–9 (1999): 47–57. It is interesting that Royce refers to these kinds of time-lapse experiments, although not in regard to determining free will, in his discussion of the experimental in psychology in *Outlines.* He writes, "Very important results have also flowed from the careful noting of the various time rela-

tions of any or of all the foregoing classes of facts [particular nervous conditions and particular mental states] as they occur when exact experimental conditions have been established. . . . [H]ow long a given mental process takes, and how this time element varies with given variations in the situation, is one of great interest to the psychologist." *Outlines of Psychology,* 19.

80. Van Inwagen, *Essay on Free Will.* This is the assumption of this exposition. In *The World and the Individual,* vol. 2, Royce defines the principle of the "uniformity of nature" as *"We conceive every natural event as preceded by a group of events such that whenever that group as a whole recurs, that same consequent must follow."* Royce also criticized Kant for assuming "causality" as fundamental to human consciousness.

81. Royce, *The World and the Individual,* 2:197.

82. Royce, *The Conception of God,* 319–30.

83. Ibid., 320.

84. Royce, *Religious Aspect,* 77.

85. Ibid., 79–80.

86. Ibid., 85.

87. Josiah Royce, "A New Study of Psychology," *International Journal of Ethics* 2 (1891): 143–69, 143.

88. Royce, "John Fiske."

89. Royce, *The Conception of God,* 290.

90. Ibid., 292.

91. Taylor, *Sources of the Self,* 39.

92. Alasdair MacIntyre, *After Virtue* (Notre Dame, Ind.: Notre Dame University Press, 1981).

93. Christine M. Korsgaard, "Personal Identity and the Unity of Agency: A Kantian Response to Parfit," *Philosophy and Public Affairs* 19 (1989): 101–32.

94. *CNN Presents: God's Warriors:* (1) "God's Muslim Warriors," 22 August 2007; (2) "God's Christian Warriors," 25 August 2007; and (3) "God's Jewish Warriors," 29 August 2007. Christiane Amanpour, CNN chief international correspondent.

95. In the interview with Amanpour, Sondra Oster Baras, an American-born Orthodox Jew now living in Israel, who lobbies Christian Evangelicals on behalf of Israel, expresses these views when she says: "I am a daughter of Abraham and I believe when Jews live in the Holy Land, Jesus and God will come" ("God's Jewish Warriors").

96. See John Hagel, *Jerusalem Countdown,* rev. ed. (New York: Frontline, 2007). Hagel is pastor of a church in San Antonio, Texas. He believes the Bible supports Israel. He had a replica of the Jewish Wailing Wall built for his church. In his book he envisions a war led by Iran and Russia with Arab allies who will invade Israel. In the Armageddon battle Jesus will return to slay nonbelievers and the Jews will recognize him as the Messiah.

97. From "God's Jewish Warriors," *CNN Presents.*

98. Royce, "What Is Vital in Christianity," 109.

99. Ibid., 116.

100. Ibid., 117.

101. Cornel West, *Democracy Matters: Winning the Fight against Imperialism* (New York: Penguin Group, 2004), 175, 174.

102. Within Islam, particularly in its fundamentalist forms, there is also a perceived opposition between religion and science, a view that science is heresy. In an extensive study of the 57 nations of the Organization of the Islamic Conference by Pakistani physicist Pervez Amirali Hoodbhoy, it was found that Islamic countries have only 8.5 scientists per 1,000 population, compared to a world average of 40.7. Production of scientific articles is also low, and spending on science is only about 0.3 percent of gross national product, compared with a global average of 2.4 percent. This was reported in "Islam vs. Science," by Jay Tolson, *U.S. News and World Report,* 10 September 2007, 48–49. The strongest advocate for an intellectual argument for the compatibility of science and traditional Islamic thought is Iranian-born philosopher of science Seyyed Hossein Nasr, a professor of Islamic studies at George Washington University. See his 1970 book, *Science and Civilization in Islam* (New York: New American Library).

103. Royce, "What Is Vital in Christianity?" 167, 169.

104. Royce, "Monotheism," 820–821.

105. Royce, "Self-Consciousness, Social Consciousness, and Nature," 203.

106. Royce, *The Problem of Christianity,* 2:430.

107. See Kegley, *Genuine Individuals and Genuine Communities,* chapter 5, 106–28.

108. See Richard Shusterman, "Pragmatism and Liberalism: Between Dewey and Rorty," *Political Theory* 22, no. 3 (August 1994): 391–413.

109. Shibley Telhami, *The Stakes: American and the Middle East* (Boulder, Colo.: Westview Press, 2003 and 2004).

110. Telhami, "Of Power and Compassion," 70–80.

111. Ibid., 77 and 79.

112. Orosco, "Cosmopolitan Loyalty and the Great Global Community," 210.

113. Ibid.

114. Robert B. Reich, "Capitalism and the Death of Democracy," *Foreign Policy* (September–October 2007): 38–43, 38.

115. Ibid.

116. Ibid.

117. Ibid., 39.

118. Ibid.

119. Ibid.

120. Ibid., 40.

121. Ibid.

122. Ibid.

123. Ibid., 42.

124. Ibid., 38.

125. West, *Democracy Matters,* 21.

Bibliography

Anderson, Douglas. *Philosophy Americana: Making Philosophy at Home in American Culture.* New York: Fordham University Press, 2006.

Auxier, Randall. *Papers in Honor of Josiah Royce on His Sixtieth Birthday.* Thoemmes Library of American Philosophy. Chippenham, England: Thoemmes Press, 2003.

———. *Time, Will and Purpose: Living Ideas from the Philosophy of Josiah Royce.* La Salle, Ill.: Open Court Press, 2008.

Ayer, A. J. "A Critique of Ethics." In *Language, Truth, and Logic.* London: Gollanza, 1946.

Baldwin, James Mark. *Mental Development in the Child and in the Race.* New York: Macmillan, 1895.

Bishop, Robert C. "Chaos, Indeterminism, and Free Will." In *The Oxford Handbook of Free Will,* ed. Robert Kane. New York: Oxford University Press, 2004.

Blakewell, Charles M. "Novum Itinerarium Mentu in Deum." *Philosophical Review* 24, no. 3 (1816). Reprinted in Randall E. Auxier. *Papers in Honor of Josiah Royce on His Sixtieth Birthday.* Thoemmes Library of American Philosophy. Chippenham, England: Thoemmes Press, 2003.

Blanshard, Brand, et al. *Philosophy in American Education: Its Tasks and Opportunities.* New York: Harper, 1945.

Brown, Rollo Walter. *Harvard Yard in the Golden Age.* New York: Current Books, 1948.

Brown, Stuart Gerry. "From Provincialism to the Great Community: The Social Philosophy of Josiah Royce." *Ethics* 59, no. 1 (October 1948): 14–34.

Buranelli, Vincent. *Josiah Royce.* New Haven: Twayne, 1964.

Cabot, Richard C. "Josiah Royce as a Teacher." *Philosophical Review* 25, no. 3 (1916): 466–72.

Campbell, James. *A Thoughtful Profession: The Early Years of the American Philosophical Association.* Chicago: Open Court, 2006.

Chapman, John Jay. "Portrait of Josiah Royce, the Philosopher." *Outlook* (1919): 372, 377.

Chudacoff, Howard P. *Children at Play: An American History.* New York: New York University Press, 2007. Reported by Patricia Cohen in *New York Times,* 14 August 2007.

Churchland, Patricia, and T. J. Sejnowski. *The Computational Brain.* Cambridge, Mass.: MIT Press, 1992.

Churchland, Paul. *The Engine of Reason, The Seat of the Soul: A Philosophical Journey into the Brain.* Cambridge, Mass.: MIT Press, 1995.

Churchland, Paul, and Patricia Churchland. *On the Contrary.* Cambridge, Mass.: MIT Press, 1998.

Clendenning, John, ed. *The Letters of Josiah Royce.* Chicago: University of Chicago Press, 1970.

———. *The Life and Thought of Josiah Royce.* Rev. and exp. ed. Nashville, Tenn.: Vanderbilt University Press, 1999.

CNN Presents: God's Warriors. "God's Muslim Warriors" (22 August 2007); "God's Christian Warriors" (25 August 2007); "God's Jewish Warriors" (29 August 2007). Christiane Amanpour, CNN chief international correspondent.

Cotton, Harry. *Royce on the Human Self.* Cambridge, Mass.: Harvard University Press, 1954.

Dawkins, Richard. *The God Delusion.* Boston: Houghton, Mifflin, 2007.

Dennet, Daniel. *Breaking the Spell: Religion as a Natural Phenomenon.* New York: Penguin, 2007.

———. *Elbow Room: Varieties of Free Will Worth Wanting.* Cambridge, Mass.: Harvard University Press, 1997.

Dewey, John. "Problems of Men." In Blandshard et al. Quoted in Campbell, 289.

Dijksterhuis, Ap. "Why We Are Social Animals: The High Road to Imitation as Social Glue." In Hurley and Chater, 2:266–82.

Ede, Sian. Review of *Making Up the Mind: How the Brain Creates Our Mental World* by Chris Frith. *Nature* 448, no. 30 (August 2007): 995.

Farah, Martha J. "Emerging Ethical Issues in Neuroscience." *Nature Neuroscience* 5, no. 11 (2 November 2002): 1123–29.

Frith, Chris. *Making Up the Mind: How the Brain Creates Our Mental World.* New York: Blackwell, 2007.

Fuss, Peter. *The Moral Philosophy of Josiah Royce.* Cambridge, Mass.: Harvard University Press, 1965.

Galston, William A. "Religious Violence or Religious Pluralism: Islam's Essential Choice." *Philosophy and Public Policy Quarterly* 25 (Summer 2005): 12–17.

Gazzaniga, Michael S. *The Bisected Brain.* New York: Appleton-Century-Crofts, 1970.

———. *The Ethical Brain.* New York: Dana Press, 2005.

Glannon, Walter. *Bioethics and the Brain.* New York: Oxford University Press, 2007.

Goldman, Alvin I. "Imitation, Mind Reading and Simulation." In Hurley and Chater, 2:79–93.

——. "Interpretation Psychologized." *Mind and Language* 4 (1989): 161–85.

Gray, John. *Men Are from Mars, Women Are from Venus: The Classic Guide to Understanding the Opposite Sex.* New York: Harper and Row, 2004.

Hackman, George W., Charles W. Kegley, and Viljo K. Nikander. *Religion in Modern Life.* New York: Macmillan, 1957.

Hagel, John. *Jerusalem Countdown.* Rev. ed. New York: Frontline, 2007.

Hartshorne, Charles. *The Divine Relativity.* New Haven: Yale University Press, 1948.

Hine, Robert V. *Josiah Royce: From Grass Valley to Harvard.* Series editor Richard Etulain. Norman: University of Oklahoma Press, 1992.

Hocking, Ernest, ed. *Josiah Royce. Metaphysics: His Philosophy 9 Course of 1915–1916 as Stenographically Recorded by Ralph W. Brown and Complemented by Notes from Byron E. Underwood.* Albany: State University of New York Press, 1998.

Hodgson, David. "Quantum Physics, Indeterminism and Free Will." In *The Oxford Handbook of Free Will,* ed. Robert Kane. New York: Oxford University Press, 2004.

Hurley, Susan, and Nick Chater, eds. *Perspectives on Imitation: From Neuroscience to Social Science.* 2 vols. Cambridge, Mass.: MIT Press, 2005.

Iglesias de Orro, Josefina. "The Role of Psychological Theories in the Development of Royce's Ethical Concept of the Human Self." Ph.D. diss., Columbia University, 1988.

James, William. *The Varieties of Religious Experience.* New York: Longmans, Green, 1902, 1916.

Johnson, Mark. *Moral Imagination.* Chicago: University of Chicago Press, 1993.

Kane, Robert, ed. *The Oxford Handbook of Free Will.* New York: Oxford University Press, 2004.

Kegley, Jacquelyn Ann K. "Community, Autonomy, and Managed Care." In *Pragmatic Bioethics,* ed. G. McGee. Nashville, Tenn.: Vanderbilt University Press, 1999 and 2004.

——. *Genuine Individuals and Genuine Communities: A Roycean Public Philosophy.* Nashville, Tenn.: Vanderbilt University Press, 1997.

——. "Josiah Royce: Anticipator of European Existentialism and Phenomenology." In *Doctrine and Experience,* ed. Vincent G. Potter. New York: Fordham University Press, 1988.

——. "Josiah Royce on Self and Community." *Rice University Studies* 66 (1980): 4.

——. "Josiah Royce's Theory of Knowledge." *Dissertation Abstracts International* 33, no. 1 (1972): 1954.

——. "A New Bioethics Framework for Facilitating Better Decision-Making about Genetic Information." In *Public Health Policy and Ethics,* ed. M. Boylan. The Netherlands: Kluwer Academic Publishers, 2004.

——. "Peirce and Royce on Person: New Directions for Ethical Theory." In *Peirce and Value Theory,* ed. Herman Parret, 17–26. Amsterdam: John Benjamin's Publishing, 1994.

——. "Peirce and Royce on the Betrayal of Science: Scientific Fraud and Misconduct." Paper read at the annual meeting of the Society for the Advancement of American Philosophy, Columbia, S.C., March 2007.

Korsgaard, Christine M. "Personal Identity and the Unity of Agency: A Kantian Response to Parfit." *Philosophy and Public Affairs* 19 (1989): 101–32.

LeDoux, Joseph. *The Emotional Brain.* New York: Simon and Schuster, 1996.

———. *The Synaptic Self: How Our Brains Become Who We Are.* New York: Viking, 2002.

Libet, Benjamin. "Do We Have Free Will?" *Journal of Consciousness Studies* 6, no. 8–9 (1999): 47–57.

Loewenberg, Jacob. Introduction. In Josiah Royce, *Fugitive Essays.* Freeport, N.Y.: Books for Libraries Press, 1920.

———. "Royce's Synthetic Method." *Journal of Philosophy* 53, no. 3, "In Memoriam of Josiah Royce, Born November 20, 1855" (2 February 1956): 63–72.

———. *Thrice Born: Selected Memories of an Immigrant.* New York: Hobbs, Dorman, 1968.

———. [Tribute to Josiah Royce]. *Harvard Alumni Bulletin* 51 (29 January 1949): 350–51.

MacIntyre, Alasdair. *After Virtue.* Notre Dame, Ind.: Notre Dame University Press, 1981.

McDermott, John. *The Basic Writings of Josiah Royce.* New York: Fordham University Press, 2005.

Mead, George Herbert. "Josiah Royce—A Personal Impression." *International Journal of Ethics* 27 (1917): 168.

Merleau-Ponty, Maurice. *La Structure du comportement.* Paris: Presses Universitaires de France, 1942.

———. *The Structure of Behavior.* Trans. Alden Fisher. Boston: Beacon Press, 1963.

Midgley, Mary. *Science as Salvation: A Modern Myth and its Meaning.* London: Rutledge, 1992.

Nasr, Seyyed Hossein. *Science and Civilization in Islam.* New York: New American Library, 1970.

Nygren, Anders. *Agape and Eros,* part 2: *The History of the Christian Idea of Love.* Trans. Philip S. Watson. London: Society for the Promotion of Christian Knowledge, 1939.

Ogden, C. K., and I. A. Richards. *The Meaning of Meaning.* New York: Harcourt, Brace and Jovanovich, 1923.

Oppenheim, Frank M. "Josiah Royce's Intellectual Development: An Hypothesis." *Idealistic Studies* 6 (1976): 85–102.

———. *Reverence for the Relations of Life: Reimagining Pragmatism via Josiah Royce's Interaction with Peirce, James, and Dewey.* Notre Dame, Ind.: University of Notre Dame Press, 2005.

———. "A Roycean Road to Community." *International Philosophical Quarterly* 10 (1970): 341–77.

———. "Royce's Community: A Dimension Missing in Freud and James." *Journal of the History of the Behavioral Sciences* 13 (1977): 173–90.

———. *Royce's Mature Ethics.* Notre Dame, Ind.: University of Notre Dame Press, 1993.

———. *Royce's Mature Philosophy of Religion.* Notre Dame, Ind.: University of Notre Dame Press, 1987.

———. *Royce's Voyage Down Under: A Journey of the Mind.* Lexington: University Press of Kentucky, 1980.

Parret, Herman, ed. *Peirce and Value Theory.* Amsterdam: John Benjamin's Publishing, 1994.

Phillips, J. B. *Your God Is Too Small.* New York: Touchstone, 1957; 2004.

Prinz, Jesse J. "Imitations and Moral Development." In Hurley and Chater, 2:266–82.

Putnam, James Jackson. *Human Motives.* New York: Little Brown, 1915.

Reich, Robert B. "Capitalism and the Death of Democracy." *Foreign Policy* (September–October 2007): 38–43.

Rose, Steven. *The Twenty-First Century Brain: Explaining, Mending, and Manipulating the Mind.* London: Cape, 2006.

Royce, Josiah. "The American University Gymnasium: Its Influence on Academic Life." *Alma Mater* 17 (February 1900): 135–38.

———. "Axiom." In *Encyclopedia of Religion and Ethics,* vol. 2, ed. James Hastings. New York: Charles Scribner's Sons, 1910.

———. "Before and Since Kant." *Berkeley Quarterly* 2 (1881): 136.

———. *California from the Conquest in 1846 to the Second Vigilance Committee in San Francisco [1856]: A Study of American Character.* Boston: Macmillan, 1886.

———. "Can Psychology Be Founded upon the Study of Consciousness Alone, or Is Physiology Needed for the Purpose?" In *Proceedings of the International Congress of Education of the World Columbian Exposition.* New York: National Education Association, 1894.

———. "The Carnegie Foundation for the Advancement of Teaching, and the Case for Middlebury College." *School and Society* (1915): 145–50, 147.

———. "The Case of John Bunyan." *Psychological Review* 1 (1894): 21–33, 134–51, 230–40.

———. *The Conception of God.* New York: Macmillan, 1897. Reprint, with an introduction by Randall Auxier. Bristol, England: Thoemmes Press, 2000.

———. *The Conception of Immortality.* Boston: Houghton, Mifflin, 1900.

———. "The Conflict of Loyalties." *Pittsburgh Lectures on the Doctrine of Loyalty,* Lecture I, 1908. Harvard Archive Royce Papers, Folio 82, 13–14.

———. "An Extension of the Algebra of Logic." *Journal of Philosophy, Psychology, and Scientific Methods* 10 (1913): 617–33.

———. "The External World and the Social Consciousness." *Philosophical Review* 3, no. 5 (1894): 513–45.

———. *The Feud of Oakfield Creek: A Novel of California Life.* Boston: Houghton and Mifflin, 1887.

———. "Football and Ideals." *Harvard Illustrated Magazine* 10 (1908): 40–47.

———. "The Freedom of Teaching." *Overland Monthly* n.s. 2 (1883): 235–40.

———. *Fugitive Essays.* Freeport, N.Y.: Books for Libraries Press, 1920.

———. "George Eliot as a Religious Teacher." *Californian* 3 (1881): 300–10.

———. *Herbert Spencer: An Estimate and Review, by Josiah Royce; Together with a Chapter of Personal Reminiscences by James Collier.* New York: Fox, Duffield, 1904.

———. *The Hope of the Great Community.* New York: Macmillan, 1916.

———. "Immortality." *Hibbert Journal* 5 (1907): 724–44.

———. "Impressions of Australia." *Scribner's Magazine* 9 (1891): 75–87.

———. "The Imitative Functions, and Their Place in Human Nature." *Century Magazine* n.s. 26 (May 1894): 137–45.

———. "The Intention of the Prometheus Bound of Aeschylus: Being an Investigation in the Department of Greek Theology." Thesis, University of California, Berkeley, 1875. Printed in *Bulletin of the University of California, Berkeley* (June 1875).

———. "Is There a Philosophy of Evolution?" *Unitarian Review* 22, no. 1 (July 1889): 1–12, 97–113.

———. "Is There a Science of Education?" *Educational Review* 1 (1891): 15–21, 121–32.

———. "John Fiske: His Work as a Philosopher and Teacher." *Boston Evening Transcript* (13 July 1901): 14–24. Reprinted as "John Fiske as Thinker." *Harvard Graduates' Magazine* 10 (1901–1902): 23–33.

———. "Joseph Le Conte." *International Monthly* 4 (1901): 324–34.

———. *Josiah Royce's Late Writings: A Collection of Unpublished and Scattered Works.* Ed. Frank M. Oppenheim. Bristol, England: Thoemmes Press, 2001.

———. "Kant's Doctrine of the Bases of Mathematics." *Journal of Philosophy, Psychology, and Scientific Methods* 2 (1905): 197–207.

———. "The Knowledge of Good and Evil." *International Journal of Ethics* 4 (1893): 48–80.

———. "The Life-Harmony." *Overland Monthly* 15 (1875): 157–64.

———. "Loyalty and Individuality." Third Pittsburgh Lecture, 1910. Harvard Archive Royce Papers Folio 82, no. 1, 11–12.

———. "Mind." In *Encyclopedia of Religion and Ethics,* vol. 8. New York: Scribner's Sons, 1916.

———. "Monotheism." In *Encyclopedia of Religion and Ethics,* ed. James Hastings. New York: Charles Scribner's Sons, 1916.

———. "A New Study of Psychology." *International Journal of Ethics* 2 (1891): 143–69.

———. "On Certain Psychological Aspects of Moral Training." *International Journal of Ethics* 3, no. 4 (July 1893): 413–36, 423.

———. "Originality and Consciousness." *Harvard Monthly* 24 (1897): 133–42.

———. *Outlines of Psychology: An Elementary Treatise with Some Practical Applications.* New York: Macmillan, 1903.

———. "The Pacific Coast: A Psychological Study of Influence." *International Monthly* 2 (1900): 555–83.

———. *The Philosophy of Loyalty.* New York: Macmillan, 1908.

———. "The Practical Value of Philosophy." *Ethical Record* 2 (1889): 9–22.

———. "Preliminary Report on Imitation." *Psychological Review* 2, no. 3 (May 1895): 225.

———. "Present Ideals of American University Life." *Scribner's Magazine* 10 (1891): 376–88.

———. "Primitive Ways of Thinking with Special Reference to Negation and Classification." *Open Court* 27 (1913): 577–98.

———. *The Problem of Christianity.* 2 vols. New York: Macmillan, 1913; Chicago: Regnery, 1968.

———. "The Problem of Job." *New World* 6 (1897): 261–81.

———. "Provincialism." In *The Basic Writings of Josiah Royce.* Ed. John J. McDermott. Chicago: University of Chicago Press, 1908, 1969.

———. "The Psychology of Invention." *Psychological Review* 5, no. 2 (1898): 113–44.

———. *Race Questions, Provincialism and Other American Problems.* New York: Macmillan, 1908.

———. "Recent Logical Inquiries and their Psychological Bearings." *Psychological Review* 9 (1902): 105–33.

———. "Reflections after a Wandering Life in Australasia." *Atlantic Monthly* 63, no. 379 (May 1889): 675–86; no. 380 (June 1889): 813–28.

———. "The Relation of the Principles of Logic to the Foundations of Geometry." *Transactions of the American Mathematical Society* 24 (1905): 353–414.

———. *The Religious Aspect of Philosophy: A Critique of the Bases of Conduct and of Faith.* Boston: Houghton, Mifflin, 1885.

———. *Royce's Logical Essays: Collected Logical Essays of Josiah Royce.* Ed. Daniel S. Robinson. Dubuque, Iowa: William C. Brown, 1951.

———. "The Sciences of the Ideal." *Science* n.s. 20 (1904): 449–62.

———. "Self-Consciousness, Social Consciousness, and Nature." *Philosophical Review* 4 (1895): 465–85.

———. *Some Relations of Physical Training to the Present Problems of Moral Education in America.* Boston: Boston Normal School of Gymnastics, 1908.

———. *The Sources of Religious Insight.* New York: Charles Scribner's Sons, 1912.

———. *The Spirit of Modern Philosophy: An Essay in the Form of Lectures.* Boston: Houghton, Mifflin, 1892; reprint, New York: Dover Publications, 1983.

———. *Studies of Good and Evil: A Series of Essays upon the Problems of Philosophy and of Life.* New York: D. Appleton, 1898.

———. *Topics in Psychology of Interest to Teachers.* Lecture I: "What Is a General Idea?" Lecture II: "General Ideas and the Theory of Habits." Lecture VI: "Apperception, Attention, and the Theory of an Orderly Acquisition of Ideas?" 1893. Harvard Archive Royce Papers, Folio 64.

———. "The Twofold Nature of Knowledge: Imitative and Reflective." Peter Fuss, ed. *Journal of the History of Philosophy* 4 (1966): 326–37, 334.

———. Urbana Lectures. Folio 76, lecture 3. Peter Fuss, ed. *Journal of the History of Philosophy* 5 (1967): 60–78, 269–86.

———. *War and Insurance.* New York: Macmillan, 1914.

———. "What Is Vital in Christianity?" *Harvard Theological Review* 2 (1901): 408–45.

———. "What Should Be the Attitude of Teachers of Philosophy towards Religion?" *International Journal of Ethics* 13, no. 3 (April 1903): 280–85.

———. "The Will as the Principle of Philosophy." Unpublished papers. 1879(?). Harvard Archive Royce Papers, Folio 79.

———. *William James and Other Essays on the Philosophy of Life.* New York: Macmillan, 1912.

——. *The World and the Individual.* 2 vols. New York: Macmillan, 1900–1901; reprint, New York: Dover Publications, 1959.

——, et al. *The Conception of God: A Philosophical Discussion Concerning the Nature of the Divine Idea as a Demonstrable Reality.* New York: Macmillan Co., 1897.

Royce, Katharine. Foreword to *A Frontier Lady: Recollections of the Gold Rush and Early California.* Ed. Ralph Henry Gabriel. New Haven: Yale University Press, 1932.

Royce, Sarah. *A Frontier Lady: Recollections of the Gold Rush and Early California.* Ed. Ralph Henry Gabriel. New Haven: Yale University Press, 1932.

Santayana, George. "The Spirit and Ideals of Harvard University." *Educational Review* 7, no. 4 (April 1894): 313–25.

Sax, Leonard. *Why Gender Matters: What Parents and Teachers Need to Know about the Emerging Science of Sex Differences.* New York: Broadway, 2006.

Searle, John R. *Freedom and Neurobiology: Reflections on Free Will, Language and Political Power.* New York: Columbia University Press, 2007.

Shusterman, Richard. "Pragmatism and Liberalism: Between Dewey and Rorty." *Political Theory* 22, no. 3 (August 1994): 391–413.

Skrupskelis, Ignas. "Royce and the Justification of Authority." *Southern Journal of Philosophy* 8, no. 2–3 (1970): 165–70.

Smith, B. "Analogy in Moral Deliberation: The Role of Imagination and Theory in Ethics." *Journal of Medical Ethics* 28 (2002): 244–48.

Smith, John E. "The New Need for a Recovery of Philosophy." In *The Spirit of American Philosophy.* Rev. ed. Albany, N.Y.: SUNY Press, 1981, 223–42. Quoted in Campbell, 290.

Starr, Kevin. "The Gold Rush and the California Dream." *California History* (Spring 1998): 57–67.

Stenger, Victor J. *God: The Failed Hypothesis.* New York: Prometheus, 2007.

Strauss, Erwin. *The Primary World of Senses.* Trans. J. Needleman. London: Free Press of Glencoe, 1963.

Taylor, Charles. *Sources of the Self: The Making of Modern Identity.* Cambridge, Mass.: Harvard University Press, 1989.

Telhami, Shibley. "Of Power and Compassion." In *The Philosophical Challenge of September 11.* Ed. Tom Rockmore, Joseph Margolis, and Armen Marsobian. London: Blackwell, 2004.

——. *The Stakes: America and the Middle East.* Boulder, Colo.: Westview Press, 2003, 2004.

Tillich, Paul. *The Courage to Be.* New Haven: Yale University Press, 1952.

——. *The Dynamics of Faith.* New York: Harper and Bros., 1957.

Tolson, Jay. "Islam vs. Science." *U.S. News and World Report,* 10 September 2007, 48–49.

"Tribute to Josiah Royce." *Science* n.s. 44 (1 December 1916): 773.

Tunstall, Dwayne. *Encountering Josiah Royce's Ethico-Religious Insight.* New York: Fordham Press, forthcoming.

Urban, William Marshall. "Progress in Philosophy." *Journal of Philosophy* 23 (1925): 40–41. Quoted in Campbell, 282.

Van Inwagen, Peter. *Essay on Free Will.* Oxford, England: Clarendon Press, 1986.

Walter, Henrik. "Neurophilosophy of Free Will." In *The Oxford Handbook of Free Will.* Ed. Robert Kane. New York: Oxford University Press, 2004.

West, Cornel. *Democracy Matters: Winning the Fight against Imperialism.* New York: Penguin Group, 2004.

Whitehead, Alfred North. *Process and Reality.* New York: Macmillan, 1927–28.

Wilson, Woodrow. Letter to Ellen Axon Wilson. 5 February 1884. In *The Papers of Woodrow Wilson.* Vol. 18. Ed. Arthur S. Link. Princeton, N.J.: Princeton University Press, 1974.

Zinn, Maxine Baca, Pierette Hondagneu-Sotelo, and Michael A. Messner, eds. *Gender through the Prism of Difference.* New York: Guilford Press, 2005.

Index

Jacquelyn Ann K. Kegley

is Professor of Philosophy and Chair
of the Philosophy Department at
California State University,
Bakersfield.